THE TERRORIST IN SEARCH OF HUMANITY

Crises in World Politics
(Centre of International Studies, University of Cambridge)

TARAK BARKAWI • JAMES MAYALL • BRENDAN SIMMS
editors

GÉRARD PRUNIER
Darfur—the Ambiguous Genocide

MARK ETHERINGTON
Revolt on the Tigris

FAISAL DEVJI
Landscapes of the Jihad

AHMED HASHIM
Insurgency and Counter-Insurgency in Iraq

ERIC HERRING & GLEN RANGWALA
Iraq in Fragments—the Occupation and its Legacy

STEVE TATHAM
Losing Arab Hearts and Minds

WILLIAM MALEY
Rescuing Afghanistan

IAIN KING AND WHIT MASON
Peace at any Price: How the World Failed Kosovo

CARNE ROSS
Independent Diplomat

FAISAL DEVJI

The Terrorist
in Search of Humanity
Militant Islam and Global Politics

Columbia University Press
New York

Columbia University Press
Publishers Since 1893
New York

Library of Congress Cataloging-in-Publication Data

Devji, Faisal.
  The terrorist in search of humanity : militant Islam and global politics / Faisal Devji.
      p. cm. — (Crises in world politics)
  Includes bibliographical references and index.
  ISBN 978-0-231-70060-3 (cloth : alk. paper)
  1. Islam and politics—Islamic countries. 2. Qaida (Organization). 3. World politics—1989–
I. Title.
  DS35.69.D48 2008
  320.5'57—dc22
                                    2008038064

⊛
Columbia University Press books are printed on permanent and durable acid-free paper.
This book is printed on paper with recycled content.
Printed in India

c 10 9 8 7 6 5 4 3 2 1

References to Internet Web sites (URLs) were accurate at the time of writing. Neither
the author nor Columbia University Press is responsible for URLs that may have expired
or changed since the manuscript was prepared.

CONTENTS

Amidst the wilds of Tartary and Russia, although he still evaded me, I have ever followed in his track. Sometimes the peasants, scared by this horrid apparition, informed me of his path; sometimes he himself, who feared that if I lost all trace I should despair and die, often left some mark to guide me. The snows descended on my head, and I saw the print of his huge step on the white plain.

Mary Shelley, *Frankenstein; or, The Modern Prometheus*

ACKNOWLEDGEMENTS

This book could not have been written without the advice and assistance of numerous friends and colleagues. I want to thank Arjun Appadurai and Carol Breckenridge in New York for their unfailing support; Michael and Rachel Dwyer in London for the quality of their understanding and the constancy of their hospitality; and Christophe Carvalho for once again giving me the time and space to write in Mumbai. This book is in substantial ways a product of the many conversations I've enjoyed with friends old and new. And it is for the pleasure of their company as much as for their arguments and insights that I want to thank Shane Brighton, Jean Comaroff, Nick Frayn, Meenakshi Ganguly, Thomas Keenan, Naveeda Khan, Mark Lacy, Uday Mehta, Satya Pemmaraju, Omar Qureshi, Vyjayanthi Rao, Sudipta Sen, Thorvald Sirnes and Neguin Yavari. I am also grateful to the Christian Michelsen Institute in Bergen, and especially to Kari Telle, for allowing me to revise my manuscript in the most beautiful location imaginable. This volume was written in association with the project on Comparative Ethics of War at the International Peace Research Institute Oslo (PRIO).

New York, June 2008   F.D.

PREFACE

Though it was an illegal practice under the Taliban, photographs continued to be taken in secret studios across Afghanistan during their rule. With the country's invasion by coalition forces following the 9/11 attacks, many of these studios and their rolls of negatives came to light, courtesy of an enterprising German photojournalist who published the previously illicit images of ordinary Afghans and even Taliban fighters posing against elaborate backdrops.[1] Dressed in street clothes and equipped with guns of various sorts, men and boys are depicted in such photographs standing or sitting before Swiss chalets and other pastoral settings, both European and Asian, with bunches of plastic flowers making up the rest of the décor. One such image appears on the cover of this book. However criminal they might have been, these portraits are not in the least idiosyncratic, illustrating despite their display of firearms a set of standard poses and generic backgrounds familiar across wide swathes of South and Central Asia. Indeed the Alpine scenes so popular among the Taliban's subjects are sold in glossy and outsize formats on the streets of African and Asian cities, their originals having been filmed as settings for many a Bollywood romp.

So common are these pastoral scenes that they form a significant part of militant imagery as well, especially on video and websites commemorating suicide bombers and other martyrs, whose portraits are frequently set amidst verdant landscapes and surrounded by flowers.[2] Such depictions no doubt invoke traditional Muslim visions of paradise, but they are also examples of kitsch as a global form that belongs to no par-

---

1   Thomas Dworzak, *Taliban* (London: Trolley, 2003).

2   For a collection of these images see "The Islamic imagery project: visual motifs in jihadi Internet propaganda", Combating Terrorism Center, Department of Social Sciences, United States Military Academy at West Point, March 2006 (http://www.ctc.usma.edu).

ticular religion. There is an intimate relationship between the Taliban fighter photographed before a Swiss chalet and pictures, popular since the nineteenth century, of Jesus knocking at the door of a similar building. Interesting about all these images is the fact that none of their subjects belong to the settings in which they seem to have strayed. Whether it is Jesus in a German village, Indian film stars on a Swiss mountainside or a Saudi martyr in a landscape with waterfalls, these figures are all set apart from their surroundings. While it might appear at first glance as if this merely reinforces the fantasmatic nature of such backdrops, a closer look reveals that exactly the opposite is true: it is everyday reality that these terrorists, martyrs and men about town seem detached from, with their clothes, guns and demeanour alienated from quotidian use in studied poses.[3]

For the most part such armed figures manage to avoid the action-hero mannerisms popularized by Hollywood, also departing the latter's ideals of masculinity by their limpid expressions and sometimes androgynously painted or retouched faces. This is the ideal not only of the Afghan men photographed in clandestine studios, but also of Al-Qaeda's martyrs, who are meant to be more beautiful in death than they ever were in life. If smiling lads point pistols at each other in these photographs, or militants appear on videotape firing semi-automatic weapons, this does little to alter the curious repose that marks such images. Many of the Taliban photographs, for instance, portray gunmen clasping hands or looking into the camera with hands over their hearts in poses of humble welcome. Yet this departure from Hollywood stereotypes by no means indicates the presence of some alternative aesthetic in the wilder reaches of the Hindu Kush, since such local histories of the Muslim imagination have become globalized in the form of kitsch, which now provides a powerful medium for the transmission of militant as well as pacific ideals. Of course not all of these ideals take the form of kitsch, though each moves horizontally, connecting people separated by history, geography and language through media in the way that fashion

---

3   For discussions of the history and significance of this aesthetic, see Arjun Appadurai, "The colonial backdrop", *Afterimage*, vol. 24, issue 5, March/April 1997, pp. 4-7, and Christopher Pinney, *Camera Indica: The Social Life of Indian Photographs* (London: Reaktion, 1997).

or advertising does, and not vertically by the kind of indoctrination that requires a hierarchically controlled environment to function.

Whatever the local context of militant practices, they possess a global form facilitated by the random connectivity of technology and spectacle, whose history passes through the printing presses, studios and cinema sets of the last two centuries as much as it descends through the Quran and its commentaries. However ephemeral these connections, their consequences for militant behaviour are as significant as those of media and advertising upon consumer behaviour worldwide, itself by no means a trivial matter. Partisans of Al-Qaeda are mindful of the global form their practices take, and try hard to lend them planetary significance. But unlike communism or even fundamentalism in the past, this significance does not lie in the attempt to create an alternative model of political and economic life on a global scale, given that the moral virtues favoured by militants neither presume nor require a revolutionized society for their instantiation. Instead these men speak from within the world of their enemies and seem to possess no place outside it. Like the kitsch forms they often take, militant ideals subvert our political reality from the inside, if only by exceeding it with the violent lustre of their hyperreality. So despite the exotic appearance of its minions, it is only natural that Al-Qaeda should lack a utopia of its own.

If Osama bin Laden speaks so familiarly of his foes, it is because he employs the same categories as they do, in particular those of humanism, humanitarianism and human rights. By invoking such terms the men associated with Al-Qaeda signal their interest in the shared values and common destiny of mankind. Indeed militant rhetoric is full of clichés about the threats of nuclear apocalypse or environmental collapse posed by the arrogance and avarice of states and corporations that happen also to threaten Muslims around the world. Those who defend Muslims, then, automatically protect the common interests of the human race. Once the threat supposedly levelled at Muslims by the United States and its clients is defined in these familiar terms, militant rhetoric can no longer remain something traditional or foreign. In fact its global influence is based precisely on stereotypes that are shared across the planet. This book is about the globalization of militancy by way of such planetary ideals. It focuses on humanity as the ideal that permits terrorism to stake its claim to a global arena in the most powerful way.

1

SLEEPING BEAUTY

Osama bin Laden and his lieutenant Ayman al-Zawahiri have repeatedly offered a truce to countries anywhere in the world that cease attacking Muslims, for instance by withdrawing from the coalitions engaged in the invasion and occupation of Afghanistan or Iraq. The proposed truce was first announced on 15 April 2004 by way of a video communiqué smuggled out of Afghanistan on an audiotape and later broadcast on the pan-Arab television stations Al-Jazeera and Al-Arabiyya:

So I present to them this peace proposal, which is essentially a commitment to cease operations against any state that pledges not to attack Muslims or interfere in their affairs, including the American conspiracy against the great Islamic world. This peace can be renewed at the end of a government's term and at the beginning of a new one, with the consent of both sides. It will come into effect on the departure of its last soldier from our lands, and it is available for a period of three months from the day this statement is broadcast.[1]

On the one hand such a truce was rightly dismissed as media rhetoric in the West, largely because it had no institutional backing—Al-Qaeda's leaders being inaccessible and possessing no party, army or state that might be negotiated with. After all the movement's founders were themselves in hiding and incapable of exerting any control over the suicide bombers they inspired.[2] But on the other hand by taking the

---

1   Bruce Lawrence (ed.), *Messages to the World: The Statements of Osama Bin Laden* (London: Verso, 2005), p. 235.

2   I know terms like "suicide bomber", "terrorist" or "fundamentalist" are not generally used by the people they define and often possess a polemical rather than scholarly character. They also belong to different histories that bear little resemblance to the one with which I am concerned. Thus "fundamentalist" comes from the history of American Protestantism, where it names churches dedicated

trouble to reject Bin Laden's offer formally, European governments lent his words a degree of credibility and even a kind of nameless reality, recognizing in this way that their politics could no longer be confined to its traditional forms and institutions. Since then calls by senior political and military figures in Europe to "negotiate" with Al-Qaeda have proliferated, alongside furious denunciations of any such attempts at "appeasement", and all this despite the fact that there is nothing and nobody to talk to—apart from a great many disconnected persons and a small number of media personalities.[3]

While it used the language of traditional politics, Al-Qaeda's truce represented something quite new. Bereft of institutional features like negotiation, arbitration and contractual guarantees, it was a truce that had lost one kind of political meaning without having gained another, since trust was the only thing that either side had to offer. It was as if such everyday terms had come to serve as the bridge to a new, and yet unknown politics that took for its arena the globe in its entirety. Notwithstanding its dismissal by Western governments, the groundless trust upon which this truce was based achieved an ambiguous political reality in the public debate that followed Al-Qaeda's offer, with Spain's withdrawal of troops from Iraq after the Madrid bombings that year

---

to a direct and literal reading of the Bible. Similarly "terrorist" no longer retains its original reference to Europe's secular and indeed antireligious revolutionaries. I continue nevertheless to use these terms here because they have become commonplace and cannot therefore be divorced from those used by militants themselves, with which they now possess a conjoined history. For not only do the Muslims so described routinely invoke these names if only to dispute them, thus turning their own terms into oppositional ones, they sometimes even accept these nominations in however qualified a fashion. This is true of the word fundamentalist as much as it is of terrorist. In any case replacing bad terms with good ones often results in nothing more than the wholesale transfer of the former meaning into the latter, insofar as both are deployed as stereotypes. This is what has happened with the word Islamist, now used even in popular culture to replace fundamentalist, which at least had the virtue of naming practices across religious lines. Islamist, of course, has no comparative reference. The stereotyped terms I use, on the other hand, retain their passionate and oppositional quality, which is exactly what I am interested in, while their everyday definitions are at the same time belied by the use I make of them. And so while I am sympathetic to the cause of correct definitions, I am not interested here in the politics of naming, leaving this task for those more qualified than myself.

3   For a detailed sociological study of Al-Qaeda's institutional fragmentation see Marc Sageman, *Leaderless Jihad: Terror Networks in the Twenty-First Century* (Philadelphia: University of Pennsylvania Press, 2008).

widely being seen as an acceptance of Bin Laden's terms. Indeed Spaniards seemed to have accepted this truce even before it was offered when they elected an anti-war government three days after the blasts on 11 March 2004. While the new Spanish government, in other words, had reasons for withdrawing from Iraq that had nothing to do with Osama bin Laden's truce, his videotape hijacked the politics of this European state by inserting it into another kind of global narrative.

But what kind of truce was this in which neither institutions nor discussions were involved—since Al-Qaeda's political invisibility robbed even the Spanish state of its institutional character by appearing to force its withdrawal of troops from Iraq on the basis of trust alone? The extraordinary spectacle of a European state coerced into acting out of good faith by a terrorist on the run somewhere in the Hindu Kush was made possible by the global media, which did not simply represent or even influence politics but actually took its place. For in the absence of institutional forms like negotiations and guarantees, not even behind the proverbial scenes, publicity served as the only medium for Osama bin Laden's truce, which it also guaranteed in a purely declarative way. In other words it was precisely the authority of a warrior incapable of engaging in battle, and living in fear of his life, that gave his words credibility in the eyes of friends and enemies alike. Osama bin Laden's peace proposal is important as an example of militancy trying to found a global politics outside inherited forms and institutions. For with the dispersal of its founders during the Anglo-American invasion of Afghanistan, Al-Qaeda has itself outgrown whatever institutional form it once possessed to become the trademark for a set of ideas and practices that are franchised by militants the world over.[4]

Having dispensed with the parties, armies and states of old for dispersed networks trademarked by the Al-Qaeda logo, our militants lack even an ideology. Indeed we shall see how their fighters jettison Islamic law itself as a political model to make an individual duty out of it, for however international their claims, ideologies have classically been focused on the nation state. Without the grounding provided by such

---

4   The global dispersal of militancy into a "phantom" or "imaginary" organization in which unconnected units are tied together by a name, method and manifesto has received ample theoretical justification by jihadists. For a detailed study of one such theoretician see Brynjar Lia, *Architect of Global Jihad: The Life of Al-Qaeda Strategist Abu Mus'ab al-Suri* (London: Hurst, 2007).

a state, they begin to fragment, and one is left with lines of thinking rather than a system of thought. This precisely is the case of Al-Qaeda's franchise, which has lost ideology to the degree that it has abandoned the nation state and with it Islamic law as a model, claiming territory only in the abstract terms of a global caliphate. By this I do not mean to downplay local or traditional forms of militancy, only to suggest that the global reach of militant networks associated with the brand name Al-Qaeda increasingly gives even such regional practices their radical meaning and mobility. So the authors of a report on Iraqi insurgent media point out that even the most localized and nationalist of militant outfits there, including those that set themselves against Al-Qaeda, take the sophisticated media products of such global jihad movements as their visual and rhetorical models. Given the parlous state of Iraq's infrastructure, the collectively and sometimes transnationally produced websites or videos these outfits release are not even targeted at a domestic audience, which therefore gains access to them only by way of news media based outside the country.[5]

Local forms of Islamic militancy are therefore increasingly mediated by global conditions rather than the other way around, for however traditional their aims, such militant practices end up losing their political meaning in a global arena that bestows on them an existential dimension in return. Thus a number of militant groups in Pakistan or Afghanistan appear to rely increasingly upon Al-Qaeda's name and technique to achieve both their global reputations and connections, however local their aims and operations might in fact be.[6] And it is exactly the existential dimension of such globalization that is deserving of scrutiny, because it signals the political fragmentation of militancy in a planetary arena whose lack of institutional forms ends up diverting its violence into the practices of everyday life, whether in the form of ordinary individuals plotting jihad online, or school friends concocting bombs in suburban basements. These disconnected and unrelated participants in Islam's long-distance militancy do not simply serve as

---

5   See Daniel Kimmage and Kathleen Ridolfo, *Iraqi Insurgent Media: The War of Images and Ideas* (Washington: Radio Free Europe/Radio Liberty, 2007).

6   See for instance Syed Saleem Shahzad, "The rise and rise of Al-Qaeda, part I: militants make a claim for talks", *Asia Times Online*, January 18, 2008 (http://www.atimes.com/atimes/South_Asia/JA18Df02.html).

the sympathetic supplements of some short-range politics, but instead reach out beyond the latter's calculations and transform its practices, constituting the local by the global in ways that no longer permit the former's politicization in any traditional way.

The importance of a global arena to militancy is demonstrated by the fact that terrorist outfits of the most varied description, even those in places like Iraq that deal with explicitly local causes, very commonly describe themselves by using an Arabic word, *alam*, that has come to define the globe as opposed to the world or *dunya*, this latter still being linked to the old religious idea of worldliness and so aligned with politics as a profane activity while at the same time being juxtaposed to the afterlife.[7] For the globe represents not worldliness but rather existence as such, including that of humanity as a whole, and so cannot be partitioned between friend and enemy, or the material and the spiritual, in any old fashioned way. The earth or *ardh* is similarly discarded in militant rhetoric, only appearing in some quotations deployed from the Quran, its reference as a ground for the action of human or divine subjects having been replaced sometimes by a vision of the globe as pure geometry and at other times by the planet as an object of conquest. In its sheer gigantism, therefore, the planet that militants describe appears to have stretched beyond the language of politics as much as religion, so that the logos and emblems of jihadi groups frequently represent it as an abstract and completely foreign entity to be conquered and assimilated into the experience of Muslim life. Entirely typical instances of this are images of the globe planted with a flag bearing the Islamic credo or skewered by a scimitar like some monstrous kebab.

Unlike Muslim politics of a previous generation, the new militancy is concerned neither with national states nor with international ideologies, though like other global movements dedicated to the environment or peace it does not seek to overturn these, taking instead the globe and all who inhabit it for sites of action. This is perhaps why Al-Qaeda's advocates often recast the geography of Islam, replacing political references like Iraq or Afghanistan with historical ones, like Mesopotamia

---

7   Of course the word *alam* also possesses religious meaning, being used in the Quran to describe cosmic worlds and multiple universes. But in modern times this word's plural form, so important in the holy book, tends to be infrequently deployed, and then too in a prosaic and metaphorical sense, while its singular form has come to refer to the globe as an existential totality.

and Khurasan, that fall between rather than within political boundaries. And even when countries are mentioned or depicted by militants, it is often in an explicitly global context where the US is viewed as part of a planetary crusader axis, and Iraq a portion of the global Muslim community under attack. Thus images of maps on jihad websites tend to locate particular countries in a planetary context, represent them floating in space like moons with the earth as a background, or portray them bleeding from wounds like parts of a global body.[8] For alongside the environmentalists or pacifists who I will argue are their intellectual peers, the men and women inspired by Al-Qaeda's militancy consider Muslim suffering to be a "humanitarian" cause that, like climate change or nuclear proliferation, must be addressed globally or not at all. So these militants take the whole planet as their arena of operations, shifting their attention from one site of Muslim suffering to another as if in a parody of humanitarian action, which indeed provides the paradoxical model for their violence.[9]

But the globalization of militancy has resulted in its fragmentation, this loss of institutional politics being compensated for by the invocation of humanity as both the agent and object of a planetary politics yet

---

8   See "The Islamic imagery project: visual motifs in jihadi Internet propaganda".

9   The philosopher Adi Ophir describes the relationship between terrorists and humanitarians like this: "The structural similarities between these two phenomena are striking (and embarrassing). Let us mention them briefly: transnational networks lacking a center (or having a center that is contingent and temporary); exemplary models of voluntary, heroic action that are quickly reproduced and distributed across the globe, breeding imitators and enjoying the admiration of large audiences that are not directly involved in the context where the model of action originated; the sacrifice and expenditure of resources taken out of regular cycles of commercial and political exchange for the sake of a goal that it portrayed as higher than the usual goals of everyday political or economic action; nomad practices and mobility that make it possible to land and sojourn for both short and long periods anywhere on the globe, combined with an in-depth interest in a particular locality, carefully chosen and meticulously studied; a special interest in bare life and a more or less systematic tendency to depoliticize the victims' bodies; a certain changing balance between spectacular and clandestine aspects of the operation; a certain indifference—in theory, if not always in practice—to the territorial and symbolic borders of the nation-state; and, finally, the use of religious discourse, which is not peculiar to terrorists, and even traditional philanthropic practices and organizations associated with religious institutions". See Ophir's "The Sovereign, the Humanitarian, and the Terrorist" in Michel Feher, Gaelle Krikorian and Yates McKee (eds.), *Nongovernmental Politics* (New York: Zone Books, 2007), p. 175.

to come. Indeed we shall see that Osama bin Laden, Ayman al-Zawahiri and the scattered flock they inspire refer almost obsessively to humanity in its modern incarnation as the sum total of the world's inhabitants, whose well-being is measured by the twin practices of humanitarianism and human rights. In the eyes of these men, Muslims are not members of a religious group so much as the contemporary representatives of human suffering. And so those who go under the name Al-Qaeda do not for the most part target their enemies for holding mistaken religious beliefs or godless secular principles, but instead for betraying their own vision of a world subject to human rights. Whatever bad faith is involved in such an accusation, the crucial role it plays in the rhetoric of terrorism needs to be accounted for, given that arguments about humanity take precedence in this rhetoric over the scriptural citations whose medieval exoticism has seduced so many of those studying Al-Qaeda.

Anchored though they may legally be in the nation-state, human rights and humanitarianism in general provide militants with the terms by which to imagine a global politics of the future. In this way our terrorists have done nothing more than take up humanity's historical role, which in earlier times was linked to the civilizing mission of European imperialism. In fact the promotion of human rights as a global project emerged within such empires while at the same time providing their justification. One has only to think of the abolition of slavery and Britain's attempt to enforce its proscription outside her jurisdiction, along with the suppression of barbaric customs more generally, to realize that imperialism was in addition to everything else a humanitarian enterprise ostensibly dedicated to securing the lives and wellbeing of human beings in general.[10] Indeed given that the language of citizenship was largely absent from colonial rule, it is perhaps no accident that its place there was taken by that of humanity instead. It is possible even in our own times to see imperialism at work as a global project in the steady replacement of the citizen by the human being, whose biological security now routinely trumps his rights of citizenship in anti-terror measures at home and humanitarian interventions abroad.

If imperialism broke the ground for a new kind of global politics based on humanitarianism, its foundations have been laid by the hu-

---

10   I am grateful to Sudipta Sen for drawing my attention to this point.

manitarian interventions of post-colonial states, which include not only the great powers but even former colonies like India, whose intervention in the Pakistani civil war of 1971 represented one of the early forms that such a politics took. For its own part Pakistan was a pioneer in the invocation of humanitarian language to describe both militant "self-defence" in the valley of Kashmir and the "violations" to which India subjected its people.[11] Since neither colonial nor postcolonial states have been able to instantiate a global humanitarian order, not least because they have been unwilling to sacrifice the politics of national and other interests for its sake, I will make the case that militants today aim at their unfulfilled goal. And in this way they are no different than the plethora of non-governmental agencies dedicated to humanitarian work. Indeed the accusation common among militants and NGOs, of the West being hypocritical in its promotion of human rights, is meant not to discredit but rather complete the latter's globalization. These examples illustrate how intimately terrorist practices are linked with those of their enemies, whose humanitarian interventions also invariably kill some civilians in the name of protecting others.

My object in this book is to argue that a global society has come into being, but possesses as yet no political institutions proper to its name, and that new forms of militancy, like that of Al-Qaeda, achieve meaning in this institutional vacuum, while representing in their own way the search for a global politics. But from environmentalism to pacifism and beyond, such a politics can only be one that takes humanity itself as its object, not least because the threat of nuclear weapons or global warming can only be conceived of in human rather than national or even international terms. And so militant practices are informed by the same search that animates humanitarianism, which from human rights to humanitarian intervention has become the rhetorical aim and global signature of all politics today.[12] This is the search for humanity as an agent and not simply the victim of history. While they possess different meanings and genealogies deriving from eighteenth-century revolutions on the one hand to nineteenth-century colonialism on the

11   I want to thank Meenakshi Ganguly for pointing this history out to me.

12   Yet to be published, Brendan O'Neill's richly suggestive new work is devoted precisely to examining this connection between the practices of militancy and those of humanitarian aid.

other, we shall see that words like human rights and humanitarianism have since the Cold War been predicated of humanity as a new global reality, one whose collective life we can for the first time contemplate altering by our deeds either of omission or of commission. So for the militants among us, victimized Muslims represent not their religion so much as humanity itself, and terrorism the effort to turn mankind into an historical actor—since it is after all the globe's only possible actor. For environmentalists and pacifists as much as for our holy warriors, a global humanity has in this way replaced an international proletariat as the Sleeping Beauty of history.

A global history of militant ideals

Al-Qaeda's Spanish truce allows us to see how it is that globalization might provide the very substance of militant practices while still lacking an institutional politics. Yet globalization is the most ambiguous of processes, which, despite its current celebrity, remains curiously undefined as an analytical or historical category. On the one hand it seems to evoke the primacy of movement, whether of people, goods, ideas or money, that has supposedly increased to an unprecedented level both in rapidity and in extent. On the other hand globalization evokes a theory of capitalism that would enclose all the social possibilities and experiential implications of such movement within a singular history of economic reach. In either case this movement is supposed to be made possible in large part by new technologies, which thus mediate it as a kind of ever-renewed present, globalization as the newest of the new.

The problem with conceiving of globalization as a movement mediated by technology into some ever-renewed present is that it ceases to have a past, properly speaking. And this is because the difference between its form of movement and any other is one of degree rather than of kind. For instance how is the Internet more illustrative of globalization than the telegraph, or today's virtual economy more global than yesterday's finance capitalism? No matter how radical their repercussions, do the new technologies mark new beginnings, or do they simply exist in the wake of older ones? This problem of historical and analytical regress exists only because accounts of globalization tend to be seduced both by the narcissism of the present, and by the glamorous novelty of its objects or experiences, in the process quite dispensing with the term's intellectual genealogy. But it is precisely this genealogy that may allow us to lend the globe some historical as well as conceptual substance.

When was it that the globe, and therefore the possibility of globalization, ceased to be a classroom model or a geographical abstraction and became real? At what point did the globe part company with the notion of world, itself connected to a particular religious history in terms like worldliness, to mark a new beginning? Languages like French, of course, continue to derive globalization (*mondialisation*) from the older notion of world (*monde*), thus linking it back to another kind of history. The earth, too, continues to be used as a synonym for the globe, though its frame of reference is the solar system rather than humanity's political or ecological existence.[13] Nevertheless there is a point when we can say that the globe subordinates all these competitors and becomes, as it were, global, a point we can for our purposes locate during the Cold War. The latter made today's militancy possible by lending political reality to previously abstract categories like the global Muslim community, which is why Al-Qaeda's acolytes very self-consciously derive their jihad from its last great battle in Afghanistan. For it was during the Cold War that two great ideals shaping the practices of both militants and their enemies, the globe as well as the humanity that inhabits it, achieved an ambiguous political reality.

The Cold War had for the first time put the globe itself at stake in the practice of politics, by dividing it into two rival hemispheres.[14] Moreover two of its greatest technological events, the atom bomb and the moon landing, permitted us not only to grasp and see the globe as such, but also and in the same moment to conceive of its destruction and abandonment. In this way Cold War technology simultaneously consolidated and transformed the earlier but more abstract experience afforded us by the globe's circumnavigation. The earth, then, like some gigantic commodity, is known only in the moment of its consumption as something capable of being destroyed or abandoned. This apocalyptic manner of knowing the planet allows thought in general, and religious

---

13   I am indebted to Carol Breckenridge for pointing this fact out to me.

14   For the globe's emergence as a new kind of political arena, see Carl Schmitt, *The Nomos of the Earth*, trans. G.C. Ulmen (New York: Telos Press, 2003).

thought in particular, to contemplate as real something that had been denied legitimacy for two centuries—the end of the world. It is in the rapture of apocalypse that the world is destroyed and the globe born, even if only as the ghost of this world.

The birth of the globe during the Cold War did not go unnoticed, its implications being noted by the philosopher Hannah Arendt among others. In an essay on her colleague and friend Karl Jaspers, who had himself expounded the phenomenology of a nuclear apocalypse, Arendt wrote about the ironic global unity that the atom bomb had made possible:

It is true, for the first time in history all peoples on earth have a common present: no event of any importance in the history of one country can remain a marginal accident in the history of any other. Every country has become the almost immediate neighbor of every other country, and every man feels the shock of events which take place at the other side of the globe. But this common factual present is not based on a common past and does not in the least guarantee a common future. Technology, having provided the unity of the world, can just as easily destroy it and the means of global communication were designed side by side with means of possible global destruction.[15]

The question Hannah Arendt tackles in her essay is not the practical one of how to prevent an apocalypse, but rather one that interrogates the new experience that its destructive possibilities brings into being. Apocalypse, in other words, refers in her essay not to the brute fact of nuclear destruction, nor to the ecological holocaust that is its heir. It names rather the new experience of the globe and thus of humanity also that the very possibility of this destruction brings to light. So according to Arendt the unity of the globe that technology produces is purely negative because it is based neither on a common past nor on a common future, relying instead on the experience of an evacuated present in which disparate histories mingle promiscuously. The reality of globalization, in other words, is premised upon an apocalypse that has not occurred, something that lends its experience an anticipatory though not necessarily a millenarian character, as its cause is human and not divine.

Yet the experience of a possible apocalypse is a manifestly inhuman one, since the globe's desolation can only be conceived from a point

---

15   Hannah Arendt, "Karl Jaspers: citizen of the world?" in *Men in Dark Times* (San Diego, New York and London: Harcourt Brace Jovanovich, 1995), p. 83.

of view set outside it, and therefore outside human reality as well. In theory modern science had accepted the inhumanity of such an experience well before the Cold War, by repudiating both geocentric and anthropocentric points of view, so that nuclear physicists had no hesitation in splitting the atom the moment it became possible to do so.[16] But it took the atom bomb and the moon landing to make this experience part of everyday reality. To see the globe, and the humanity that inhabits it, as if from outer space, is to abandon a humanistic point of view by abandoning the scale at which human beings live, defined as this is by the horizon of their senses.[17] From such a distance the globe and its inhabitants can only be approached in a technical way, by interventions of constructive as much as destructive import, whose agents end up losing their own humanity in the process. To be capable of approaching the globe and its inhabitants technically is to be almost divine. The globe is therefore strictly speaking an inhuman reality, or rather one that renders humanism and its point of view redundant.

The globe becomes real at the same time as humanity, which serves both as the agent and the victim of its possible demise. For mankind is now no longer an ideal or an abstraction, but a reality too insofar as it is capable of being destroyed.[18] Indeed in this sense humanity achieves reality in the same way as the human being, by recognizing its own mortality, though humanity's gigantic reality is of course as inhuman as that of the globe. It is the technology of destruction and abandonment that permits humanity to emerge as an historical actor for the first time by undoing the particularity of its own origins. Thus it is mankind, rather than the United States of America, which became the true agent of global events like the atom bomb or moon landing.

The Cold War provided the origins of globalization as this term is used today, and in particular as it lends substance to new forms of militancy by making the Muslim community into a global reality for the first time along with the humanity it represents. It did so by replacing the world with the globe and man by mankind, all within the horizon demarcated by an apocalyptic technology, whose power subordinated

---

16   See for this Hannah Arendt, "The conquest of space and the stature of man" in *Between Past and Future* (New York: Penguin Books, 1993), p. 276.

17   Ibid. p. 278.

18   Arendt, *Men in Dark Times*, p. 82.

all links with the past to the false unity of a global present in which distinct historical traditions come to be juxtaposed with one another. In the process globalization came to replace internationalism, which had been the ideology both of the European empires and of the Communist bloc. These orders were international because they were based on the expansion of a substance (civilization, justice, freedom and the like) in territories that were connected either by geographical or by historical contiguities. Globalization, on the other hand, depends neither on the diffusion of a substance, nor upon historical and political links, but precisely on the unintended effects and consequences that constitute its universal present.

The apocalyptic tone of Cold War thinking might have dissipated today, but its spirit continues to haunt globalization. So the atom bomb has been replaced by ecological and other threats that all take on the characteristics of an explosion, insofar as they are capable of wreaking havoc upon a humanity made interdependent by technology. Such bombs need not even destroy human lives to mimic and indeed foreshadow the global effect of their nuclear cousins. Media, for example, continually ape the apocalyptic effect of an empty present, because they bring together widely scattered constituencies in the contemplation of an event deemed newsworthy even if it occurs in some remote corner of the world with which these audiences have no real connection, and which does not even represent a substance spread by connections of geography or history. The rupture with internationalism here is absolute because the global effect of the media's information bomb is not due to consequences that go beyond particular intentions, but rather to the false unity of a present made possible by ideas, events and fashions that can only function randomly once separated from local histories.

It is the apocalyptic nature of globalization that might explain why Al-Qaeda's mobile and dispersed militants are not linked vertically, by a common origin, organization or purpose, but horizontally by sartorial, linguistic and terrorist practices made available through the media much like fashions in dress, music or behavior are. However local their aims and origins, therefore, such men are connected by global practices that lend them an existential rather than historical or political unity. In the spring of 2008, for instance, revelations that an American soldier in Iraq had used a copy of the Quran for target practice led to demonstrations in Afghanistan at which three protesters were killed. While it is clear that these demonstrations had little connection with anything going on in Iraq, it is also evident that the protests could not be confined to their locality. Such practices are global not merely because they happen to be dispersed across the planet, but also because they are meant to appropriate and even colonize it as a site of militant activity by the creation of violent spectacles.[19] Rather than existing for these terrorists as some imaginary and in any case predefined arena of operations, the globe is both produced and inhabited by them in the form of televised events.

The shape of things to come

How is it possible to be a political actor in the false unity of a globalization with no common past or future—one in which mankind has replaced man as the agent and victim of history? This precisely is the problem of militancy, whose votaries know that while everyone today speaks of a single world and a single humanity, neither one nor the other has a political life of its own. At most there exists the partial humanity of aid and relief work, defined in numerical terms as a mass of victims who cannot all be ministered to. Humanitarianism thus operates by a calculus in which the lesser number of victims must be sacrificed for the greater. Like terrorism, in other words, it depends upon sacrificing the few for the many—which also means sacrificing those suffering smaller afflictions in order to attend to bigger ones. And just like Al-Qaeda's militants, humanitarian agencies have abandoned previously exempt subjects like women and children to this calculus of sacrifice, thus bringing humanity into being in the same way as an atomic holocaust, by number alone. Here, then, is a fine example of the inhuman nature of gigantic realities like humanity, which can only be approached by technical means.

The experience of globalization made possible by the atom bomb defines the humanity that both militants and humanitarians are concerned with in quite specific ways. Writing after the First World War, for example, the jurist Carl Schmitt had argued that the emergence of humanity as a political category entailed the appearance of its opposite as well. The very idea of fighting a war for humanity, after all, makes the enemy into

---

19   I am grateful to Luc Boltanski for making this point clear to me.

someone not quite human who might be sacrificed without scruple.[20] For Schmitt, then, humanity becomes real only by practising the most inhuman cruelty. Putting this argument in another way, the philosopher Etienne Balibar has noted that attempts to instantiate humanity tend to be racist in character because they result in a hierarchy of those who are more and those who are less human, this process of exclusion providing the only way by which humanity might become manifest.[21] The atom bomb, however, produces a truly inclusive form of humanity, whose suicidal potential no longer allows its inhuman or subhuman opposite to remain external to itself, instead absorbing them into its own gigantic reality. The idea of a suicidal humanity became a political truism in the atomic age, and now defines the victims of other potential holocausts, whether environmental or even terrorist. For is not the suicide bomber only the miniaturized version of a suicidal humanity?

My comparison of today's suicide bomber with yesterday's suicidal humanity is not a casual one, for we shall see that neither is able to externalize its inhuman opposite, since in both cases the human lives alongside the inhuman and dies a collective death with it. This inability to isolate the enemy from oneself has made suicidal violence into a technical procedure internal to humanity rather than yet another way of eliminating an alien threat. After all the atom bomb has replaced the old threats of blood, race and demography that had once put a biological conception of humanity at risk from "Jews", "Blacks" or "Asians", and continues to do so in the regional politics of xenophobia or genocide. Even the global spectre of a biological holocaust, in pandemics and panics about AIDS, SARS or avian flu, continues to shed racial particularity and become a threat internal to humanity itself, from which no-one is immune, and for which no-one can be blamed. Like the carrier of such a virus, the suicide bomber can no longer be differentiated from other human beings by his ethnicity, language or country, but only by a religion that, as with communism in the past, is threatening precisely because it cannot be biologically determined. The militant's own enemy

---

20   Carl Schmitt, *The Concept of the Political*, trans. George Schwab (The University of Chicago Press, 1996), p. 54.

21   Etienne Balibar, trans. James Swenson, "Racism as universalism" in *Masses, Classes, Ideas: Studies on Politics and Philosophy Before and After Marx* (New York and London: Routledge, 1994).

is biologically even less determined, and includes Muslims as well as infidels to constitute a cross-section of humanity.

Technology rather than biology provides the threat of nuclear, environmental and terrorist destruction, not least because the gigantic reality that is global humanity cannot be grasped except by technical means such as wars of humanitarian intervention or donations of humanitarian relief, whose chief products in either case are mortality statistics. And this is because everything that is global is also inhuman, or at least beyond the ken of humanism. For the suicide bomber, however, this technology has for the first time ceased to be prosthetic, something whose danger was derived from mankind's loss of control over it. Having domesticated the technology of destruction in the shape of cell phones, household chemicals and public transportation, the suicide bomber is feared for his willingness to die and not because he might accidentally set off a chain reaction, or inadvertently cause an ecological apocalypse. While the destructive potential of terrorism, in other words, is minor and even insignificant in comparison with other kinds of technological holocaust, it is more obviously suicidal than the latter and can therefore stand in for them. This is probably what accounts for the extraordinary fear and hatred felt by some in the West for militant Islam, such widespread passions having last been seen in the anti-communist hysteria of the Cold War.

Great efforts are made, on the part of militants as well as of their enemies, to link the nightmare of an ecological or nuclear apocalypse with Al-Qaeda by talk of things like weapons of mass destruction. However opportunistic these identifications, they do indicate a deliberate effort to make the struggle with Islamic terrorism into the Cold War's heir. The suicide bomber's act gains some of its notoriety from the suicidal character of politics itself in the atomic age, whose great novelty it is to weaken the instrumental logic of technical action by putting its own agent at risk. After all, gigantic realities like the globe and humanity not only push the subject who would grasp them out of a geocentric or anthropocentric point of view, they also end up making his own existence impossibly abstract. No longer a humanist subject, the individual serves as an example of humanity itself as a global fact, one which cannot provide a mere backdrop for this individual, having stepped to the foreground and overwhelmed him. This is why the humanist subject no longer provides the model for humanity, which was once seen as an aggregation of such individuals. Instead the species is anthropomorphised as a subject in its own right, one that turns all individuals into its exemplars. Any individual who would approach the globe and its inhabitants by technical means ceases to be properly human, for the only entity that might survive this encounter is humanity itself in all its gigantic reality. By bringing a global humanity to the fore, the atomic age sacrifices humanism and even the human being. Indeed the latter is asked to sacrifice himself for the former just as the suicide bomber sacrifices himself for the global Muslim community that I will argue represents humanity as such.

Once it becomes possible for humanity to commit suicide, politics of a traditional sort starts to lose meaning, giving way to a logic of sacrifice that might set the stage for a new political life at the planetary level, but that does not yet possess institutional form, if only because the possibility of a global apocalypse represents a risk quite beyond the calculus of interests that defines statecraft. For any politics that results in mutually assured destruction loses its character to become a sovereign and even capricious act of risk and sacrifice. This at least is the thesis that Karl Jaspers propounds in a celebrated book on the nuclear brinkmanship of the Cold War, in which he tells us how sacrifice has come to dominate political life today.[22] The possibility of nuclear war, claims Jaspers, confronts us with two choices—the sacrifice of humanity for the sake of politics or of politics for that of humanity. In either case, humanity now becomes manifest in sacrifice alone.[23] This fact is fully recognized by those who campaign against nuclear war as much as against global warming, depending as they do upon a language of sacrifice to prevent sacrifice. Thus sacrificing a politics dedicated to the acquisition of wealth and power in the form of deforestation or carbon emissions is seen as being essential to preventing the sacrifice of humanity itself in an atomic or environmental apocalypse.

Environmental and pacifist movements today can only describe a global politics of the future using the vocabulary of sacrifice—more precisely that of yesterday's politics both national and international.

22   Karl Jaspers, *The Future of Mankind*, trans. E.B. Ashton (Chicago: The University of Chicago Press, 1961).

23   Ibid., pp. 171-2.

Occurring as it does in the wake of these great sacrificial movements, militancy derives much of its rhetorical charge by partaking of their effects. Moreover Osama bin Laden and his acolytes mention the threat of a nuclear or environmental catastrophe frequently, and very deliberately place the supposed threat that the West poses Muslims in their context. This threat, in other words, is seen to take as its object neither Islam nor any particular Muslim population, but the Muslim community itself as a global fact. Yet the Muslim community's biological survival is never put in question by militants, only that of the human race as a whole in a nuclear or environmental conflagration. In this sense Muslims are indeed conceived as representing humanity, with their acts of sacrifice seen as attempts to prevent a far greater sacrifice and turn humanity into the master of its own destiny. However the point of this sacrifice, as Jaspers would have it, is that while not political in any normative sense, it serves as an invitation to a politics of the future. I shall return to this statement in a subsequent chapter of this book, though whatever else it might be, a sacrificial practice like suicide bombing is not only a transitional phenomenon, but one possessing an existential dimension that cannot be reduced to politics in its institutional and instrumental form.

Karl Jaspers points to Gandhi as the chief and indeed only global example of modernity's sacrificial logic, though he well knew that the Mahatma's practice of sacrifice preceded the Cold War.[24] This latter-day apostle of nonviolence commented rather frequently on the place of sacrifice in an atomic age during his last years, though Jaspers did not cite him on the subject. Gandhi had come to embody sacrifice in its global form, not only because he inspired its practice among so many others to make for a movement of truly planetary import, but also because of what Jaspers calls the "suprapolitical" character of his sacrifice, which resided in the purposeful withdrawal from institutional politics and so in a certain sense from political rationality itself.[25] Of course for the Mahatma sacrifice was as much subpolitical as it was suprapolitical, since he thought of it not as something that overreached everyday life but instead as the very sign of normality. Thus his use of everyday examples, like that of parents, children or spouses sacrificing themselves for each other in a range of ways that included dying. It was rather

---

24   Ibid., pp. 36-40.

25   Ibid.

the self-interested individual who Gandhi thought was an aberration—produced only after much individual and collective effort.

In its everyday sense sacrifice represents human freedom not only because it is disinterested in the most literal way imaginable, but also because it escapes the chain of cause and effect which binds all political calculation. For the paradoxical thing about sacrificial action is that it attends to its human instrument just as much as, if not more than, it does to any principle or cause, thus leaving its object forever in doubt by emphasizing individual action over collective politics. While for Gandhi such practices of sacrifice, which ran the gamut from fasting and celibacy to non-cooperation and passive resistance, had clear links to traditional Hinduism as well as to Christianity and Islam, to say nothing of Jainism and Buddhism, they were at the same time consummately modern in nature—not least because directed against the political institutions of the state. But even when Gandhi directed these sacrificial practices at citizens who defied the state in using violence against their fellows, he did so to compel or convert them into another kind of politics, though only ever by suprapolitical means. Such were his famous fasts unto death, whose object was precisely to divert attention from some general political cause to the very particular suffering of his own body, which therefore served as the medium through which one kind of politics was transformed into another.

Although he was of course the very antithesis of a terrorist in his espousal of nonviolence, the Mahatma resembles Al-Qaeda's militants by his suprapolitical deployment of sacrifice, which like them he glorified in the form of a willingness to die for principles. So Gandhi, like Bin Laden, very regularly used the Islamic word for martyrdom, *shahadat*, to describe this sacrifice, and as frequently expressed the desire that a million innocent lives be willingly surrendered to achieve India's freedom and cement its unity with their blood. It can even be argued that the Mahatma's sacrificial practices were inspired by his Muslim employers in South Africa, developed as these were under their patronage, and first manifested in the grounds of Johannesburg's Hamidia mosque.[26] Having been founded within the borders of Gandhi's India, and as we

---

26 I am indebted to Jonathan Hyslop for drawing my attention to this fact, which Gandhi himself was quick to acknowledge. See, for instance, his book *Satyagraha in South Africa*, trans. Valji Govindji Desai (Madras: S. Ganesan, 1928).

shall see at the very site of one of his great sacrificial experiments, Al-Qaeda's violence has come to partake in the history of the Mahatma's nonviolence, if only by joining the latter's sacrificial practices with its own in the most unexpected way. But this precisely is the fate of local histories in a global arena, knocking against one another to find accidental points of contact and construct new trajectories. For in this arena such histories can no longer grow like trees from some original seed, but must proliferate by the logic of coincidence as networks do.

Like the stories of European explorers being welcomed by Central Americans or South Sea islanders as gods whose coming had long been foretold, terrorist practices of sacrifice are perhaps recognized by the people among whom they occur as a fulfilment of their own past, with Osama bin Laden playing the role of a Cortez or a Cook in the uncharted spaces of our global present—though perhaps more appropriate as a model for the Hindu Kush is Kipling's character Daniel Dravot in "The Man who Would be King". In anthropology this kind of phenomenon is called a cargo cult, and refers to the way in which persons and objects are freed from one kind of history and appropriated by another through media and markets. It is this logic of coincidence that brings together different histories of violence in the making of a new trajectory for Islamic sacrifice. Gandhi, for example, comes in this way to provide a precedent for militant Muslims not by reason of his own engagement with Islam, but because he addressed political parties and states without ever assuming the membership of such institutions, or making of them the framework for his own actions. And as with today's militants, the Mahatma's sacrificial actions were justified precisely on religious rather than political grounds. We should also not forget that today's apostle of nonviolence was for the best part of his career seen by the guardians of law and order as an anti-modern Oriental who abetted large-scale and even terrorist violence to threaten the civilizing mission of a great Occidental empire.

Gandhi himself would probably have welcomed the comparison between his methods and those of Osama bin Laden, whose practices he might have seen as the evil perversion of his own. For the Mahatma believed good and evil to be reversible principles rather than distinct and opposed ones, famously holding that evil was only made possible with the help of goodness.[27] Not only did good people support evil out of habit or cowardice, in other words, evil itself depended upon goodness because it could only survive with the aid of virtues like selfless loyalty and altruistic sacrifice among its own supporters. And since it was goodness that imparted strength to evil, virtue consisted in withdrawing support from it. This is why Gandhi always claimed to understand if not to support terrorist forms of sacrifice, which he sought simply to convert to nonviolent ends. In any case placing Al-Qaeda's suprapolitical practices alongside the Mahatma's allows us to shift our gaze from the familiar concerns of Western security and Middle Eastern policy to address the globalization of Muslim militancy as a properly intellectual problem—one that is moreover tackled from a location outside Europe or America.[28] So for Jaspers, also addressing the globalization of violence as an intellectual problem, Gandhi's sacrifice was unparalleled in its modernity because the popular mobilization it effected was detached from the practices of traditional sacrifice, which had been confined to castes of religious or military specialists.[29]

If Gandhi, like Al-Qaeda, made the exaltation of sacrifice possible for ordinary people by inculcating what he repeatedly called the "art of dying" among them, this was because traditional specialists could no longer embody it. Modern warfare in general, says Jaspers, and nuclear warfare in particular, has by its technological means denuded the soldier of his sacrificial virtue, making victims precisely of ordinary people

27   Perhaps his most elaborate examination of the intimate relationship between good and evil is to be found in the Mahatma's lectures of 1926 on a celebrated Sanskrit text. See M.K. Gandhi, *The Bhagvadgita* (New Delhi: Orient Paperbacks, 1980).

28   I invoke Gandhi in this book for both methodological reasons, to dissociate militant Islam from the interpretive carapace of Middle Eastern policy and Western security, and substantive ones, to associate it with historical movements outside Europe and America. As a historian of South Asia I hope by this invocation not only to offer a new perspective on militant Islam, but also to point out how important South Asia in fact is to this phenomenon, comprising as it does the world's largest Muslim population together with some of the chief sites of Islamic militancy today. In addition to providing the world with a powerful new vernacular of resistance, whose sacrificial and suprapolitical forms interest me here, Gandhi, I will argue, is crucial to the modernization as well as the globalization of South Asian Islam, without which Al-Qaeda could never have been founded in the region.

29   Jaspers, pp. 36-40.

and indeed of humanity itself.[30] Thus civilians rather than soldiers now come to embody sacrifice, the latter being, after all, less vulnerable than the former in modern warfare. And indeed Gandhi quite deliberately sought to instantiate the sacrificial vocation of traditional soldiering in the civilian practice of nonviolence. Thus sacrifice is no longer linked to the state, since it no longer occurs within a political institution like the army, and is therefore no longer dedicated to the country in some inevitable way. Just as the Mahatma drew on Hindu as well as Muslim tradition to create a modern, suprapolitical form of sacrifice, so too do Al-Qaeda's militants draw their practices from an Islamic past. The point being that both types of sacrifice, though different in many respects, are truly modern in their attempt to found a new politics, which in the case of militancy today is nothing less than the elevation of humanity into the agent of global history.

Writing about the limits of traditional politics in the global reality of the Cold War, Karl Jaspers only echoed Gandhi in defining humanity by its capacity for sacrifice:

But sacrifice is the inescapable foundation of true humanity. If its soldierly form disappears, it will assume others. What renunciations, self-denials, ventures, lie on the road to a new reason cannot be specified in advance. Only this much is certain: without sacrifice we are not truly human. [...] Sacrifice would not only make peace possible; it would fulfil it. A lasting peace could only be achieved if the greatness, the strength, and the valor of the sacrifice hitherto shown in history by the soldier would now materialize in no lesser form.[31]

Very little thought is required to recognize that the suprapolitical movements of our time, from environmentalism to jihad, all depend upon a language of sacrifice that goes well beyond its military or even traditionally religious origins, however lasciviously Al-Qaeda's minions might flirt with metaphors of soldiering and holy war. Opposed as these movements may be to one another, they address themselves to the same problem, that of calling humanity into being through sacrifice. Surely it is this temptation, and not some impossibly political identification with the suffering of unknown Muslims in unknown lands, that rallies European or American militants to Al-Qaeda's banner? And is such vicarious

---

30   Ibid., p. 49.

31   Ibid., pp. 55-6. Parenthesis mine.

identification with the suffering of others not a perversely humanitarian impulse that links terrorism to its opposite? It might well be that this intimacy between the terrorist and the humanitarian is what lends militant Islam its popularity, and poses therefore its greatest threat as well.

2

THE PERFECT VICTIM

While in the holy city of Qom some years ago, I wandered through shops selling religious souvenirs alongside posters of wrestlers and Swiss chalets. But all these items, including footballing memorabilia from Iran's victory over the USA in the 1998 World Cup, seemed negligible compared with the extraordinary audio and video recordings whose sounds emanated from the stalls in a cacophony. There were sermons by leading ayatollahs, including by the late Imam Khomeini, as well as elegies chanted to commemorate the martyrdom of the Prophet's grandson Husayn. This event of the seventh century, an unequal battle in which Husayn's small band gave their lives for the cause of justice, represents the death of virtue at the hands of tyranny.

Amidst the mingled sounds of religious commentary and ritual lamentation were films being shown in complete silence. These depicted scenes from the long and brutal Iran-Iraq war of the 1980s. A fallen Iranian soldier would appear on the television screen, lying with his dead and dying comrades on the field of some battle already lost or won. The camera held perfectly still on the soldier's grievously wounded form, as if meditating upon his congealing blood, cracked lips and the flies astir his half-open eyes. I was viewing the last moments in the life of this new martyr, marking every laboured breath, each softer and slower than the one before, until his death.

What struck me about these scenes of contemporary martyrdom was neither their depiction of death, nor the political cause such depictions were meant to serve. I was taken rather by the fact that the videotapes came to an end abruptly, at the same time as the soldier's life, differing in this respect from the literary and theatrical representations of

Husayn's martyrdom, which dwell on the aftermath of his death and the fate of those who survived the Battle of Karbala.[1] For unlike the martyr of history, the dying soldier of Qom was anonymous and bereft of any personality. He was the very image of that Unknown Soldier who lies entombed in memorials around the world.

At the heart of these films lay anonymity, which deprived their subjects of a past as much as a future by focussing so ferociously upon the men's last moments. It is as if these moments were so important that they robbed the soldiers of their own biographies, and even of the commemoration normally brought about by death. Trapped between life and death, the subject of such a film was not a personality of any sort, neither soldier nor citizen, but a generic human being. For can humanity be more perfectly embodied than in the figure of an individual deprived of everything but life itself?[2]

As displays of humanity, the videotapes of Iranian martyrs that I watched in Qom were familiar enough. Did they not mimic footage used by humanitarian agencies to depict the victims of every natural or man-made disaster for precisely the same reason, to emphasize their humanity by purifying it of all dross? If humanity can only be embodied by people denuded of every other thing—as if it were the lowest common denominator that we all share—this is because the idea was never meant to take human form. Traditional definitions of humanity, inherited from classical antiquity by Christians as well as Muslims, were focussed on immaterial things like speech that deliberately sought to transcend the body. Our efforts at giving bodily shape to what for centuries had been an ideal have ended in the irony of human beings become bloodless abstractions.

Humanity becomes embodied during the twentieth century, when it is given biological as well as juridical form in debates about the status of the unborn, the comatose, the criminal and the insane.[3] But conjur-

---

1 That many representations of Iran's revolutionary soldiers continue to follow the traditional script of martyrdom made the videotapes I saw even more notable.

2 For the paradox of humanity becoming manifest in bare life, see Hannah Arendt's "The Decline of the Nation-State and the End of the Rights of Man" in *The Origins of Totalitarianism* (San Diego: Harcourt Brace and Co., 1973), pp. 267-302.

3 The work of the historian Michel Foucault is indispensable for detailed studies

ing him up in the language of medicine as much as of human rights transforms man into a kind of monster whose humanity is never quite fulfilled, since it cannot be embodied in an ideal way, but only manifested in a greater or lesser degree. In other words the embodiment of humanity presupposes that of the inhuman as well.[4] Like the monster in Mary Shelley's *Frankenstein*, modern man's humanity remains abstract and dislocated, despite the fact that every part of him is human. But in the victim reduced to bare life, humanity finally comes to light in its minimal form, as if violence itself were searching for man's essence by mortifying his monster's flesh.[5]

Is it to discover the elusive humanity represented by bare life that such victims are so frequently tormented by a cruelty that exceeds "rational" motives like resentment or retribution? Excessive cruelty is so frequently called "irrational" because it goes well beyond individual expressions of hatred and fear, as much as collective expressions of nationality and religion, to torture its victims in a laborious yet unproductive way. In other words it is the kind of cruelty whose existential aspect cannot entirely be confined to the motives and passions of our political vocabulary.[6] The anthropologist Arjun Appadurai describes such gratuitous and therefore non-rational practices as disembowelment during religious violence in India as being experimental and even epistemological in nature, because their painstaking and almost surgical cruelty appears to be in search of something like the inhuman essence of enmity within the victim's otherwise ordinary body.[7] To this we might add that such violence can just as well be in search of man's common humanity hidden inside a foreign body.

---

of the ways in which criminals, the insane, and other categories of persons have come to define humanity—or its absence.

4   See for this Balibar, trans. James Swenson, "Racism as Universalism" in *Masses, Classes, Ideas: Studies on Politics and Philosophy Before and After Marx* (New York and London: Routledge, 1994), pp. 191-204.

5   For the humanity of bare life see Giorgio Agamben, trans. Daniel Heller-Roazen, *Homo Sacer: Sovereign Power and Bare Life* (Stanford: Stanford University Press, 1998).

6   See for this Etienne Balibar's illuminating essay, "Violence, Ideality and Cruelty" in *Politics and the Other Scene* (London: Verso, 2002), pp. 129-145.

7   Arjun Appadurai, "Dead Certainty: Ethnic Violence in the Era of Globalization", *Public Culture*, Winter, vol 10 no. 2 (1998), pp. 225-47.

Among the earliest victims of this sort, neither the criminal and insane who were submitted to experiments for the good of humanity, nor
the refugees and stateless persons who first bore the legal title of human
being—because they had come to possess only human rights—looked
upon their status with equanimity. Indeed they wanted to relinquish
this status as soon as possible.[8] And all those who were not victims of
one sort or another were asked to recognize a common humanity in
what must often have appeared to be the most wretched specimens of
the race. The victim's humanity represents a revolt against traditional
notions of the human being, which saw in the free, robust and refined
man its best example. Yet there is something undeniably Christian in
the shape humanity takes in our time—that of the poor, the sick and
the vulnerable. In this form it announces a universal community founded upon the principle of humanitarianism. Humanity, therefore, not
only differentiates its embodiments of misery from other men, it also
requires these latter to identify with them.

It is clear that the Iranian martyrs whose last moments I witnessed on
videotape partook of humanity in its modern conception, though they
did so in a very particular way. While these soldiers had become generic
in their suffering, like all the victims of humanitarian pity, the nobility
of their sacrifice could not be grasped by easy reference to some already
known "human spirit". It was precisely this absent spirit that the films
sought to capture in Qom, their cameras lying in wait for its fugitive
appearance, something that had to be tracked down because it was so
elusive. In other words this was not a humanity already given to the
Iranian filmmaker, but one that had to be trapped like a rare bird.

The search for humanity in its modern form defines much of Islamic
militancy today; indeed the violence of militant Islam cannot be understood without this quest. This was already evident in Khomeini's
Islamic Revolution, as well as during the Iran-Iraq war, the source of the
footage I watched in Qom. It is startling how often the words human,
humanity and human being were used in the Islamic Republic over the
course of both these events. This usage was startling because humanity
seemed to have replaced properly theological identifications like Shiism,

---

8   Arendt, "The Decline of the Nation-State and the End of the Rights of Man",
        pp. 267-302.

Islam or even religion in general, so that in texts like Khomeini's last testament it becomes a synonym for all three.

The Ayatollah's testament can in fact be read as a parable of humanity lost and found. Its narrative is framed by a commentary on words that Shiites in particular attribute to Muhammad. According to this tradition, the Prophet left two weighty trusts behind him, the Quran and a line of successors called imams. These two were never to be separated until they returned to Muhammad on the Day of Resurrection—though in the Shiite view of history they were in fact separated by tyranny, resulting in the Quran's corruption and the imam's disappearance. Khomeini ends his commentary on this tradition by depicting both trusts as victims, each suffering what the other did, until they come together at heaven's lake. At this point he identifies the trusts with humanity itself as the eternal victim in a striking departure from conventional exegesis:

The Prophet of God, peace be upon him and his descendants, said "I leave two things with you, the book of God and the descendants of my household; indeed they shall not be separated until they return to me at heaven's lake [...]. Perhaps the phrase "they shall not be separated until they return to me at heaven's lake" might be an indication of the fact that after the holy existence of the Prophet of God, peace be upon him and his descendants, whatever is suffered by one of these two is also suffered by the other, and the neglect of one is the neglect of the other, until these two neglected entities return to the Prophet of God at heaven's lake. And whether this lake is the place that joins multiplicity to unity and droplets in the sea, or anything else, can it be grasped by the mind and soul of man? And it must be said that the cruelty which tyrants have done these two trusts left behind by the gracious Prophet, peace be upon him and his descendants, has also been inflicted upon the Muslim community, and indeed upon mankind, so (much so) that the pen cannot transcribe it.[9]

Having raised the possibility of heaven's lake being a reference to spiritual union, Khomeini goes on to suggest that the trusts left behind by Muhammad will be united each with the other, as well as with the Muslim community and mankind itself on the Day of Resurrection. Humanity, then, which has been smuggled into this tradition alongside the Muslim community that serves to represent it, is to find release

---

9   Ruhallah al-Musavi Khomeini, *Akhirin Payam* (Tehran: Sazman-e Hajj-o Awqaf-o Umur-e Khayriyyat, 1361), pp. 1-2. Parentheses mine.

from suffering and achieve its fulfillment at the end of time. As of yet it exists only in a negative way, a victim rather than an agent of history.

Such a view of humanity, as a potential to be fulfilled, was not peculiar to Khomeini but is characteristic of modern thinking, from which Islamic movements of every kind have adopted it. This is a view that continues to inform a great deal of Muslim militancy, though in rather different ways, such that waiting for the Day of Resurrection is no longer required for humanity's instantiation. We shall see that for many militants today turning humanity from victim into agent provides not the justification so much as the very content of their violence. After all in global forms of jihad like that pioneered by Al-Qaeda, this violence is no longer confined to specific persons and places but encompasses humanity itself, of which Muslims now serve as the privileged example. The Muslim community, in other words, has broken its theological bounds to stand in for humanity, but by doing so it has also created bonds with all the world's people, who are no longer asked simply to convert to Islam, but rather identify with Muslim suffering to achieve their own potential humanity.

Islam converted

On the fifth anniversary of 9/11 a jihadist website posted a long interview with Osama bin Laden's lieutenant, Ayman al-Zawahiri, in which he described Muslim militancy as offering an opportunity for all the world's oppressed, whether or not they converted to Islam:

[Interviewer] Speaking of the plunder of resources, grievances, and the oppressed ones in the world, in recent statements by Al-Qa'ida of Jihad calls for supporting the oppressed in the world have been repeated. Is this a new Al-Qa'ida approach?

[Al-Zawahiri] No, this is a confirmed jurisprudence-based law. God, the exalted, said in [a] Hadith Qudsi: "O my servants, I have forbidden oppression for myself, and forbidden it for you, so do not oppress each other."

[...]

I invite all of America's victims to Islam, the religion which rejects injustice and treachery. If they don't convert to Islam, then they should at least take advantage of Muslims' defensive campaign to repel America's aggression against them and overcome them, each under his own banner, and with whatever is at his disposal.[10]

This is a novel interpretation of Islam's universality, and one that has transformed the language of religious conversion itself. The American convert Adam Gadahn, for example, whose name within Al-Qaeda circles is Azzam al-Amriki or Azzam the American, invites his compatriots to accept Islam in a videotape released in 2006 by the terror network's media arm. Prefaced by a testimonial from Zawahiri, Gadahn's performance is dedicated to giving proselytism a radically new meaning:

We invite all Americans and other unbelievers to Islam, wherever they are and whatever their role and status in Bush and Blair's world order. And we send a special invitation to all of you fighting Bush's Crusader pipe dream in Afghanistan, Iraq, and wherever else 'Dubya' has sent you to

[...]

Finally, some will ask how we expect to attract converts to Islam after having spilled so much non-Muslim blood, albeit in defense of our religion, liberty and lives. We might ask the same question to those who kill Muslims by the millions for the crime of being Muslim, and then foolishly hope to win their hearts and minds. But we will suffice by pointing to the sharp spike [in] conversions to Islam after September eleventh, which, as we've mentioned, is giving the enemy many a sleepless night.[11]

Echoing Bin Laden's comments in the aftermath of the 9/11 attacks, Gadahn points out that these had led to a sudden rise in global interest about Islam, as well as a spike in conversions to the religion. Personal forms of missionary activity that would attract converts to a particular religious tradition, in other words, are dismissed for an impersonal

---

10   "Al-Zawahiri calls on Muslims to wage 'war of jihad', reject UN resolutions", *United States Central Command* (http:// www.centcom.mil/sites/uscentcom1/ What%20Extremists%20Say/Al-Zawahiri%20Calls%20on%20Muslims%20 to%20Wage%20'War%20of%20Jihad'%20,Reject%20UN%20Resolutions. aspx?PageView=Shared), p. 14. Parenthesis mine.

11   "Al-Qaeda operative Adam Gadahn, aka 'Azzam the American': 'The truth of Islam is sweeping across America and constitutes a fearsome challenge to the security, identity, and survival of the crusader state [America]'; time is running out to convert to Islam before you meet the dismal fate of thousands before you", *Middle East Media Research Institute* special dispatch series, no. 1281, September 6, 2006 (http://memri.org/bin/opener.cgi?Page=archives&ID=SP128106), pp. 2-3. Parenthesis mine.

and in fact inadvertent proselytism by way of spectacular events whose purposes might have been altogether different. Moreover the Islam to which such converts are led is completely open as far as sect, school or tradition is concerned, these particulars being left to the discretion of the converts themselves.

Gadahn's invitation to Islam discounts doctrine and practice for something so generic as to be human in nature. The examples he gives of American soldiers turning Muslim rely not upon their discovery of Islamic scripture so much as their identification with the suffering, endurance and sacrifice of America's Muslim victims. Thus Gadahn reproaches critics of the War on Terror like the British MP George Galloway and the journalist Robert Fisk for not taking the final step to accept Islam. Conversion for him has become a sign chiefly of identification with victims in general, who, whether or not they happen to be Muslim, are represented at this historical juncture by Islam. This is why Al-Qaeda's spokesmen can deploy the language of identification in secular as well as religious ways.

For those who adopt the brand name Al-Qaeda, non-Muslims who identify with Muslim victims become human and Muslim at the same time, even if their conversion remains in the realm of potentiality, since the criteria for both humanity and Islam are the same. The breadth of Islam's humanity is such that even its greatest enemies, according to Gadahn, could be forgiven and treated as brothers if only they would repent of their actions. Unlike the rhetoric used in the War on Terror, which is determined to punish Islamic militants for crimes committed, that used in Al-Qaeda's jihad would forgive US President Bush and Britain's former Prime Minister Blair for crimes as great if only they were to repent. However preposterous, Al-Qaeda's rhetoric is more Christian than that of its Western enemies.

Given that militants today routinely invoke the plight of suffering Muslims in exactly the same way as humanitarians do of victims in general, the identification of Islam and humanity is hardly surprising. Indeed humanitarian interventions even serve as the model for militant ones in the contemporary rhetoric of jihad, so that Ayman al-Zawahiri recommended attacks upon infidels in the same breath as he counseled assistance to those injured and displaced by the devastating earthquake that hit Pakistan in 2005. Indeed Zawahiri not only identified the earthquake's victims as martyrs, as if, like Al-Qaeda's militants, they had died for their faith, he also accused America of making war against Islamic charitable work, thus very deliberately conflating militant with humanitarian action:

We have sadly received the news of the disaster that befell the Pakistani Muslim people following the earthquake that struck the region [...] We ask Allah to grant those killed in the earthquake the positions of martyrs and pious people. My brothers and myself wish to be among you, our dear brothers, on this day. However, agents of America are standing in our way to help our Muslim brothers in their distress. Today, I call on Muslims in general, and on Islamic relief organizations in particular, to go to Pakistan and help their Pakistani brothers and withstand the troubles and harm they face for this purpose. We all know the raging American war against Islamic charitable work.[12]

Such identifications are made even less surprising when we realize that one of the great themes of contemporary Islam, characterizing liberals as well as fundamentalists and pacifists as well as militants, has to do with its supposed naturalness. Islam is justified as the natural religion of humanity, one that some Robinson Crusoe might well discover by purely rational means on his desert island. Its history therefore serves as a carapace for Islam's essentially human nature rather than providing believers with truth of a doctrinal sort as in Christianity. So believers today have reworked traditional notions like that of Islam as mankind's original faith, one that Muhammad simply cleansed of time's corruption, by predicating them of humanity's modern manifestation in biological as well as juridical terms. Thus a tradition describing Islam as the religion of all children, who are only subsequently turned by their parents into Jews or Christians, has led to the development of novel terms like "reverts" for English-speaking converts.

The modern identification of Islam with humanity has a varied and substantial history, one that reached its apogee in the early years of the last century. Exemplary of this identification between the Muslim and the human was the work of the Indian divine Abul Kalam Azad, an important political and religious figure whom I shall return to in a later chapter. Azad argued that Islam itself, to say nothing of theological

---

12   "Al-Zawahiri urges Pakistan quake aid", *Al-Jazeera*, 23 October 2005, (http://english.aljazeera.net/NR/exeres/E36CCE01-95E6-41C6-B4C7-DC9131E65733.htm), p. 1. Parenthesis mine.

categories like jihad, did not belong to Muslims alone but was the common inheritance of all human beings fighting for justice. Indeed Muslims themselves might well fall behind infidels in upholding Islam, with Azad arguing that Hindus were doing more to manifest Islamic virtues like jihad than Muslims by following Gandhi's methods to claim their freedom.[13] Though Muslims might risk losing possession of Islam by its identification with humanity, this latter category remained for Azad a theoretical rather than historical one, since it served only to illustrate the universality of the Quran's teaching. But globalization has transformed the character of Islam's universality by making its identification with the human race into a properly historical phenomenon. And this it has done by turning humanity into the potential subject of history instead of being its inevitable object.

If humanity in its biological and legal forms came to be embodied by individuals at the beginning of the last century, with globalization it became a collective reality well before that century was out. For humanity is the globe's only subject, being the true agent as well as the victim of crises like global warming or nuclear warfare. The worldwide Muslim community or *ummah* has become a global cause on the same pattern as a humanity threatened by global warming or nuclear war. And in fact the Islamic community literally takes the place of humanity in modern times. It does so by claiming the status of global victim, the purity of whose suffering serves as an equivalent of its pure humanity. In times past this *ummah* was viewed not as a body of people existing in the historical present, but as a transhistorical community made up of the dead, the living and the yet unborn. Such a conception of the Muslim community can still be seen in the passage cited above from Khomeini's political testament. By the time Osama bin Laden made the following statement to a conference of Pakistani divines in 2001, however, this community had come to represent nothing but human life itself under attack:

Honorable scholars, I write these lines to you at a time when every single inch of our *umma*'s body is being stabbed by a spear, struck by a sword, or pierced by an arrow.[14]

---

13   Irfan Ahmed, "A preliminary outline of Abul Kalam Azad's cosmopolitan theology", unpublished paper, 2007.

14   Lawrence (ed.), *Messages to the World: The Statements of Osama Bin Laden* (London: Verso, 2005), p. 96.

It is only when the Islamic community becomes a merely contemporary reality that it can become a political one— either as an agent or a victim. Yet today all global figures, the environment and humanity included, exist in rhetoric and reality only as victims. Which is to say they exist only as the potential subjects of politics. The task of militancy is to fulfil this potential and make them into actors. But for the moment there is no such thing as a global politics properly speaking, though it is possible that the militants and their enemies will bring it into being by their combined efforts. But until that happens global movements of an environmentalist, pacifist and religious bent will continue to pose certain limits for politics traditionally conceived. Indeed such limits arise from humanity itself as a reality bereft of reality. It was this humanity that Hannah Arendt, writing in the aftermath of the Second World War, described as a reality made possible by the very shame of its absence:

For many years now we have met Germans who declare that they are ashamed of being German. I have often felt tempted to answer that I am ashamed of being human. This elemental shame, which many people of the most various nationalities share with one another today, is what finally is left of our sense of international solidarity; and it has not yet found an adequate political expression.[15]

Is it too much to say that the negative humanity Hannah Arendt defined by the word shame provides the starting point for Muslim militants today? Insofar as these militants claim to participate in a universal struggle and not a specifically Muslim one, such a conception of humanity does inform their actions. For Islam has come to represent this humanity in its status as global victim. Yet the Nazi attempt to eliminate European Jewry, which serves to exemplify humanity's victimization in the political and juridical culture of the West, merits no special mention among Muslim militants. But unlike the anti-Semitism that would either deny the Jewish holocaust, or claim an equivalent victimhood for itself, Al-Qaeda's votaries tend to acknowledge it only as one example of the violence they claim is characteristic of Western civilization. In doing so our terrorists end up rejecting the final identification of humanity with victimhood, and discounting the apocalyptic language of genocide for Muslims themselves. In this sense militancy

---

15   Hannah Arendt, "Organized guilt and universal responsibility", in *Essays in Understanding* 1930-1954 (New York: Harcourt Brace and Co., 1993), p. 131.

is faithful to the idea of Islam's victorious and immortal future, being concerned not with the victimization of humanity so much as with its transformation into a global agent.

What then are the implications of identifying Muslims with humanity as far as militant acts are concerned? Arendt suggests that "the terror of the idea of humanity" resides in the universal responsibility it implies:

For the idea of humanity, when purged of all sentimentality, has the very serious consequence that in one form or another men must assume responsibility for all crimes committed by men and that all nations share the onus of evil committed by all others. Shame at being a human being is the purely individual and still non-political expression of this insight.[16]

In what remains of this chapter I want to explore the implications of identifying Islam with humanity by focussing precisely on the universal responsibility that its militants so loudly proclaim in suicidal attacks on civilian populations the world over. My thesis, let us recall, is that the search for humanity, or rather the attempt to realize it, lies at the heart of militant action. While Al-Qaeda's terrorists may begin by identifying Muslims with the passive victims who embody humanity in the discourse of human rights and crimes against humanity, their aim is to transform this humanity from the inside, not least because their sacrificial practices deny the possibility of any position external to it. These militants are not interested in saving Muslim victims by humanitarian missions, but in remaking humanity itself by abandoning the technical language of humanitarianism and human rights—which is invoked in their rhetoric only to be condemned as hypocritical.

From humiliation's heart

Arendt's shame has turned into a humiliation broadcast by one militant after another. And while this language of humiliation has not gone unnoticed by those studying movements like Al-Qaeda, its importance is generally stated more than it is examined. At most shame and humiliation are seen as providing the psychological determinants of militancy. Humiliation exists here as a collective as well as an individual fact. Indeed its rhetorical usage makes humiliation a social as much as

---

16   Ibid.

a psychological category, as its central place in the argumentation of militancy makes clear. Zawahiri describes the humiliation of a humanity unachieved in the following passage from a video posted on the Internet on 23 December 2006, in which he goes so far as to compare the Muslim victims of Western domination to animals:

O my Muslim Ummah, you must choose between two choices: the first is to live on the margins of the New World Order and international law and under the control of the enemies of Islam, dishonoured, humiliated, plundered and occupied, with them meddling in your beliefs and true religion, sticking their noses in all your domestic and foreign affairs, and you living the life of a vassal, lowly, disgraced and defiled.

And the second choice is that you rely on your Lord, renew your Tawheed (worship of the one God), rise up with your true faith, follow the revealed religion of Allah, and stand with it in the face of the arrogant criminals, as your truthful and trustworthy Prophet (peace be upon him), his righteous companions, and his purified family (Allah was pleased with them all) stood in the face of the world, inviting, giving the good news, warning and performing Jihad in order that Allah's Word be made the highest and the word of the infidels the lowest. And there is no third choice.

The Crusaders and Jews will only be pleased with the Muslim Ummah if it is satisfied with vassalage, humiliation and repression. If, however, the Ummah sets about repelling the aggression which has been committed against it for centuries, it gets nothing but bombing, destruction, torture, occupation, abuse and infringement, because in that case it is not eligible for human rights, due to it being a species of animal which has attacked its Western masters.[17]

Not one militant has attributed his radicalization to any personal humiliation, whether arising out of foreign domination, racism or discrimination of some other kind, though to do so would not compromise his motives in the least. On the contrary these men explicitly reject such motives, which remain nevertheless the stock in trade of "expert" analyses regarding their militancy. Not their own humiliation, but that of others shames them, whose acts are therefore committed out of pity for the plight of others. This is the same abstract and vicarious emotion that characterizes the actions of pacifists or human rights campaigners,

---

17   "Website Posts Latest Video of Al-Zawahiri, English Text" *United States Central Command* (http://www.centcom.mil/sites/uscentcom1/What%20Extremists%20Say/ZawahiriVideoDecember2006.aspx?PageView=Shared), pp. 5-6.

and as we have seen, Zawahiri himself attributes the humiliation of Muslims to their deprivation of human rights. Taken together, these expressions of pity belong to the language of humanitarianism and therefore to humanity itself.

That such a language need not be pacifist is demonstrated by its common use in Al-Qaeda suicide bombings as much as in the air strikes of humanitarian intervention. Hannah Arendt was perhaps the first to identify pity as an emotion born from the womb of humanity and characteristic of a violent humanitarianism in modern phenomena like revolutions. She argues that unlike charity in its Christian form, or compassion more generally, pity presupposes a vast gulf separating those who give and receive it, not least because it moves beyond the limited circle of people we know to apply itself to an abstract and unknowable humanity. Rather than choosing to share in the suffering of others, pity seeks to destroy this suffering together with the unbearable shame it produces among its possessors, precisely in acts of revolutionary and other violence. [18]

Osama bin Laden is probably the most eloquent orator of Muslim humiliation today, his rhetoric setting the standard for militant expositions of shame more broadly. But for Bin Laden shame and humiliation are by no means the expression of Islam's defeat or oppression by the West as has generally been assumed. Such an inference would indeed be an odd one to make for someone who glories in the wholesale martyrdom of Muslims. The martyr, after all, is technically a defeated person, like the dying Iranian soldier I began this chapter with. Whether death leads to the victory of the martyr's cause is neither here nor there as far as his elevated status is concerned. So in the case of the Prophet's grandson Husayn, who provides the archetype of Muslim martyrdom, victory was most emphatically not the outcome of his death. Or as Bin Laden, referring to Al-Qaeda's martyrs, puts it in a video broadcast by Al-Jazeera on 26 December 2001:

No Muslim would ever possibly ask: what did they benefit? The fact is that they were killed—but this is total ignorance. They were victorious, with the

---

18   See Hannah Arendt, "The Social Question" in *On Revolution* (London: Penguin Books, 1990), pp. 59-114.

blessings of God Almighty, and with the immortal heavens that God promised them. Victory is not material gain; it is about sticking to your principles.[19]

If martyrdom represents a victory in its own right, one that transcends defeat on the political plane, then humiliation, too, becomes a category transcending politics. Osama bin Laden's sermons of shame have little, if anything to do with the political, economic or religious subordination of the Muslim world to the West, and are concerned rather by the duties of courage and sacrifice that Muslims neglect, and of whose absence defeat and oppression are only the signs. Far from being negative phenomena, defeat and oppression are seen positively, as heaven-sent opportunities to make humanity manifest. They serve as counterparts to the Biblical trials imposed by God upon an Abraham or a Job.

Martyrdom is noble not because it will result in the political, economic or religious triumph of Islam so much as because it allows Muslims to exhibit the fundamentally human virtues of courage and sacrifice, thus doing their duty to represent humanity itself as a global agent rather than victim. The coalescence of the traditional virtues of martyrdom with modern conceptions of humanity is manifest in Bin Laden's rhetoric, for example in the following extract from his 2001 message to a gathering of Pakistani divines:

I write these lines to you at a time when even the blood of children and innocents has been deemed fair game, when the holy places of Islam have been violated in more than one place, under the supervision of the new world order and under the auspices of the United Nations, which has clearly become a tool with which the plans of global unbelief against Muslims are implemented. This is an organization that is overseeing with all its capabilities the annihilation and blockade of millions of Muslims under the sanctions, and yet still is not ashamed to talk about human rights![20]

The link forged between Islam and modern conceptions of humanity in the passage I have just quoted is far from arbitrary. For one thing Islam's victimization is seen as a properly global phenomenon and put in the context of human rights violations. And for another the virtues of courage and sacrifice, as well as the aims of peace and security that mili-

---

19   Lawrence (ed.), *Messages to the World*, p. 154.

20   Ibid., p. 96.

tant acts like suicide-bombings supposedly uphold, are human in their generality and cannot be limited to Muslims. Indeed specifically Islamic virtues like honouring the Prophet or attesting to the unity of God are remarkable by their absence from the rhetoric of martyrdom, though Muslim authorities are certainly invoked to support the sanctities of a wider humanity. But theological justifications apart, Islam has come to represent humanity by the sheer extent of its apparent victimization. Not only Bin Laden and his acolytes, but also the liberal or fundamentalist Muslims who oppose Al-Qaeda need only count up the victims of conflict globally to obtain an overwhelmingly Muslim quorum. Thus the importance of such lists in the narrative of militancy: Bosnia, Kosovo, Chechnya, Kashmir, Palestine, Iraq, Lebanon, Afghanistan, Somalia and more.

Whether it is accurate or not, such counting is in fact used to make the connection between Islam and the victimized humanity it has come to represent. It is as if the very size and dispersal of the Muslim *ummah* are enough to guarantee the stability of this connection, whoever is responsible for the victimization that brings Islam and humanity together. Strictly speaking such causes are secondary to the identification of Muslims as human beings, though their seeming diversity poses a problem for militants, who must subsume them all under increasingly abstract labels like "the Crusader-Zionist axis". The enemy of Islam and humanity, in other words, is a constantly morphing presence that can be joined or abandoned at will. For the moment Israel and the United States account for two of this hydra's heads, but not so long ago the Soviet Union or Serbia were far more important. The point being that this enemy's abstraction permits militants to move past international politics and establish themselves in the global arena that is proper to humanity. This is why Osama bin Laden, in his videotaped statement of 4 January 2004, regards jihad as something providential and not simply an unfortunate necessity:

This confrontation and conflict will go on because the conflict between right and falsehood will continue until Judgment Day. Such a confrontation is good for both the countries and peoples. God says: "If God did not drive some back by means of others, the earth would be completely corrupt [...]"[21]

---

21   Ibid., p. 217. Parenthesis mine.

Similarly in a video posted on the Internet on 22 January 2007, Zawahiri welcomed President Bush's move to send some 20,000 additional troops to Iraq, even asking him to send the entire US army, so that it might vie with the militants in virtue as much as vice. Seen as part of a providential design, the battle between faith and infidelity makes these enemies into partners striving to exhibit the truth of their cause and destroy its evil. The first words blazoned on the videotape, in English, are the following:

So send your entire army to be annihilated at the hands of the Mujahideen, to free the world from your evil and theirs.[22]

Militant acts serve to make humanity manifest by transmuting the shame of its negative existence into the pride of an identity achieved as if in some alchemical precipitation. Such an achievement is properly human because it has little to do with defeat or victory in a political sense, constituting rather the display of universal virtues by individuals and groups of all descriptions. The only victory on this battlefield is that of courage and the only defeat that of cowardice. And for this an enemy is necessary while being at the same time quite incidental. In vogue with the dispersed networks of Sunni militancy as well as among the hierarchies of Shiite radicalism, this conception of struggle differs markedly from the collective ideals that serve as traditional military goals. Whether fighting for his freedom, his country or even his material interests, the conventional soldier anticipates a result whose attainment lies beyond his powers in an undefined future. Such self-realization as he achieves in battle never becomes part of the struggle and is relegated to his letters and anecdotes, his memories and his dreams.

The militant however fights for self-realization of the most immediate kind, one whose individuality is simultaneously a realization of humanity itself. Such acts of militancy, moreover, reach out to humanize their enemy in the moment of violence, for only in this way can the humanity claimed by Islam fulfil its universal destiny. It is no longer the universality of conversion that militant Islam seeks, but an identification that puts everyone, Muslim or non-Muslim, friend or foe, in

---

22   "Al-Zawahiri Video on Bush's Iraq Security Plan" *United States Central Command* (http://www.centcom.mil/sites/uscentcom1/What%20Extremists%20Say/Al-ZawahiriVideoonBush'sIraqSecurityPlan.aspx?PageView=Shared), p. 1.

the quintessentially human position of global victim. This might seem a far-fetched argument to make, but it is borne out by the character of militant activity. For example it is clear from Osama bin Laden's statements that he considers acts of terror necessary so that the West might experience the equivalent of Muslim suffering. But far from being a form of revenge, such equivalence is meant to permit both sets of victims to identify with and indeed speak to each other. Thus the following statement of Bin Laden's, which was broadcast by Al-Jazeera on 12 November 2002:

If it pains you to see your victims and your allies' victims in Tunisia, Karachi, Failaka, and Oman, then remember that our children are murdered daily in Palestine and Iraq. Remember our victims in the mosques of Khost, and the deliberate murder of our people at weddings in Afghanistan. If it pains you to see your victims in Moscow, then remember ours in Chechnya.[23]

In statement after statement, Al-Qaeda's soldiers describe their attacks as a "language", in fact as the only one that America or the West understands. In other words these men define violence as a mode of conversation and persuasion, the common language they share with their enemies. Murder has therefore become a medium of exchange for Islam's global militants, representing in this way the intimate relationship they enjoy with the infidel. However its true purpose is pedagogical, to school these unbelievers in the forgotten language of ethics and principles, thus serving as the clearest example of militancy as a form of hospitality. This is how Ayman al-Zawahiri puts it in an interview released on the Internet on 11 September 2006:

The materialistic Crusader western civilization knows not the language of ethics and principles but understands the language of punishment and retribution. So, if they taste some of what they are inflicting on our women and children, then they will start giving up their arrogance, stubbornness, and greed and will seek to solve the problem between them and the Muslims.[24]

The language of violence, then, belongs to the infidel as much as it does to the faithful, allowing one's vice to compete with the other's vir-

---

23   *Messages*, p. 175.

24   "Al-Zawahiri Calls on Muslims to Wage 'War of Jihad', Reject UN Resolutions", p. 2.

tue in such a way as to bring the ethics and principles of humanity back to political life in the most spectacular of ways.

Blood brothers

Osama bin Laden's rhetoric has consistently voiced a desire for global equality, in this case, that between Muslims and Christians, or between the Islamic world and the West. Having accused America of hypocrisy as far as its advancement of this equality is concerned, Bin Laden turns his attention to the only form in which he thinks such freedom is possible: the equality of death. This is why he has repeatedly emphasized the need for an equivalence of terror between the Muslim world and the US, as if this were the only form in which the two might come together and even communicate one with the other. For Al-Qaeda terror is the only form in which global freedom and equality are now available. It therefore functions as the dark side of America's own democracy, as inseparable from it as an evil twin. So in the aftermath of the 2004 Madrid bombings, Bin Laden issued a statement in which he defined terrorism as an effort to universalize security as a human right, if only by refusing to accept its monopolization by the West. For equality demanded that security should be enjoyed by all or by none:

It is well known that security is a vital necessity for every human being. We will not let you monopolize it for yourselves [...][25]

In all this Bin Laden has done nothing more than recognize the unity of a globe in which no man can be separated from any other, each one being held responsible for his fellows, with whose suffering he must identify. Such is the humanitarian logic that characterizes global movements like environmentalism and pacifism as well. But this unity is made manifest by violence, which builds a bridge between enemies by demonstrating that all men are equal if in death alone. It is as if this macabre equivalence has replaced the equality that is supposed to exist between men and unite them as part of a single humanity. The militant's violence, then, ironically links the world's people together in a web of mutual obligation and responsibility. It is this web of univer-

25   *Messages*, p. 234.

sal complicity, after all, that allows American or British civilians to be killed in recompense for the killing of Muslims in Iraq.

The worldwide web of war spun by Al-Qaeda exists as a kind of spectre of our global interrelatedness, one that has as yet no specific political form of its own. And the militant's obsessive demands for equal treatment within this world, even if it be only in the form of a reciprocity of violence, represents the dark side of humanity's global brotherhood, whose reality is the product of our increasingly interconnected universe. But this means that the same web of responsibilities and obligations linking the holy war to its enemies, also links them together as a community, even as a community of brothers. For are not Al-Qaeda's victims said to be merely the counterparts of innocent Muslims killed elsewhere? They are therefore in some perverse way brothers at one remove, made even more like brothers by dying alongside suicide bombers and mingling blood.

In the global perspective adopted by militant Islam, the peoples of the world are bound together in a web of mutual relations and complicities. For the moment this intimacy expresses itself in the most murderous way, though even here it represents what I have referred to as the dark side of another, more benign kind of relationship, like that of universal brotherhood. Indeed Al-Qaeda's actions and rhetoric continuously invoke the spectre of a global community that has as yet no formal existence of its own. And this is what allows its war to draw upon the forms and even the vocabulary of other global movements such as environmental and pacifist ones, all of which are concerned with the fate of humanity as a whole. In his more ironical moments, Osama bin Laden takes this language of global community so far as to put Al-Qaeda and its American enemy on the same side of their mutual war, saying in a 2004 video that the Bush administration's invasion of Iraq for power and profits contributed to the terror network's own aims:

To some analysts and diplomats, it seems as if we and the White House are on the same team shooting at the United States' own goal, despite our different intentions.[26]

---

26   Ibid., p. 242.

It truly shows that al-Qaeda has made gains, but on the other hand it also shows that the Bush administration has likewise profited.[27]

Islamic militants exhibit a perverse humanity by addressing their victims in the language of intimacy, reciprocity and equivalence. That this is not a merely rhetorical gesture becomes evident when we consider that such militancy, unlike all previous forms of terrorist or insurgent action, refuses to set up an alternative utopia for itself, something that even anarchists are not immune to. Unlike the members of religious cults or fringe political groups, few of Al-Qaeda's killers display signs of entering some closed ideological world by cutting themselves off from their families or everyday life. This suggests that the Islam they seek to defend is not conceived as an ideology at all because it does not provide a complete or alternative vision of the world into which the would-be bomber can retreat as into a fortress. Thus Bin Laden defines his own militancy merely as the obverse of the violence he attributes to the West, his refusal to claim autonomy for jihad making for a curious identity between Muslims and their enemies:

Since we have reacted in kind, your description of us as terrorists and of our actions as terrorism necessarily means that you and your actions must be defined likewise.[28]

Apart from strictly operational agreements, there is little unity of doctrine even between an Osama bin Laden and his lieutenant, Ayman al-Zawahiri, while the religion they follow possesses no established tradition, being made up of fragments snatched from differing Islamic authorities. There are at most very general patterns of thought that are neither codified nor propagated in any systematic way. We shall see in the following chapter that instead of being recruited to a well-defined movement the jihad's disparate soldiers franchise Al-Qaeda's expertise and brand name for a variety of equally disparate causes that exist comfortably within the structures of everyday life. Rather than offering an alternative to the world as it exists, these militants would transform it by a kind of internal convulsion, bringing forth its latent humanity by their acts of sacrifice.

---

27 Ibid.
28 Ibid., p. 234.

Earlier movements of resistance or terror had advanced critiques of existing conditions, such as capitalism or imperialism, and offered alternatives to them. This was the case with communists and anarchists as well as of nationalists and fundamentalists. Like the more pacific global movements that are its peers, Al-Qaeda offers no real criticism of existing conditions (apart from inveighing against them) and possesses no alternative to take their place. Deprived of the political and ideological unity available to regional or national movements, these latter-day militants live scattered among their enemies, whom they accuse only of heedlessness and hypocrisy. So Americans, as we shall see, are accused not so much of believing in the wrong religion or ideology, as of being heedless and hypocritical about the beliefs they do hold. Global movements like Al-Qaeda's want not an alternative to America so much as the fulfilment of America's promise of freedom for all. Indeed by dying alongside their victims, Islam's militants demonstrate that they exist in the same world as these latter, and as members of the same humanity.

Murder most equivocal

Militant rhetoric is marked most forcefully by the logic of equivalence: you kill our civilians so we kill yours, because we suffer so must you. This logic is so rigorous that it makes equivalence into the touchstone of humanity itself. Yet the logic of equivalence comes apart at its rhetorical heart, the suicide bombing otherwise known as a martyrdom operation. The propagandistic power of a suicide bombing, its heroism as much as its horror, derives from the fact that the killer is willing to die alongside his victims. I have already pointed out the relations of intimacy and reciprocity that this willingness creates between militants and their enemies, though it is increasingly obvious that the suicidal portion of the bombing is not equivalent to its murderous part. The militant's sacrifice, in other words, carries so much of the bombing's power as to reduce his victim's death to relative insignificance. It is this breakdown in the logic of terrorist equivalence that I want to explore, because, I contend, it represents the shift from a statistical to an existential conception of humanity.

Gandhi's is not a name to be uttered alongside that of Osama bin Laden, though he, too, spoke of the necessity of bloody sacrifice in the cause of justice. In doing so the Mahatma was in the early days of his career responding to the Indian terrorists whose arguments, as he recounted them, bear a remarkable similarity to those that "experts" of all kinds attribute to the jihad movements of our own time:

At first, we will assassinate a few Englishmen and strike terror; then, a few men who will have been armed will fight openly. We may have to lose a quarter of a million men, more or less, but we will regain our land. We will undertake guerrilla warfare, and defeat the English.[29]

To this political argument Gandhi offers the following religious response, which to my mind is far closer to the response that suicide bombing offers us today:

That is to say, you want to make the holy land of India unholy. Do you not tremble to think of freeing India by assassination? What we need to do is to kill ourselves.[30]

If the Mahatma so frequently advocated killing oneself for a just cause, this was not because he thought it an effective and ethical way of achieving some end, but rather because sacrificing one's life could not in fact be an instrumental act and was thus thrown back upon itself to become not a means so much as an end unto itself. Choosing death therefore transformed political acts into religious ones by demonstrating their unworldly and disinterested nature. Gandhi was quite clear that the terrorists of his day partook of sacrifice in its religious form, though they did so in a perverted way. Referring to one such suicidal assassin he wrote:

Dhingra was a patriot, but his love was blind. He gave his body in a wrong way; its ultimate result can only be mischievous.[31]

By the time Gandhi's movement of nonviolence had achieved maturity, the mutual violence between Indians had far outstripped their combined violence against the British. But this only made the Mahatma more determined on sacrifice. While not advocating the killing even of noisome insects, in other words, he was willing to countenance the

---

29   M.K. Gandhi, *Hind Swaraj and Other Writings* (Cambridge: University Press, 2003), p. 77.

30   Ibid.

31   Ibid., p. 78.

voluntary sacrifice of a million human lives for righteous ends. Indeed towards the end of his own life Gandhi longed for as many such Hindu and Muslim deaths as possible, so that these rival communities might cement their unity in blood. As it turns out Gandhi, who was assassinated by a Hindu militant, ended up shedding his own blood to mix the cement of this unity.

Gandhi's practices of sacrifice were meant to retrieve another sense of the human from the idea of humanity that informed terrorist as much as humanitarian acts. After all it was no accident that the Mahatma's assassin described his own act of violence as a "humanitarian" one, since he had already identified Hinduism with a statistical conception of humanity well before Islam came to occupy its place:

For, is it not true that to secure the freedom and to safeguard the just interests of some thirty crores of Hindus constituted the freedom and the well-being of one-fifth of [the] human race?[32]

Faced with the increasingly murderous enmity between Hindus and Muslims in the India of the 1940s, the Mahatma determined to transform this violence, not by futile pleas for harmony, but by turning it inwards in acts of sacrifice that would invite if not compel a different kind of response from those spoiling for a fight. The purpose of this sacrifice, which Gandhi had also mobilised against the British rulers of India, was to lay claim to the noblest of human virtues, like courage and fearlessness, and so provoke the collapse or conversion of those who were bent on violence. All this was to be achieved not by prating about nonexistent ideals, but instead by separating the already existing practice of sacrifice from that of murder, and this by emphasizing it to such a degree that the courage and fearlessness of sacrifice were turned into gestures of hospitality. If the Mahatma's extraordinary career demonstrated the truth of his methods, however temporary or partial it might have been, the amplification of a language of martyrdom and sacrifice in militant Islam suggests that such a truth is yet possible.

It is not difficult to imagine a suicide bombing, say against infrastructure like buildings or transport networks, which does not kill anyone other than the militant himself. And this in fact is the case with a large

---

32   Nathuram Godse, *Why I Assassinated Mahatma Gandhi* (Delhi: Surya Bharti Prakashan, 1998), p.26. Parenthesis mine.

number of terrorist attacks from Kabul to Glasgow. Such attacks aim precisely at infrastructure, along with the people associated with it, so that it is unclear which of the two is indispensable as a target. Is it possible to imagine a suicide bombing in which the only life taken is the militant's own? While a perversely Gandhian act of sacrifice such as this might seem inconceivable among the members of movements like Al-Qaeda, it is certainly true that the victim is becoming more and more a symbolic presence in the practice of militancy, one often dispensed with altogether.

As if mimicking the symbolic character of such terrorism, counter-terrorist security measures are equally symbolic in nature, though doubtless for very different reasons. As an example we can look at the ruinously costly, disruptive and, it must be added from anecdotal evidence ineffectual security measures that were instituted at British airports following the discovery of an alleged plot by a number of its Muslim citizens to blow up transatlantic airliners in July 2006. These checks and restrictions were not matched by anything even remotely similar on trains or buses, despite the fact that the only successful Islamic attacks in Britain had occurred precisely on ground transportation. That such blanket security was obviously impossible meant that the measures taken at airports were all the more symbolic, though even these were so insupportable that they soon had to be relaxed. Perhaps inevitably, the would-be intentions of terrorist as much as counter-terrorist acts have become incidental to the complex economy of global speculation and risk-management in which states, companies and individuals are all involved, and in which image is often more important than substance.

Earlier forms of terrorism like hijacking, hostage taking, and assassination were concerned with threats to life in particular, while its more recent forms like suicide-bombing are fixated on the infrastructure that makes such life possible. For humanity becomes manifest in a form like a crowd or a people, a mass or a nation, precisely in the public spaces and conveyances made possible by infrastructure. The people attacked in such places, after all, are victimized precisely as anonymous human beings rather than as the adherents of a particular religion, the residents of a particular neighbourhood or even the citizens of a particular state. Commuters are attacked because they provide a statistically random sample of humanity, and trains targeted because they do not belong to any locality but are quite literally the vehicles of this humanity.

Violence against infrastructure thus targets life in the abstract, its victims having lost the capacity to become personalities both in their own right, and as the individual representatives of particular nations or religious groups, being quite unlike the hostages of old in this respect. Indeed militants and their victims seem even to have changed places, with the latter drifting into generic anonymity at the same time as the former achieve a posthumous celebrity as victims of their own devising. Of course the two forms of terror I have been describing do not always occur in isolation from one other, but if anything their mixture, too, tells us that there has been a sea change not only in the organization, methods and motives of terrorism, but in its existential dimension as well.

The infrastructure of humanity

What does it mean to attack infrastructure? Apart from the rationality of such actions, which we are told are meant to cause the maximum amount of death, injury, panic, cost and disruption, they possess an existential dimension that is independent of terrorist intentions. Indeed these intentions are the least obvious factors of such events, since terrorists are not constituted to profit from the disruption, etc. they cause in any military, economic or even political sense, not least because attacks on the Al-Qaeda model offer support only to the most global of political demands, and none at all to political parties with which governments can negotiate. This older model of terrorist politics, which had characterized groups like the PLO or the IRA, has been replaced by one in which it is no longer necessary even to claim responsibility for attacks. At most such attacks participate in political life by fomenting panic, thus forcing some very general and unpredictable reaction from citizens and their governments, of which the terrorists can take little or no advantage.

But to create panic militants need not attack infrastructure, as if it were a military or economic target, and might in fact succeed far more by attacking residences instead. After all, what could be more panic-inducing than the random and practically uncontrollable targeting of domestic spaces? Isn't this what traditionally organized armies and militias do all the time? It is even possible to say that the exercise of force by legitimate armies, as well as by their illegitimate copies in the form of militias, is increasingly being extended to private life, while terrorism quite irrationally confines itself to the public spaces created by infrastructure. And this to the degree that terrorism appears to sanctify private spaces and reinforce domestic life as zones of security and comfort. In this way militant operations against infrastructure mirror similar American, British or NATO attacks on cities like Baghdad or Belgrade, both kinds of intervention having become "humanitarian" by their targeting of command, control or logistics capabilities to secure a regime's compliance with human rights codes. With suicide bombers taking the place of "smart bombs" one can argue that terrorist attacks on infrastructure represent another instance of the logic of equivalence that marks militancy so strongly as to discount fears of an assymetrical threat, for instance that posed by the use of weapons of mass destruction.[33]

But maybe it is also the idea of the public, of a people, and even of the humanity infrastructure represents that terrorists are attacking. The economic and other costs incurred by attacks on infrastructure are undeniably of little or no profit to these militants, being as abstract in this respect as the idea of humanity, though far less significant than it. Whatever their motives, however, the men who target infrastructure must, out of necessity, perceive and approach their victims in a particular way. The anthropologist Vyjayanthi Rao has explored the particularity of such terror in an essay on the militant practice of multiple bombing in Mumbai. Distinguishing the novelty of such attacks from the old-fashioned religious riot, which emerged out of local conditions and disputes to spread across the city, Rao points out that the serial bombing of Mumbai's infrastructure targets the city in its entirety to redress grievances that are themselves global and abstract.[34] There exists therefore no locality of grievance or epicentre of violence in Mumbai's serial blasts, of which there have been three instances since 1993.

In order to attack infrastructure like Mumbai's railway stations, commuter trains, road transport, stock market, airline offices and hotels, the city must be seen as urban planners and military tacticians see it, which

---

33   I am grateful to Shane Brighton for bringing this issue to my attention.

34   Vyjayanthi Rao, "How to Read a Bomb: Scenes From Bombay's Black Friday" *Public Culture*, vol. 19 no. 3 (2007), pp. 567-592.

is to say from above and in the abstract form of a map. In such a view, and from such a height, the people who are meant to use this infrastructure, or be attacked within it, can only be seen as a set of statistics, certainly not as individual victims. Setting off multiple and simultaneous blasts across the city, moreover, interrupts the time by which men live, as well as the time it takes for them to move from place to place, with the abstract and synchronous time by which urban or military planning operates. In other words attacks on transportation networks, like those of Mumbai in 2006, London in 2005 or Madrid in 2004, are conducted according to the very procedures that permit such infrastructure to function in the first place. Whether or not they were carried out by suicide bombers, then, such attacks can be seen as suicidal because in them infrastructure is destroyed by its own hand.

The fact that terrorists who attack infrastructure must adopt the very procedures by which it operates provides yet another example of the intimacy that is entailed in such violence. Like the suicide bomber who dies alongside his victims, and by sharing blood with them brings to light a common humanity, if only in death, the bomber who attacks infrastructure discovers a kind of humanity in its destruction too. His violence, indeed, seems to break through the generic and statistical definition of humanity that infrastructure makes possible, in the form of passengers or pedestrians, to reach the human being inside. After all by destroying infrastructure, the militant brings to a halt its task of constituting humanity as mass or volume; as the infinite flow of numbers eternally in motion; as a people, nation or public displaying itself in the streets, trains and cinema halls of a city.

The destruction of infrastructure does not cease to produce life in the abstract, in this case the statistics of those who have been killed and injured, but these no longer constitute the kind of humanity made possible by road, rail or recreation. The dead and injured are no more manifestations of a people or a nation because they are no more a crowd of passengers, pedestrians or onlookers. In fact terrorism's temporary suspension of humanity, at least in its public and collective forms, leaves private persons as its only survivors. And while we cannot attribute to terrorists the aim of retrieving a more authentic humanity from the masses and volumes that infrastructure makes of people, their inadvertent achievement of this end is not without its irony. Gandhi, for example, had famously attacked modern infrastructure, and the railways in particular, precisely because it brought into being a new kind of humanity that he considered false and malign.

Railways have indeed provided the infrastructure of an abstract humanity for much of India's modern history. From the famous story of Gandhi being subjected to racial attack and thrown off a moving train in South Africa, to the many stories of trains arriving in Pakistan or India with all their passengers massacred during the subcontinent's partition in 1947, railways have made possible the abstraction of people into Indians and Pakistanis or Hindus, Muslims and Sikhs. In 2002, for example, the setting alight of a train carrying Hindu pilgrims led to large-scale massacres of Muslims in the state of Gujarat. And in 2007 a Pakistan-bound train, this time filled with Muslims, was set alight in a very similar way killing some sixty-six passengers. The train massacre has therefore become a stereotyped way of mobilizing masses and volumes of people. Though he wrote before the train massacres of 1947, the Mahatma nevertheless began his exordium against railways by pointing out the inhuman implications of infrastructure:

It must be manifest to you that, but for the railways, the English could not have such a hold on India as they have. The railways, too, have spread the bubonic plague. Without them, the masses could not move from place to place. They are the carriers of plague germs. Formerly we had natural segregation. Railways have also increased the frequency of famines, because, owing to facility of means of locomotion, people sell out their grain, and it is sent to the dearest markets. People become careless, and so the pressure of famine increases. They accentuate the evil nature of man. Bad men fulfil their evil designs with greater rapidity. The holy places of India have become unholy. Formerly, people went to these places with very great difficulty. Generally, therefore, only the real devotees visited such places. Nowadays, rogues visit them in order to practice their roguery.[35]

To the argument that infrastructure can promote good as much as it does evil, Gandhi responded in the following way:

Good travels at a snail's pace—it can, therefore, have little to do with the railways. Those who want to do good are not selfish, they are not in a hurry, they know that to impregnate people with good requires a long time. But evil has wings. To build a house takes time. Its destruction takes none. So the railways

---

35   Gandhi, *Hind Swaraj*, p. 47.

can become a distributing agency for the evil one only. It may be a debatable matter whether railways spread famines, but it is beyond dispute that they propagate evil.[36]

As for the statistical forms of humanity, and of humanitarianism, that infrastructure makes possible, they met only with criticism from the apostle of nonviolence:

I am so constructed that I can only serve my immediate neighbours, but, in my conceit, I pretend to have discovered that I must with my body serve every individual in the Universe. In thus attempting the impossible, man comes in contact with different natures, different religions, and is utterly confounded. According to this reasoning, it must be apparent to you that railways are a most dangerous institution.[37]

Gandhi took a dim view even of the sense of national, and we might today also say global, unity that is the product of modern infrastructure, claiming that it sought to smooth out differences that were of its own creation:

Only you and I and others who consider ourselves civilised and superior persons imagine that we are many nations. It was after the advent of railways that we began to believe in distinctions, and you are at liberty now to say that it is through the railways that we are beginning to abolish those distinctions. An opium-eater may argue the advantage of opium-eating from the fact that he began to understand the evil of the opium habit after having eaten it.[38]

One need neither be a Luddite, nor favour retreating into a commune, to recognize a certain justice in Gandhi's arguments. And if I have dwelt on these at such length, it is to show that the use made of infrastructure has unintended consequences for the idea as well as the experience of humanity. The Mahatma's homespun philosophy, moreover, tells us how such consequences can be made available for popular thought as much as action. Without betraying any consciousness of this philosophy, militant attacks on infrastructure nevertheless bring about a Gandhian resolution to the problem posed by an abstract humanity. It goes without saying that such a resolution is far from nonviolent and would not have met with the Mahatma's approval, but it is also evident

---

36   Ibid., pp. 47-8.

37   Ibid., p. 51

38   Ibid., p. 49.

that these attacks participate in his enterprise of reducing an abstract humanity to a multiplicity of concrete individuals.

In the suicide bombing an abstracted humanity is destroyed at the same time as the infrastructure that makes it possible. Indeed it is the very form of this humanity that commits suicide in the blast, which joins together terrorists and victims in a death from which only individuals can escape. For the militant desire to fulfil the promises of a statistical humanity by making the whole world responsible for Muslim suffering, as well as by turning the equality of life into the equivalence of death, end in nothing so much as the production of its opposite. After all, the martyr produced by the suicide bombing is human precisely in his nonequivalence. This is so because his humanity no longer resides in biology or jurisprudence, but rather in the virtues of courage and sacrifice that he manifests, existential virtues whose production completely overpowers the statistical logic of equivalence that the militant had initially espoused.

These are the very virtues that Gandhi himself lauded, especially in the traditional figure of the soldier, who, unlike the doctors and lawyers whom the Mahatma famously castigated, was unable to turn his vocation into an instrumental quest for money and power because he was obliged to risk his life in its prosecution. Doctors and lawyers, who stood behind the biological and juridical definitions of humanity, in fact deprived their clients of humanity as an existential fact by assuming control over it in a purely technical way. So while he did not of course approve of war, Gandhi saw soldiering as one of the few professions in which virtues like courage, honour and sacrifice had managed to survive for their own sake, and this because it put the individual's life at risk. These very virtues also make the militant human, if only posthumously, which is to say only when he has dispensed with the physical and juridical body that had once tied him to the statistical form of humanity characteristic of humanitarianism and human rights.

But we might go further than this militant critique of an aggregated humanity by suggesting that with prosthetics and genetic engineering it is no longer possible to locate the human essence even in bare life, since from the test-tube baby to the patient on life-support, increasing numbers of such lives can only be described as posthuman in their combination of technical and biological parts, being in this respect the all too real descendants of Frankenstein's imaginary monster.[39] And indeed the cyborg as a sign of the posthuman future is nowhere more clearly made flesh than in the figure of the suicide bomber who transforms his own body into an explosive device. Can the human and nonhuman parts of this cyborg be distinguished from one another so that we can say which does the killing and who does the dying? In this situation the human in either its individual or collective form ceases to have a foothold in life, however bare, to become instead a project in the instantiation of virtue. And while such a project harks back to earlier ways of conceiving humanity, it is resolutely modern in the rejection of life as the zero-point of politics. But having been annihilated by the posthuman future, the life of humanity's past makes a posthumous return, in the shape of those ghostly individuals who speak to us from martyrdom videotapes.

So the anonymous Iranian soldiers I beheld dying on videotape in the holy city of Qom have been replaced by a new breed of martyrs whose humanity has finally acquired a posthumous presence in the form of relics like the videotaped testaments they leave behind. Whether it has been lost or found, in other words, the martyr's humanity manifests itself as a ghost haunting the world's television screens in snippets of footage whose life is as brief and as explosive as that of its subject. And if in the moment of death these men achieved a common humanity with their victims by mingling blood, as the posthumous subjects of television they do so by mingling with film stars and others who inhabit that medium as the subjects precisely of "human interest" stories. For martyred militants belong not in the group of politicians on television but in that of "media personalities" whose doings are of interest because they represent the virtues and vices of humanity in its existential rather than statistical or biological form. In becoming a human being the militant has also become a celebrity.[40]

39   The classic text of posthumanity is Donna Haraway's *Simians, Cyborgs and Women: The Reinvention of Nature* (New York: Routledge, 1991).

40   I am indebted to Thorvald Sirnes for drawing my attention to this possibility.

3

LAWS OF UNCERTAINTY

On July 7, 2005, as I was going through airport security in New Delhi, en route to Mumbai, four bombs ripped through London's mass transit network. Just before being herded onto the plane, I saw images of the carnage on a television monitor in the departure lounge. Among these were shots of the bus that Hasib Hussain had blown up in Tavistock Square, directly in front of a pedestrian walkway that led to my flat. Waiting to get more news of the suicide attacks till reaching Mumbai, I was left thinking not only of how close I had come to being one of its victims, but also of how I had equally become a potential suspect in the process. Of course I was only one of millions of possible victims and suspects in a global struggle that seemed to explode the idea of responsibility itself by extending it to the ends of the earth.

In her essay on Karl Jaspers and the atomic age, Hannah Arendt locates this transformation of political responsibility in the new global arena produced by the Cold War. She suggests that the expansion of such responsibility to a global arena had the consequence of depriving it of political meaning altogether:

Our political concepts, according to which we have to assume responsibility for all public affairs within our reach regardless of personal "guilt," because we are held responsible as citizens for everything that our government does in the name of the country, may lead us into an intolerable situation of global responsibility.[1]

Intolerable about the globalization of responsibility is not only the conversion of every man into his brother's keeper, but also the disappearance of responsibility as such by reason of its very universality. If as

---

1   Arendt, *Men in Dark Times*, p. 83.

citizens we are responsible for the consequences of our country's actions in the furthest reaches of the globe, or if as polluters we are responsible for the suffering caused by climate change among unknown people in unknown lands, then such responsibility may continue to pose ethical claims upon us, but it has ceased to have political meaning. For having been discovered everywhere this responsibility is to be found nowhere in particular.

It is this problem that Muslim militants grapple with when trying to locate responsibility within the global arena of their operations. For these men, as we know, the globalization of responsibility means that anyone anywhere can be found guilty of British or American actions in Iraq and Afghanistan, including any Muslim sympathetic to or accepting of such actions. While locating culpability among civilians abroad or collaborators at home has long been the stock in trade of guerrilla and resistance movements, I wish to suggest that transposing this search from a state to the globe changes it into something quite different. For one thing a responsibility that can be assigned to every person and place in the world soon becomes politically invisible, and in doing so makes punishment indiscriminate by its very universality. And for another the militant confronted by this universality is as likely to be concerned with renouncing his share of the responsibility as with finding it in another.

Perhaps the universalization of such responsibility is what allows it to be claimed only by, or on behalf of, suicide bombers, while the non-suicidal attacks that terrorists had once so eagerly claimed now often remain anonymous, lacking even the enunciation of a cause. By letting responsibility slide into global abstractions like "jihad" that lack any local cause, such anonymous acts deprive terrorism of its old-fashioned political meaning as a collective enterprise, while simultaneously turning the suicide bomber's purely individual claims of responsibility into acts of renunciation. For the suicide bomber claims and disclaims responsibility in the same move, by releasing a videotape acknowledging his action on the one hand, and on the other by attributing all responsibility for this act to his enemy, who is said to have left the martyr-murderer no other choice. Indeed the random killing of civilians is very frequently seen as doing nothing more than holding up the mirror to infidel attacks upon Muslims, thus transferring the responsibility for both to the militant's enemy. We shall see later that the only act this militant claims to possess fully is that of killing himself. In this sense murder and martyrdom belong in quite distinct registers though they tend to occur together.

In this chapter I will argue that the globalization of responsibility has not only robbed it of political meaning by predicating it of humanity as such, but that in the process acts of militant punishment work to disclaim culpability for oneself as much as they do to claim it of others. The suicide bombing, in other words, can be seen as a practice of withdrawal deriving from a religious tradition, that of renouncing the world, while transforming it at the same time. For withdrawal has now itself become a worldly act, and so one capable of giving rise to a new politics. That Gandhi happens to be the great theorist of such worldly withdrawal, as well as being its foremost practitioner, should by now come as no surprise. The Mahatma turned old-fashioned politics upside-down by sacrificing the positive instrumentality of its action for a negative practice of non-cooperation. By disclaiming responsibility in this way, Gandhi sought the collapse of a politics he considered evil without necessarily proposing some virtuous alternative to it, since his action, as Jaspers would say, was a suprapolitical one. Our militants, too, rarely propose any alternative political vision, and if their violence does appear positive or instrumental, we shall see that its effort to disclaim responsibility possesses a profoundly negative core.

How the lady vanishes

As an effort to claim responsibility for others while disclaiming it for oneself, the suicide bombing has special relevance for the citizens of countries seen by militants as posing threats to Islam. I will be discussing the terrorist acts of such men here, all European citizens, and in particular those who bombed London's public transport network on July 7, 2005. By attacking their own compatriots, these men were in fact acting as citizens who, like murderous caricatures of the conscientious objector, refused to assume responsibility for the actions of their fellows—even trying to compel the latter into righteousness by the example of their sacrifice. Given its globalization, however, this responsibility was so dispersed as to be difficult to locate politically, its universality making acts of militant violence possible and impossible at the same time. For if it was not to be indiscriminate, militant violence had to ground responsibility somewhere, since its very ubiquity made this responsibility invisible. The London bombings, I want to suggest, represented such an act of grounding.

There is nothing peculiar about this vanishing of responsibility in the London bombings, which indeed presented a very common problem in the immediate aftermath of the blasts, as one of the government reports on the attacks tells us. Despite almost immediate confirmation of the event as a terrorist attack that had long been foretold, and of a kind London had experienced many times before, rumours started circulating about other elements that might have been responsible for it, including power surges, explosions and accidents in general. Quite apart from the conspiracy theories that were also in circulation, such explanations extinguished responsibility altogether by dispersing it into an abstraction. And in fact it is now routine for accidents around the world to be mistaken for terrorist attacks, and for terrorist attacks to be mistaken for accidents, so that it requires sustained effort by politicians and experts of all kinds to set a standard narrative in place.

Rather than illustrating some mindless panic, such explanations recognize that the potential dispersal of responsibility in the complex space of a modern city renders it politically invisible, since it might be attributed to anyone and anything, not least to the city itself as an ultimate cause. For while the modern city is always spoken of in terms of construction, for example in the building of public institutions, private dignities and generalized opportunities, it can equally be defined in terms of destruction. From Haussman's Paris to Le Corbusier's Chandigarh, we know that modern cities are made possible by the kind of urban planning that involves large-scale shifts of population and the devastation of entire communities. These processes are not present simply at the city's founding, but continue to characterise its modernity in acts of zoning, development, slum-clearance and the like, which sometimes give rise to another kind of destruction in urban demonstrations and riots. But the city not only displaces and destroys in order to exist, it actually plans for its own destruction as well.

The architect and theorist of technology Paul Virilio argues that because the modern city as a product of urban planning is particularly vulnerable to wholesale destruction, whether due to natural forces, war and terror or technological malfunctions and accidents, it must also plan for these exigencies in such a way as to predict and internalize its own annihilation.[2] Because it is increasingly difficult to tell the difference between urban destruction caused wilfully and that caused by an accident, Virilio points out that one kind of disaster is frequently mistaken for another, making the subject or agent of this destruction both ambiguous and irrelevant.[3] For urban authorities have to plan for both kinds of eventuality in the same way, naturalizing and homogenizing destruction in such a fashion as to make it almost an effect of the city itself—a death foretold by urban planners and so inherent in the city from the time of its founding.

Beyond its vanishing in the accident, there exists an abundance of conspiracy theories that similarly muddy responsibility by their multiple and unknowable claims. And so the London bombings were followed by numerous reports of mysterious packages, a non-existent fifth bomber and the equally imaginary mastermind who was said to have escaped the country. Like the suicide bombers themselves, many of these theories seemed to be animated by the desire to ground an invisible responsibility somewhere by capturing and punishing some living perpetrator for it. More interesting, however, were the false claims of responsibility made by groups and individuals for reasons of publicity or advertising. Adding confusion to uncertainty, these claims, which are now commonplace in situations of accidental or planned carnage around the world, used the bombings as gigantic billboards for their causes. Indeed the terrorists themselves served merely as celebrity sponsors for such groups or individuals, who in this way forced their attacks into the everyday practices of a media-produced society.

As if realizing that their acts of claiming and disclaiming responsibility ran the risk of being hijacked by others, the suicide bombers tried very hard to place their copyright upon the attacks, though of course they could only do so posthumously by way of videotaped testaments. Yet even these were poached, with a video clip of Ayman al-Zawahiri endorsing the attacks appended to one of the tapes. And while a celebrity sponsor like Zawahiri is likely to have been welcomed by the Lon-

---

2   Paul Virilio, *The Original Accident*, trans. Julie Rose, (Cambridge: Polity Press, 2007).

3   Ibid.

don bombers, it is noteworthy that their videotaped testaments make no mention of such an endorsement, claiming only inspiration from Al-Qaeda. In an extraordinary move, the chief terrorist, Mohammad Sidique Khan, went so far as to have objects that identified him placed at three of the explosion sites, although he was only present at one of them. I suspect that Khan entrusted these bureaucratic proofs of his identity to his fellow bombers precisely so that they would be found in the wreckage of the attacks by the same bureaucracy that issued them, as if in a mockery of the equally bureaucratic practice called "return to sender".

Whether or not he meant to return his British identity to the state that issued it, Mohammad Sidique Khan was obviously very keen to claim the bombings—all the bombings—as his own by leaving his "prints" at three of its sites. If anything, this tells us how difficult it was for the terrorists to claim responsibility even for these most spectacular of their acts, since they had to, as it were, go into overkill in order to establish their own innocence alongside the guilt of their victims. Or was it also the innocence of these victims that their deaths sought to share? For despite all their bluster about guilt and innocence, the responsibility that made both these states possible remained fundamentally mysterious to the bombers, who had therefore to ground it by their acts of sacrificial violence. Indeed I will go on to show how this might account for the otherwise inexplicable uncertainty about pinpointing responsibility for terrorist killings that is to be found among so many militants prior to their attacks.

In addition to betraying no signs of militant views before his suicide bombing, Mohammad Sidique Khan spoke against the attacks of 9/11 at school.[4] Two of his accomplices, however, Hasib Hussain and Jermayne Lindsay, were known to have expressed extreme views at school, though it is not clear how a phrase like "Al Qaeda No Limits", scrawled on a school notebook, might depart from the anti-establishment culture that is common among adolescents.[5] In any case we are told that conspiracy theories regarding Al-Qaeda abounded among the bombers, and at least some of them "expressed the view that the 9/11 attacks were a plot by

---

4   *Report of the Official Account of the Bombings in London on 7th July 2005. Return to an Address of the Hon. The House of Commons dated 11th May 2006* (London: The Stationery Office, 2006), p. 17.

5   Ibid., p. 18

62

the US".[6] These facts are highly significant, as they not only demonstrate the lack of ideological uniformity among the terrorists, indeed their lack of ideology as such, but in addition tell us how uncertain the militants were about assigning responsibility for the incidents of war and terror that seemed to have engulfed so much of the Muslim world.

We should not underestimate the problem posed by this vanishing of responsibility for actual and would-be militants, since their uncertainty about assigning or disclaiming such responsibility in a global arena is not at all uncommon. So in documents released by the US government from the military hearing of a British citizen who had been captured in Afghanistan and detained at Guantánamo Bay, we find the same uncertainty regarding terrorism as well as the conspiracy theories about 9/11 that had been displayed by the London bombers. Uganda-born Feroz Ali Abbasi had been inspired by the teachings of the Kashmir-based Pakistani militant Masood Azhar, and had travelled to Afghanistan in order to join the Taliban or fight against the Indians in Kashmir.[7] While in Afghanistan he was alleged to have undergone basic training at Osama bin Laden's Al Faruq camp, and after the fall of the Taliban in 2002, was turned in to American troops by an informer.

The documents released from Abbasi's hearings at Guantánamo Bay are concerned for the most part with his efforts to claim prisoner of war status, since this would endow him with the formal and legal standing that the US administration's new classification of enemy combatant deprived him of. Remarkable about the written materials he submitted to the camp authorities, is Abbasi's almost obsessive concern with the mystery and doubt that appeared to obscure responsibility altogether in the War on Terror. Abbasi's texts on doubt and mystery are full of interest. The detainee, as he styles himself, uses two forms of reasoning to render responsibility problematic in the War on Terror. The first is highly legalistic, and has to do with the US government's inability to define what exactly Al-Qaeda is, how Abbasi was meant to have been recruited to it, and what proof it in fact had that Al-Qaeda was responsible for the 9/11 attacks. Abbasi also argues that since Osama bin Laden had

---

6   Ibid., p. 22

7   Feroz Ali Abbasi, "TO WHOM IT MAY CONCERN/RE. US9UK-000024DP's CLAIM OF THE STATUS; PRISONER OF WAR", pp. 666 and 671.

sworn allegiance to the Taliban leader Mullah Omar, Al-Qaeda must be regarded as part of the Afghan government, giving its members prisoner of war status, even if the Taliban state had not been recognized by the United States.[8] While this argument might constitute a reasonable defence in a court of law, its irrelevance to Abbasi's tribunal, of which the detainee was repeatedly made aware, deprives it of instrumentality and exposes instead Abbasi's own obsession with the claiming and assigning of responsibility. This becomes clear once he moves on to discuss 9/11 as a conspiracy:

This point is made even more heinous by the subsequent point that Usama bin Laden possessed a *fax line* with the Terrorist American government. That through that *fax line* he was *WARNED* to the similar purport of, "the Americans are going to bomb in one month's time"! Knowledge only a handful could have possessed, all I would surmise within the upper echelons of the American government itself.

Not only that the US military "telegraphed" its intentions to bomb via civilian radio transmission by telling Northern Alliance to, "Ground their planes"! Further fuel to add to the plausible suspicion that the USA's government was in cahoots with Usama bin Laden!

Therefore George W. Bush's "War on Terrorism" is nothing of the sort. It is but a puppet show pretence to truth and justice. The real war is clear to all with a sense of truth, justice, and fair play: it is a war on the Muslims, a war on Islam; a pathetic attempt at warring against Allah—a Crusade.

As to the perpetrators of the terrorist attacks of September 11th 2001 I would suggest those who truly want to know the answer to that dilemma (certainly the Americans do not) to look to those who gained the most from that crime. It certainly can not be the Muslims who have suffered greatly and can rightly be considered as the Ongoing Victims of September 11, 2001.

I end this response with a quote from Arthur Conan Doyle's "Sherlock Holmes": "The difficulty is to detach the framework of fact—of absolute undeniable fact from the embellishments of theorists and reporters. Then, having established ourselves upon this sound basis, it is our duty to see what inferences may be drawn, and which are the special points upon which the whole mystery turns."[9]

---

8   Ibid., p.644.

9   Ibid., pp. 637-8.

Relying upon the methodology of detective fiction, Abbasi's writing is consumed by the effort to establish an "absolute undeniable fact", but ends up only with inferences, chief among them being that the victimization of Muslims following the 9/11 attacks suggests the United States is their perpetrator. Far as it is from the sophisticated reasoning of a Bin Laden or a Zawahiri, this crude attempt to establish political responsibility in a global arena joins the larger stream of militant thinking in its concern with dispelling the mystery of globalization by making the conspiracy theories to which it gives rise come true. The terrorist act, in other words, substitutes itself for the missing facts in this mystery, as if in a kind of self-fulfilling prophecy, creating in this practical way the certainty that refuses to yield itself to the eyes of theory. And while such an act has a great deal in common with the tactic of "direct action" that once characterized fascist as well as communist attempts to fulfil the "logic" of history, among militants today it also possesses an existential and indeed epistemological dimension that the former lacked. This at least is what Abbasi's list of reasons for military struggle indicate:

I.   To make Allah's word the highest[10]

II. To establish Allah's law upon the land[11]

III. To protect innocent and persecuted men, women, and children[12]

IV. In the hope of being martyred for the cause of Allah[13]

V.   To purge the ranks of the hypocrites[14]

VI. To test the believers (?)[15]

The last three of these reasons for militant action illustrate the strictly individual purposes of jihad beyond any collective political cause. And if "the ranks of the hypocrites" who must be purged include the potential militant himself, as I will argue in another part of this chapter, then his act of terror claims and disclaims global responsibility in the way I

---

10   Ibid., p. 667.

11   Ibid.

12   Ibid., p. 668.

13   Ibid.

14   Ibid., p. 669.

15   Ibid.

have been suggesting it does. This conclusion is certainly provided by the final reason Abbasi gives for violent struggle, which thus functions as a test of the militant's sincerity in an existential way, while at the same time serving as a test of his truth in an epistemological one. The fact that our detainee places a question mark after the last purpose underlines my argument, since it is precisely this sort of uncertainty that his unfulfilled militant act would have resolved. I shall return to this existential and epistemological "test" that violence poses for the would-be militant, only pausing here to note that by passing it at the cost of their lives, the London bombers managed to erase the question mark that still haunts Abbasi's own.

Although Abbasi's texts are much more extensive than those of his martyred compatriots, the London bombers, and very different in style, they, too, are addressed to an abstract and anonymous audience. And while this makes sense for the video testaments that Khan and Tanweer had recorded to be distributed by the mass media, it appears bizarre in Abbasi's letter to his captors, which, as I have already pointed out, barely addresses any issue within their jurisdiction. So in the transcript of Abbasi's interview with these authorities, which is appended to his written statement, the detainee is repeatedly asked by the tribunal, and advised by the representative assigned him, to keep to the subject at hand, but entirely without success. After numerous quotations from the Quran, as well as from the executive orders of the American president, and an attempt to conduct a legal defence of the kind that might appear in a popular film or a work of detective fiction, Abbasi's hearing was finally adjourned. And indeed the detainee was not really speaking to his captors at all, but rather to an imaginary global audience, even though he had no idea at the time that his lengthy disquisition would ever leave the closely guarded precincts of Guantánamo Bay. If anything Abbasi's testimony functioned like one of the videotaped testaments left behind by suicide bombers, since in it he largely ignored his actual audience and circumstances to speak to some abstract audience in the future. It is important to note in this respect that unlike such "martyrological" testaments, militant communiqués invariably address themselves to a contemporary audience and even to individuals in the most direct form of dialogue that media can provide.

Abbasi's narrative is imagined as a media product, and this is important because the media are virtually indispensable in grounding responsibility among militants, though it does so in a way that goes beyond its traditional role of publicity and communication. Like the edifying discourse of old, or some traditional moral discipline, the media functions to build character and turn would-be militants into responsible agents. So Abbasi wrote himself into an Arthur Conan Doyle mystery in which he played a Muslim Sherlock Holmes, referring in his screed to the various incidents he encountered in captivity as if they were detective stories. Thus the " Adventures of Sherlock Holmes, Adventure XXIV— The Beardless Face Mystery", in which Abbasi claims that his testicles were "mutilated" and he was injected with a mysterious substance in order to promote the kind of beard growth that would make him appear the image of a fanatical Muslim.[16] Similarly we are told that the London bombers repeatedly watched videotapes of Muslims fighting and being killed in places like Bosnia or Chechnya in order to fire their imaginations and steel their resolve.[17] As a form of self-incitement, of course, these videotapes operated like pornography, though even here the practice of edification should not be dismissed. In any case such media did not work merely to communicate or publicize information, this latter being turned by the future terrorists to rather different existential and epistemological ends.

Closer to the tradition of character building is the way in which militants model their behaviour upon that of men like Osama bin Laden or Ayman al-Zawahiri, each with a very different style of speech and presentation in their audio and video recordings. Some of the London bombers mixed these individual styles into a generic model of militancy, as displayed in the videotaped testaments that were to be aired posthumously on Al-Jazeera. Thus Khan and Shehzad Tanweer both imitated Bin Laden's locutions as they appear in English translation, while adopting Zawahiri's more animated body language, which includes wagging a finger at the camera to emphasize his rhetorical points. Also important as a model for Khan's testament was that of a British Muslim, with the *nom de guerre* of Suraqah al-Andalusi or Suraqah the

---

16   Ibid., pp. 645-6.

17   "7 July bomber's motives examined", *BBC News*, 11 November, 2005 (http://news.bbc.co.uk/go/pr/fr/-/2/hi/uk_news/4444358.stm), p. 2.

Spaniard, who had been killed in 2002 during the American bombard-ment of Tora Bora.[18] Significant about these internal media references are two facts: not only has character building shifted its focus from living or bookish models to videotaped ones, but this visual medium functions to restrict communication to itself. Instead of serving as the media by which living persons might communicate, television footage and video clips increasingly communicate only with one another in militant testaments, which after all make no distinction between the living and the dead.

Paul Virilio points out that the "real time" within which media tech-nologies now operate replaces the nocturnal-diurnal temporality of our everyday lives with a "world time" measured by the global incidence of disasters like earthquakes, assassinations, terrorist attacks and the like.[19] An example of the way in which we all live in world time is provided by the questions we ask each other: what were you doing when JFK was assassinated or when 9/11 happened? Militant actions are also struc-tured according to world time, their videotaped testaments talking to each other around the globe. But the self-referential way in which the media operates within militancy circumvents communication as much as directing it. By taking their characters from videotapes, and using the same medium to give new characters back to the repertoire of militancy, the London bombers moved video technology away from its mediating purpose to turn it back upon itself. In so doing they were occupied by technology's ontological dimension, being concerned with its nature more than with its ordinary deployment. Since violence is the most technical of practices, depending as it does upon the use of tools both rude and sophisticated, this attention to technique in its own right is not surprising among terrorists. Extraordinary, however, is the way in which militant concern with technique diverts violence from its own in-strumentality, for example in the bit of "cartoon" animation showing a train approaching Kings Cross station that prefaced one of the London bombers' videotaped testaments.

There is something playful and experimental about the terrorist's perversion of technologies of communication, transportation and la-

---

18   *Report of the Official Account of the Bombings in London*, p. 22.

19   Paul Virilio, trans. Chris Turner, *The Information Bomb* (London: Verso, 2005), pp. 115-130.

bour to violent new ends. Thus the "technologization" of beauty products like peroxide and cooking ingredients like flour in the manufacture of bombs by African immigrants to London in 2005. These pantomime terrorists seemed more interested in technique and simulation than in any real attack, but even those who are in deadly earnest often end up robbing technology of its instrumentalism, since this is no longer tied to any traditional political project but possesses instead an existential dimension of its own. How else are we to account for the aesthetic dimension that has been lent militant websites like "Al-Ansar's Top 20" from Iraq, to which insurgents send in clips of attacks that are then competitively ranked on the model of top twenty music countdowns?[20] Naturally these video clips are ranked by their aesthetic merits rather than by anything so instrumental as the number of people killed in the attacks they depict. For if they have a utilitarian aim, it is to join militant practices to those of everyday life through mass media. Their aim, in other words, is not to depart the world so much as rejoin it.

What kind of communication do visual media make possible when one or more of the speakers are dead? Neither messages transmitted by their technology around the globe, nor publicity obtained by the same means to flatter an ego or further a cause, but rather something as old-fashioned as immortality. And what this immortality might lack by way of its historical survival as a living memory, it more than makes up for in the sheer extent of its subject's global notoriety. Like literary works in the past, or even Feroz Abbasi's narrative of mystery in the present, media today offer the suicide bomber a posthumous life, in this way constituting a medium in the occult sense, one that allows him to speak after dying. Stopping at a shop on his way to blow himself up, Tanweer is described as looking directly into a surveillance camera, as if contemplating its film's future broadcast to the world and therefore his own death and immortality. He might as well have winked at the camera, sharing with the millions who would soon see its footage, the secret that he could control both his future and theirs.[21]

Immortality is not a feature unique to the suicide bomber's videotaped testament, being a quality commonly invoked in reference to

---

20   Kimmage and Ridolfo, *Iraqi Insurgent Media: The War of Images and Ideas*, pp. 28-29.

21   *Report of the Official Account of the Bombings in London*, p. 5.

the classic films or television reruns that also depart from a simpleminded theory of communications technology. What is original about the militant's use of this medium is that he claims (and disclaims) responsibility through it. But such responsibility differs from the sort claimed by terrorists in the past, for by preceding rather than following the terrorist act, the suicide bomber's videotaped testament works to create and foreshadow his responsibility instead of merely illustrating it. Though they depend upon attacks for their resonance, in other words, these videotapes exist independently of them, such attacks serving only as references, advertisements and points of departure for a narrative about the globe and the martyr's place within it.

It is in the videotape rather than in real life that the militant comes to possess and relinquish responsibility by embedding his impending attack within an Islamic narrative. The taping of this narrative, therefore, as well as its dispatch to media outlets like Al-Jazeera, represents the coming into being of the militant more than any other act before his attack, for it lends every would-be terrorist the global countenance of a media personality by offering him up as a hostage to an anonymous audience that is both human and divine in the public confession of an act not yet committed. More than the attack itself, it is the videotape that allows the militant to become responsible in a prophetic and posthumous way, by broadcasting his impending death to ground this responsibility, while simultaneously withdrawing from its ubiquity in a dramatic act of sacrifice. Indeed the suicide bomber can only ground responsibility in this dual sense by dying for it. But this is the same thing as saying that the only good Muslim is a dead Muslim.

Shuffling off the alternative lifestyle

If it is death that makes the good Muslim, then his life is correspondingly freed up for activities other than piety. Is this why so many suicide bombers abandon their religious scruples in the days before their martyrdom to revel in the hitherto illicit pleasures of the flesh? In many cases this change is so drastic as to draw attention to the would-be terrorist rather than serving as a disguise. As for the foretaste of paradise that such pleasures are sometimes said to offer, we know of not one militant, only an imaginative journalist or two, who has described them

in this way. Whatever its motives, the important thing about such ir-
religious behaviour is the fact that it "normalizes" the lives of militants
beyond instrumental reasons like disguise, and according to the norms
of the profane society that surrounds them. In other words before his
death as a good Muslim, the suicide bomber very frequently discards
his alternative lifestyle as a religious man to rejoin the corrupt society
he will soon attack. It is almost as if the militant were preparing to die
alongside his victims by sharing their lives beforehand to acknowledge a
common humanity. Was it also this common humanity that the bombers wanted to put on display by conducting two of their operations in
areas of London known for their Muslim populations—Edgware Road
for Arabs and Aldgate East for Bangladeshis?

Some of the London bombers provide us with good examples of this
normalization, in which the militant not only dies together with his
victims, but also does so having become like them in the most egregious
of ways. This is how the official report on the attacks describes Jermayne
Lindsay in the days before they occurred:

Lindsay's behaviour thereafter became increasingly erratic, although not in a
way that would suggest he had terrorism in mind. He was sometimes violent.
He flirted openly having been very strict in contacts with women before (it
is now known that he had at least one girlfriend and sought to contact other
women over this time). He would not pray with his wife, shaved his beard and
began wearing western clothes. He began associating with petty criminals.[22]

While Lindsay's fellow conspirators did not change so drastically,
though Hussain had been cautioned for shoplifting the year before[23],
they also rejoined mainstream British society prior to attacking it—if
only by their completely unexceptional behaviour. For instance while
driving to the railway station from where they would catch a train to
London, the soon-to-be bombers stopped at a service station to fill up
with petrol. Shehzad Tanweer went in to pay, bought some snacks and
quibbled with the cashier over his change, which he would take with
him to meet death shortly afterwards.[24] Having worn a white T-shirt,
dark jacket, white tracksuit bottoms and a baseball cap when paying at

---

22   Ibid., p. 27.
23   Ibid., p. 18.
24   Ibid., p. 5.

Woodall Services, Tanweer emerged at Luton station in dark tracksuit bottoms, the official report commenting that, "There is no explanation for his change at present".[25] However the report does tell us that Tanweer "took care with his appearance, with fashionable hairstyles and designer clothing"[26], so it can be assumed that he changed because his white tracksuit bottoms had become dirty or even because of sartorial better judgement. As if hinting at Tanweer's concern with clothing and his change of clothes on the day of the attacks, Ayman al-Zawahiri, in the clip appended to Shehzad Tanweer's videotaped testament, made a very deliberate and possibly ironical point of noting that while the suicide bomber came from a wealthy family, he had always lived frugally and dressed simply.[27] No mention of Tanweer's red Mercedes-Benz. Once at the railway station the men bought return tickets, as if they had not bombs in their rucksacks but picnic hampers which they would bring back empty from London. Unlike the 9/11 hijackers, there is no evidence that the London bombers made any attempt to dignify their last moments with some ritual or prayer.

Not only does the banality of these details go well beyond disguise, their very ordinariness becomes absurd in the context of the bombings, as if the four would-be martyrs were playing at some childish game of mimicry, which included among its episodes Tanweer's participating in a cricket match on the evening before his suicide attack. Not surprisingly, such incongruous details have given rise to a number of conspiracy theories about the London bombers, though what I find interesting is their illustration of the fact that the terrorists were determined to separate their lives from their deaths, as if the two had nothing at all in common, not even in terms of cause and effect. And indeed the radically different appearance these men adopt in their videotaped testaments tells us that their true lives were posthumous, with the acts allowing them access to this life after death having been prompted not by their previous existence, so much as by the actions of other militants before them,

25   Ibid., p. 7.

26   Ibid., p. 18.

27   "American Al-Qaeda Operative Adam Gadahn, Al-Qaeda Deputy Al-Zawahiri, and London Bomber Shehzad Tanweer in New Al-Sahab/Al-Qaeda Film Marking the First Anniversary of the 7/7 London Bombings", *The Middle East Media Research Institute*, Special Dispatch Series, no. 1201, 11 July, 2006 (http://memri.org/bin/opener.cgi?Page=archives&ID=SP120106), p. 2.

all of which were circulating the globe in the form of media spectacles. For like militants before and after them, the London bombers never derived their acts from any personal experience of oppression or suffering, which is to say from their own life histories or political circumstances, but only from those of other Muslims as seen on television.

All this means that there is very little in the way of a conversion narrative, a "moment of decision", to be found in militant lives, whose radicalization thus remains profoundly mysterious. From the terrorist narratives we possess, it is clear that such moments of conversion are rare indeed, with figures as important as Osama bin Laden claiming to have been radicalized simply by watching television and not by any personal, let alone spiritual transformation. Extraordinary though militant lives can be it is their banal and everyday aspects that may possess the most weight, not least because of the haphazard and amateurish character of so many "radical" biographies. These men are not the professional terrorists of previous times, but as Western security agencies recognize, self-conscious amateurs lacking the alternative lifestyle that defines professional as much as cult behaviour. And while such amateurishness might be expected from single-act terrorists like the London bombers, it seems to characterize those hardened in the battlefields of Iraq or Afghanistan as well. Thus the bizarre videotape that came to light in 2006 depicting Abu Musab al-Zarqawi, the Jordanian head of Al-Qaeda in Mesopotamia, who was reputed to be the most ruthless fighter in Iraq. In the videotape, Zarqawi, wearing white tennis shoes with his dark "terrorist" gear, appeared unable to handle his gun and had to be helped by an assistant. This is not to suggest, of course, that militants possess no technical skills, only that such expertise does not end up defining who they are in any professional sense. Might it be their very lack of old-fashioned professionalism, as well as the collective organization and ideology sustaining it that makes these men so creative, so dangerous and so human in their commonness?

As it turns out, the rejection of an alternative lifestyle in the days before their attacks marked only the completion of the London bombers' already banal lives. Mohammad Sidique Khan, known as "Sid", was married and the father of a child. While the extended sick leave he took at the end of 2004, followed by his resignation from the primary school where he worked as a learning mentor, might indicate Khan's shift to militancy during this period, he betrayed no other signs of unusual behaviour. Indeed Khan was perfectly integrated into mainstream British society and respected by all those who knew him, as the official report tells us:

He was highly regarded by teachers and parents, and had a real empathy with difficult children. Children saw him as a role model. He was highly successful in calming situations and getting excluded children back into school. He gave an interview to the *Times Educational Supplement* in 2002 in which he spoke passionately about his work.[28]

In addition to being a bit of a dandy and driving a red Mercedes, Shehzad Tanweer did well at school, was an outstanding athlete who played for a local cricket team, and worked in his father's fish and chip shop while looking around to set himself up as an independent businessman.[29] Hasib Hussain, though a mediocre student, continued with his college education, completing it only a month before blowing himself up.[30] While all were said to be religious, of the four it was only Jermayne Lindsay, also known as Jamal, who had participated in any political activity, including, in 2002, a "Stop the War" march in London.[31] But even Lindsay's prior history of handing out leaflets supporting Al-Qaeda, or following the Jamaican preacher Abdallah al-Faisal, who had been jailed for soliciting murder and inciting racial hatred, was not out of keeping with his grittier background of a broken home, unemployment and odd jobs.[32] Indeed if anything Lindsay's activist stance over racism and the wars in Afghanistan and Iraq put him in the mainstream of British political concerns during this period.

As the official report recognizes, none of this adds up to anything as far as identifying a militant profile or locating the sources of radicalism are concerned:

What we know of previous extremists in the UK shows that there is not a consistent profile to help identify who may be vulnerable to radicalization. Of the 4 individuals here, 3 were second generation British citizens whose parents

---

28   *Report of the Official Account of the Bombings in London*, p. 17.

29   Ibid.

30   Ibid.

31   Ibid., p. 21.

32   Ibid., pp. 20-21.

were of Pakistani origin and one whose parents were of Jamaican origin; Kamel Bourgass, convicted of the Ricin Plot, was an Algerian failed asylum seeker. Richard Reid, the failed shoe bomber, had an English mother and Jamaican father. Others of interest have been white converts. Some have been well-educated, some less so. Some genuinely poor, some less so. Some apparently well integrated in the UK, others not. Most single, but some family men with children. Some previously law-abiding, others with a history of petty crime. In a few cases there is evidence of abuse or other trauma in early life, but in others their upbringing has been stable and loving.[33]

Rather than trying to locate responsibility for such militancy in the exotic or exceptional details of terrorists' lives, it should be found in the unremarkable and ordinary aspects of their existence. After all, it is precisely in the banality of everyday life that global responsibility lies, whether for environmental degradation or Muslim suffering. And if this is the case, then there is no reason for militants of either sort to fulfil their own responsibilities to Islam or to the environment out of any but the most ordinary of circumstances. Perhaps this is why the official report on the London bombings found that the would-be suicide bombers attended no mosque regularly, evidenced little Internet use at home and had no real association with any radical figure, let alone an Al-Qaeda sleeper lurking in some Islamic school or bookstore.[34] Their independence of any militant organization is also indicated by the bombers' planning and equipment, which are described as simple, cheap and local.[35] Neither the ideology nor the organization that make for an alternative lifestyle are present in this case of militancy and no doubt in that of many others as well.

The globalization of responsibility permits the terrorist to destroy his own ubiquitous share of it alongside that of his anonymous and generic victim, with the suicide bombing making his true individuality visible only posthumously and by way of videotaped testaments. This shifting of responsibility from life to death renders the ideology and organization of traditional politics irrelevant, since these militants do not seek to make a fortress of their Islam. Instead they inhabit the same world as those around them and are moved by the same concerns as those that

---

33   Ibid., p. 34.

34   Ibid., p. 19.

35   Ibid., p. 30.

dominate the headlines of mass-circulation newspapers. There is no cult behaviour on exhibit here, but the suicide of ordinariness when faced with its global responsibility. This absence of ideology and organization is equally visible in the Intelligence and Security Committee's report on the bombings, which notes that the extraordinary speed of the militants' radicalization precluded indoctrination of a traditional sort:

We have been told that the speed of radicalisation of some of those involved in the attacks was also unexpected. According to the Director-General of the Security Service, July showed that extremists could be created at any time through a very quick process.[36]

Although it is part of a larger movement linked by modes of argumentation and forms of practice, such do-it-yourself militancy is suprapolitical in its concern with the globalization of responsibility as an existential and epistemological problem. It remains unconcerned with the future utopia that ideologies are so keen on, and has nothing to do with theories of Islamic law or an Islamic state. In fact such militancy belongs to a post-ideological world, its actors possessing no sociological profile and undergoing no indoctrination—though they might well undergo some practical training. A couple of the London bombers had participated in a bit of jihad tourism in Kashmir, under the aegis of a Pakistan-based militant group, and had later made a brief and equally touristic foray into Afghanistan. But whatever inspiration they received abroad, their collective "training" occurred entirely in England, where the future bombers forged themselves into a group not in any secret hideout or religious lair, but in public places like gyms, youth clubs and rafting expeditions.[37] The official report on the London bombings has this to say about the latter:

Camping, canoeing, whitewater rafting, paintballing and other outward bound type activities are of particular interest because they appear common factors for the 7 July bombers and other cells disrupted previously and since.[38]

---

36   *Intelligence and Security Committee Report into the London Terrorist Attacks on 7 July 2005, Presented to Parliament by the Prime Minister by Command of Her Majesty* (London: May 2006), p. 29.

37   *Report of the Official Account of the Bombings in London*, p. 19.

38   Ibid., p. 20.

Such trips are varied in location and informal; there is no particular centre or centres where they are based. There is no firm evidence about how such trips might have been used.[39]

I imagine these activities were used in the same way as companies and corporations use them for their staff: to create bonds of trust and goodwill and certainly not as training for some physical prowess required at work. Indeed the public nature of such practices might well be more important than their performance, since these activities very clearly reject the privacy that marks ideological, cultic and professional practices for the publicity of everyday life. Even the unavoidable privacy of militant plotting is revealed in the suicide-bomber's videotaped testament, where it takes on a thoroughly simulated character.

Unlike the desire for some authentic private life that defines liberalism as much as any other ideology, our militants seem to prize only the simulated privacy purveyed by mass media in today's surveillance societies. For in a surveillance society, privacy increasingly resides in its global unveiling on web-cams, reality shows or Jerry Springer-style television. The simulation of such privacy occurs in the flirtatious but ultimately unfulfilled promise of revealing itself to a public audience. The suicide-bomber's videotape constitutes an unfulfilled promise not only because it speaks of an event that hasn't yet occurred, but also because it is broadcast after the event's occurrence. Like other ways in which the media simulate privacy, in other words, the videotaped testament offers us something that has either happened already or not yet happened. Its form of privacy is therefore temporal rather than spatial, the martyrdom videos teasing us for having missed the moment to which they gesture. Temporality is perhaps the last redoubt of privacy in a surveillance society, but more importantly it is also the category that structures militancy as such, since we have seen that this latter no longer depends upon the spatial obsession of traditional ideologies, being taken up instead by a world time and the coming of an Islamic victory with neither territories nor borders.

We have moved far from the ideological model of militant indoctrination through collective study and discussion here, to say nothing of plotting in smoke-filled rooms for the conquest of some utopia. So

---

39   Ibid.

before concocting their explosives and blowing themselves up, what the London bombers did together was to exercise and go rafting rather than debate or pray, though they probably did talk about Islam and current politics in the way that everyone else was doing at the time. Indeed the one thing that all of them had in common was a devotion to personal fitness, something the official report repeatedly mentions, though without drawing any conclusion from it. This practice of making and even transforming oneself physically no doubt stood the bombers in good stead when it came to the remaking of a Muslim self in the practice of martyrdom. Is it then possible to say that bodily self-improvement was as important to the making of these militants as any peculiarly religious observance?

Another way to love your enemy

By moving responsibility beyond the reach of ideology, globalization also renders it fragmentary and relativistic. For if it no longer pertains to any political or juridical system, such responsibility becomes a purely individual trust, which is why anyone can kill or be killed in its name. So militants fighting for a global Islam routinely uproot jihad from its classical status as a political obligation governed by law, known as the *farz kifaya*, and define it instead as a *farz ayn*, an ungoverned and quite personal obligation. In this way they have quite clearly taken leave of political traditions like ideology and statehood to globalize their practices without even a collective utopia in sight. At most there exists the vague and undefined global caliphate that Osama bin Laden speaks of, and otherwise nothing at all, as we see from the testaments of the London bombers and those like them.

Yet not so long ago it would have been impossible for any Muslim radical not to speak of Islamic law, an Islamic state and an Islamic revolution. Even Ayman al-Zawahiri, who participated in this earlier phase of Muslim radicalism, made it quite clear in a famous letter to Abu Musab al-Zarqawi, the head of Al-Qaeda in Mesopotamia, that his vision of a global caliphate based in Egypt or the Levant was purely a personal opinion.[40] But then the same is true of global movements more

---

40   Office of the Director of National Intelligence, "Letter from al-Zawahiri to al-Zarqawi, October 11, 2005" (http://www.dni.gov/release_letter_101105.

generally, since environmentalists and pacifists also lack an ideological utopia, concentrating like the militants on suprapolitical practices of an individual sort. The environmentalist's resolve to minimize his carbon footprint is suprapolitical because its form of sacrifice cannot possibly make a difference to climate change, no matter how many people are inspired by his example. In this sense the environmentalist's personal practices are disconnected from any political vision he might have of an ecologically friendly world. Similar are the practices of Muslim militancy, which lose political instrumentality in the global arena but gain existential meaning in the process.

Rather than being a drawback this lack of ideology and organization is actually an advantage in the global arena, where individuals can quickly be mobilized without any of the coercive mechanisms deployed by states as well as by would-be states for this purpose. The case of Feroz Abbasi, who tells us that he was inspired to go to fight in Afghanistan by the Pakistani militant Masood Azhar's book on jihad as an individual moral obligation, is quite typical,[41] as is the fact that he wasn't committed to any particular struggle in a political sense, choosing Afghanistan over Kashmir for completely accidental reasons. Not only are causes interchangeable in this global struggle, then, so are enemies, with Indians doubling for the Northern Alliance and later on for the Americans as well. Since I have dealt extensively with the ethical dimension of global militancy in a previous work,[42] I will focus here on its epistemological aspect instead—for to individualize responsibility outside a political or juridical system is also to make of it something entirely relative. Thus in his fulminations at Guantánamo Bay we find Abbasi quoting the following passage from the Quran, one that is particularly beloved among Muslim liberals and "moderates" because of its pluralistic ethos:

To each among you we have prescribed a law and an Open Way. If Allah had so willed, He would have made you a single people, but (His plan is) to test you in what He hath given you; so strive in a race in all virtues. The good of

---

html), p. 2.

41   Abbasi, p. 666.

42   See Faisal Devji, *Landscapes of the Jihad: Militancy, Morality, Modernity* (London: Hurst, 2005), especially chapter one.

you all is to Allah; it is He that will show you the truth of the matters in which ye dispute.[43]

In its emphasis on the fundamentally unknowable truth that causes people to dispute with each other, this passage plays into Abbasi's own obsession with mystery, uncertainty and doubt. And by speaking of the test that God has imposed upon these disputants, it upholds the militant practice of sacrificing to demonstrate the truth, or rather to produce it as such. But it is the relativism of this quotation that interests me here, since it is to be found mirrored in militant rhetoric more generally. Rather than subscribing to some collective ideology to which they would convert others, and by which others are to be judged, these men are content to have friends and enemies alike live by their own rules and be tested by them. While the scriptural passage above, for example, speaks of laws and seems to refer to communities that dispute the truth between them, Abbasi is concerned with individuals and their responsibility to submit to tests for the sake of the truth they profess. Indeed like his fellow militants, Abbasi does not himself belong to any of the traditional schools of Islamic law, instead picking and choosing pieces from their jurisprudence for purely personal use.

The bulk of Abbasi's narrative in the document he wrote at Guantánamo Bay is concerned with proving that the United States is breaking its own laws and flouting its own principles, not the laws and principles of Islam. Like other militants all over the world, he judges America by its own rules and according to its own terms. There is a precedent for such juridical pluralism in Muslim history, for before the emergence of modern nation-states and their uniform legal codes, religious communities were often judged by their own rules as far as personal law was concerned. And while a few elements of such juridical pluralism have survived in some places to this day, Abbasi's highly individualistic form of pluralism is not of course linked to them, being suprapolitical in nature. It is however quite explicitly linked to the word hypocrisy, which plays an important part in the Quran, where it designates those who pretend to be Muslims out of convenience while secretly plotting against Islam. We have already seen that rooting out hypocrisy is one of the duties that Abbasi, following Masood Azhar, assigns to the waging of jihad, though

---

43   Abbasi, p. 634.

in tune with militants elsewhere he extends the term so that it applies to infidels as well as Muslims—as it were "converting" the former to an Islam of the human spirit. At the same time as he differentiates people according to the principles they profess, therefore, Abbasi brings them together under a judgment that they all must equally face.

In a clip appended to Shehzad Tanweer's videotaped testament, Adam Gadahn, otherwise known as Azzam al-Amriki, expounds upon the meaning of hypocrisy in fairly typical fashion when discussing the American and British occupation of Afghanistan and Iraq:

And we haven't mentioned the fact that these actions of the Americans and British are prohibited by the same international laws and treaties, which they hypocritically claim to uphold and protect, and which they impose on others, even as they themselves violate them with impunity. And nor have we mentioned their unconditional support for the butchery and terrorism of their dear friend and ally, Israel, which I imagine everyone knows about. So after all the atrocities committed by America and Britain and their allies, which constitute terrorism in every sense of the word, you want us to observe restraint and civility in our response, or better yet—not respond at all? You want us to target their soldiers and tanks only, which as we've seen, still makes us terrorists in our [sic] eyes. And why should we target their military only—because to do otherwise would violate the precepts of that idol, that false god called international law, which we've conclusively shown, they themselves violate? No thanks, we have our own law, the law of God, who says in His book: 'And if you punish, let your punishment be proportionate to the wrong that has been done to you'.[44]

Important about this passage is that its rejection of international institutions as hypocritical creates a political vacuum, in which friends and enemies alike can only be judged pluralistically, according to their own principles and professions. This to the degree that God's law, too, which Gadahn invokes as an alternative to the hypocrisy of international law, turns out to be nothing but the legitimization of such pluralism. In the absence of a global politics, militant pluralism functions to assign responsibility according to the divergent principles of multiple actors, which is why hypocrisy becomes such a foundational category for it.

But by charging enemy practices rather than principles with such responsibility, Muslim militants refuse to see their struggle as a clash

---

44   "American Al-Qaeda operative Adam Gadahn, Al-Qaeda deputy Al-Zawahiri, and London Bomber Shehzad Tanweer in new Al-Sahab/Al-Qaeda film marking the first anniversary of the 7/7 London bombings", p. 4. Parenthesis mine.

of civilizations or ideologies, and are therefore unable to proffer any alternative civilization or ideology in their place. Thus Gadahn deprives militant attacks of all autonomy by defining them merely as proportional reactions to the violence of others. Such proportionality is invoked by the Quran, which describes acts of warfare in a situation where no common code of military conduct exists. According to the holy book, believers may respond in a strictly proportional way to any excesses perpetrated against them, though forgiveness is recommended as the best retaliation. Explicitly outside the juridical order, this form of proportionality resembles the structure of traditional feuds and even what we might call gangland ethics, where any provocative action is often matched by a strictly equivalent reaction in what sometimes becomes a classic spiral of violence. Irrespective of their justification by scriptural citation, in other words, these "reactions" are seen as being profoundly negative and therefore quite lacking in ontology, since they do no more than hold the mirror up to infidel provocations. Indeed acts of sacrifice are the only ones that possess an autonomy as well as ontology of their own in the rhetoric of jihad, which paradoxically means that martyrdom represents militancy's only positive element, even though it is a gesture of withdrawal from worldly responsibility. However self-serving this emptying out of responsibility from acts of violence, it reveals very clearly the militant's concern with such responsibility as something both claimed and disclaimed. And so Gadahn, for example, claims and disclaims responsibility by suspending principles altogether for a practice of violence with neither autonomy nor name:

I'm not saying that we should go and slaughter their women and children one by one, like they did ours, at Haditha, and Ishaqi, and Mahmudiya, and God knows where else, even if some of our legal experts have permitted that, and even if it is hard to imagine that any compassionate person could see pictures, just pictures, of what the Crusaders did to those children, and not want to go on a shooting spree at the Marines' housing facilities at Camp Pendleton. But what I am saying is that when we bomb their cities and civilians, like they bomb ours, or destroy their infrastructure and means of transportation, like they destroy ours, or kidnap their non-combatants, like they kidnap ours, no sane Muslim should shed tears for them. And they should blame no one but themselves, because they're the ones who started this dirty war, and they're the ones who will end it, by ending their aggression against Islam and Muslims, by pulling out of our region, and by keeping their hands our [sic] of our affairs.[45]

It is no exaggeration to say that hypocrisy represents an obsession for militant rhetoric, whose deployment there differs from its use among communists, for instance, by the fact that it is not meant to broach some truth alternative to capitalism. Rather than serving as an instrument to distinguish truth from falsehood, the language of hypocrisy is an acknowledgement of epistemological as well as existential pluralism, because it allows the militant to judge people only according to the principles they profess. Naturally this judgment includes in its purview the militant himself, who is therefore constantly testing his own loyalty to the principles he professes in comparison with that demonstrated by friends and enemies alike, with the final and most unanswerable of tests being the sacrifice of one's life. Bizarrely this means that militancy may be defined as a demand for people to be true to themselves. However strange, there is nothing extraordinary in the peremptory pluralism of this request, which constituted a staple element in anti-colonial rhetoric, and continues a major demand of public opinion in large parts of Asia and Africa, whether or not they happen to be populated by Muslims. For unlike the citizens of great powers, people in the rest of the world tend not to possess global missions or universal ideologies, and must by default remain pluralists both morally and politically.

Jawaharlal Nehru, who became India's first prime minister following her independence from Britain in 1947, had famously written about what he called "the two Englands", one the home of truth and liberty and the other of falsehood and oppression.[46] Nehru tried to reconcile the colonial power's two faces by asking England to remain true to herself in freeing India, and if she would not do so voluntarily, then by persuading England to fulfil her civilizing mission through political action. Gandhi, on the other hand, was more interested in testing Britain's claims to civilization by using his movements of mass sacrifice to force her into an unbearable choice: between giving India freedom on the one hand or tyranny on the other. And while Nehru might well have shared the liberal ideals that he urged England to live up to, Gandhi, who pos-

---

45   Ibid., p. 5.

46   Jawaharlal Nehru, *The Discovery of India* (New Delhi: Oxford University Press, 1999), pp. 284-288.

sessed rather different ones, asked her to remain true to these ideals as a pluralist. Like today's militant, the Mahatma was concerned with the falsehood and hypocrisy that he thought lay at the root of England's problems as much as India's. As always his aim was to detach the good of this situation from its evil, thus causing the latter to collapse, by testing both Indians and Englishmen in the ways of sacrifice.

In a video clip aired by Al-Jazeera on 29 November 2004, Ayman al-Zawahiri offers America the same choice that Gandhi had once offered Britain:

You must choose one of two paths in your treatment of the Muslims. Either you treat them with dignity and [based on] mutual interests, or you treat them as fair game in war, as land to be stolen, and as holy places to be desecrated. This is your problem, and you must make your own choice.[47]

Phrased in the same language of invitation and hospitality as the Mahatma's offer, and made compelling by the same practices of sacrifice, the choice Zawahiri demanded of the United States was also just as pluralist in character. For in the absence of a global politics Zawahiri could not rely upon any universal criterion, let alone any neutral institution to mediate between Al-Qaeda and its foe, and so appealed only to the integrity of American principles. Or rather he sought to test these principles against militant ones to see which were the more genuine. And it is this mutual testing that gives substance not only to the rhetoric of militancy but to its reality as well.

Competing in goodness

In passages much cited by Muslim liberals, the Quran appears to advocate religious and other forms of pluralism by asking different communities to compete with each other in goodness, each according to its own standard. Muslim militants, too, or at least those gathered under the sign of Al-Qaeda, seem to have taken these scriptural passages to heart, a particularly egregious example of which can be found in the testimony of the 9/11 linchpin, Khalid Sheikh Mohammed. On the one hand, competing in goodness with the enemy is only the obverse

---

47   "Al-Qaeda leader Ayman Al-Zawahiri on Al-Jazeera", *Middle East Media Research Institute*, Special Dispatch Series, no. 950, August 4, 2005 (http://memri.org/bin/opener.cgi?Page=archives&ID=SP95005), p. 3.

of competing with him in evil, which we have seen plays such a large part in militant rhetoric. But on the other hand competing in goodness goes beyond merely the mirroring of another's actions, and implies caring for the enemy's goodness as a quality that requires protection. This indeed is the closest the kind of militant I am describing comes to the Christian virtue of loving one's enemy.

In the redacted and unclassified version of his hearing at Guantánamo Bay on March 10, 2007, Khalid Sheikh Mohammed adopted the Gandhian practice of pleading guilty before a tribunal he considered illegitimate, thus turning his hearing into one for the tribunal itself, since his own guilt or innocence had ceased to be an issue for it. Indeed Mohammed's admission of guilt was so extensive as to place the charges laid against him quite in the shade by reversing the normal relationship between law and criminality, in which it is the person charged whose claims of responsibility tend to be minimal. Acknowledging guilt in this excessive way deprives it of meaning while returning such responsibility into the keeping of the law, where it remains something impersonal with which the person charged has only a formal and not an existential relationship. Perhaps this is why Khalid Sheikh Mohammed could afford to speculate upon responsibility as a theoretical category during his hearing, in which he concluded a long list of criminal claims with the following statement about the utterly conventional character of guilt:

What I wrote here, is not I'm making myself hero, when I said I was responsible for this or that. But your are military man. You know very well there are language for any war. So, there are, we are when I admitting these things I'm not saying I'm not did it. I did it but this the language of any war. If America they want to invade Iraq they will not send for Saddam roses or kisses they send for a bombardment. This is the best way if I want. If I'm fighting for anybody admit to them I'm American enemies. For sure, I'm American enemies.[48]

In one way this passage evokes my discussion earlier in this chapter on the difficulty of locating responsibility in a global arena. Thus Mohammed's lengthy list of claims threatens to spiral out of control and turn responsibility into an absurdity, so that he is finally forced to ground it by reducing these global claims into merely the illustrations of his enmity for America. But in another way this Gandhian admission

---

48   Unclassified Verbatim Transcript of Combatant Status Review Tribunal Hearing for ISN 10024, p. 21.

of guilt in someone else's language if not in one's own ultimately opens the door to a highly pluralistic vision of human relations, in which the refusal to recognize someone's legitimacy does not preclude the building of a relationship with him. The formal admission of guilt, in other words, functions like a gift that establishes relations even in the absence of recognition. This is how Khalid Sheikh Mohammed, for example, described his refusal to present evidence at his hearing under oath:

Take an oath is part of your Tribunal and I'll not accept it. To be or accept the Tribunal as to be, I'll accept it. That I'm accepting American constitution, American laws or whatever you are doing here. This is why religiously I cannot accept anything you do. Just to explain for this one, does not mean I'm not saying that I'm lying. When I not take oath does not mean I'm lying. You know very well peoples take oath and they will lie. You know the President he did this before he just makes his oath and he lied. So sometimes when I'm not making oath does not mean I'm lying.[49]

Having set the terms of engagement with his captors by offering them an admission of guilt without by that token according them any legitimacy, Mohammed went on to discuss the substance of this engagement, which for him consisted in being true to oneself. In fact he spent the whole of his hearing trying to get his American captors to be true to their own principles, which he took to be those of the promotion and protection of human rights, while at the same time treating their accusations as if they were questions regarding his own truthfulness to Islamic principles. Here, then, was an example of the testing in goodness of which the Quran spoke, and of whose pluralist character militants make so much. But while in militant rhetoric more generally it is the willingness to die for one's principles that demonstrates how true one is to oneself, in Mohammed's testimony this demonstrative role is played by the admission of guilt, which allows a relationship of mutual testing to occur between the bitterest of enemies. How else are we to explain the detainee's numerous and often carping objections to the accusations brought against him, as well as to the procedures of the tribunal at Guantánamo Bay, in light of his equally frequent admissions of guilt? It was not his innocence that Khalid Sheikh Mohammed tried to prove during his hearing, but rather the coherence and internal consistency of the charges levelled against him, which in an extraordinarily Gandhian move he sought only

---

49   Ibid., p. 21.

to correct by their own light. The first of these corrections occurs after the reading of the charges against the detainee:

Paragraph a. On the morning of 11 September 2001, four airliners travelling over the United States were hijacked. The flight hijacked were: American Airlines flight 11, United Airlines flight 175, American Airlines flight 77, and United Airlines flight 93. At approximately 8:46 a.m., American Airlines flight 11 crashed into the North Tower of the World Trade Center, resulting in the collapse of the tower at approximately 10:25 a.m. At approximately 9:05 a.m., United Airlines flight 175 crashed into the South Tower of the World Trade Center, resulting in the collapse of the tower at approximately 9:55 a.m. At approximately 9:37 a.m., American Airlines flight 77 crashed into the southwest side of the Pentagon in Arlington, Virginia. At approximately 10:03 a.m., United Airlines flight 93 crashed in Stoney Creek Township, Pennsylvania. These crashes and subsequent damage to the World Trade Center and the Pentagon resulted in the deaths of 2,972 persons in New York, Virginia, and Pennsylvania.

Paragraph b. The Detainee served as the head of the al Qaeda military committee and was Usama bin Laden's principal al Qaeda operative who directed the 11 September 2001 attacks in the United States.

Paragraph c. In an interview with an al Jazeera reporter in June 2002, the Detainee stated he was the head of the al Qaeda military committee.

Paragraph d. A computer hard drive seized during the capture of the Detainee contained information about the four airplanes hijacked on 11 September 2001 including code names, airline company, flight number, target, pilot name and background information, and names of the hijackers.

Paragraph e. A computer hard drive seized during the capture of the Detainee contained photographs of 19 individuals identified as the 11 September 2001 hijackers.

Paragraph f. A computer hard drive seized during the capture of the Detainee contained a document that listed the pilot license fees for Mohammad Atta and biographies for some of the 11 September 2001 hijackers.

Paragraph g. A computer hard drive seized during the capture of the Detainee contained images of passports and an image of Mohammad Atta.

Paragraph h. A computer hard drive seized during the capture of the Detainee contained transcripts of chat sessions belonging to at least one of the 11 September 2001 hijackers.

Paragraph i. The Detainee directed an individual to travel to the United States to case targets for a second wave of attacks.

Paragraph j. A computer hard drive seized during the capture of the Detainee contained three letters from Usama bin Laden.

Paragraph k. A computer hard drive seized during the capture of the Detainee contained spreadsheets that describe money assistance to families of known al Qaeda members.

Paragraph l. The Detainee's name was on a list in a computer seized in connection with a threat to United States airlines, United States embassies and the Pope.

Paragraph m. The Detainee wrote the *Bojinka Plot*, the airline bomb plot which was later found on his nephew Ramzi Yousef's computer.

Paragraph n. The *Bojinka Plot* is also known as the Manila air investigation.

Paragraph o. The Manila air investigation uncovered the Detainee conspired with others to plant explosive devices aboard American jetliners while those aircraft were scheduled to be airborne and loaded with passengers on their way to the United States.

Paragraph p. The Detainee was in charge of and funded an attack against United States military vessels heading to the port of Djibouti.

Paragraph q. A computer hard drive seized during the capture of the Detainee contained a letter to the United Arab Emirates threatening attack if their government continued to help the United States.

Paragraph r. During the capture of the Detainee, information used exclusively by al Qaeda operational managers to communicate with operatives was found.

Paragraph s. The Detainee received funds from Kuwaiti-based Islamic extremist groups and delivered the funds to al Qaeda members.

Paragraph t. A computer hard drive seized during the capture of the Detainee contained a document that summarized operational procedures and training requirements of an al Qaeda cell.

Paragraph u. A computer hard drive seized during the capture of the Detainee contained a list of killed and wounded al Qaeda martyrs.

And lastly, Paragraph v. Passport photographs of al Qaeda operatives were seized during the capture of the Detainee.[50]

Despite their length, these charges are in fact drawn from rather limited sources of evidence—a computer hard drive and an Al-Jazeera interview. As if offended by the meagreness of this evidence, especially given the rich detail of his own lengthy if also uncorroborated confessions, Khalid Sheikh Mohammed proceeded to criticize the charges laid against him on factual and procedural grounds, though without of course trying to claim his innocence while doing so. This made his criticism into an act of reformatory kindness very reminiscent of Gandhi's courtroom practices:

PERSONAL REPRESENTATIVE: The Detainee responds to the unclassified summary of evidence with the following key points.

PERSONAL REPRESENTATIVE: "Some paragraphs under paragraph number 3, lead sentence are not related to the context or meaning of the aforementioned lead sentence. For example, paragraph 3-a is only information from news or a historical account of events on 11 September 2001, and note with no specific linkage being made in this paragraph to me or the definition of Enemy Combatant. As another example, sub-paragraph 3-n makes no linkage to me or to the definition of Enemy Combatant."

DETAINEE: Are they following along?

PERSONAL REPRESENTATIVE: Ah, they have that in front of them for reference.

PRESIDENT: Yes.

DETAINEE: Okay.

---

50   Ibid., pp. 5-7.

PERSONAL REPRESENTATIVE: Point number 3. "There is an unfair 'stacking of evidence' in the way the Summary of Evidence is structured. In other words, there are several sub-paragraphs under parent-paragraph 3 which should be combined into one sub-paragraph to avoid creating the false perception that there are more allegations or statements against me specifically than there actually are. For example, sub-paragraphs 3-m through 3-o, which pertain to the *bojinka* plot should be combined into one paragraph, as should paragraphs 3-a through 3-h, which pertain to 9/11."[51]

Aware that much of the evidence adduced against him was derived from a computer hard drive and an Al-Jazeera interview, in which he was said to have claimed to be the head of Al-Qaeda's military committee, Khalid Sheikh Mohammed asked the tribunal to produce two witnesses on his behalf from among the detainees at Guantánamo Bay. One was Ramzi bin al-Shibh, who had been with him during the Al-Jazeera interview, and the other Mustafa Hawsawi, with whom he had been captured and who owned the computer from which the evidence had been drawn. Mohammed's point was that in the absence of any corroborating evidence, the statements of these two witnesses had to be taken into account, one of whom could state that Khalid Sheikh Mohammed did not in fact claim to lead Al-Qaeda's military committee, and the other that no link could be made between Mohammed and the information found on the hard drive, since the computer in question did not belong to him. The tribunal determined quite correctly that neither of these witnesses would be able to produce testimony relevant to determining Khalid Sheikh Mohammed's status as enemy combatant, and so denied his requests that they be produced. Mohammed's aim, however, was not to prove his guilt or innocence so much as to reveal the incorrectness of the hearing itself and so to call for its reformation in order that America might be true to itself as the global protector of human rights. Thus he points out that the facts used against him often don't even belong in the category of circumstantial evidence, such as, for instance finding a picture of the chief 9/11 hijacker Muhammad Atta on a computer that didn't belong to the accused. Many hundreds of thousands of Americans, said Mohammed, might well possess such a picture, which turned this particular "fact" into nothing more than a piece of general information elevated into a hollow accusation:

---

51   Ibid., pp. 8-9.

DETAINEE: most of these facts which be written are related to this hard drive. And more than eleven of these facts are related to this computer. Other things are which is very old even nobody can bring any witnesses for that as you written here if it will be ah a value for you for the witness near by you will do it. This computer is not for me. Is for Hawsawi himself. So I'm saying I need Hawsawi because me and him we both been arrested day. Same way. So this computer is from him long time. And also the problem we are not in court and we are not judge and he is not my lawyer but the procedure has been written reported and the way has mostly as certain charged against me; tell him [Arabic phrase].

TRANSLATOR: [Translating] They are only accusations.

DETAINEE: So accusations. And the accusations, they are as you put for yourself ah definition for enemy combatant there are also many definitions for that accusation of fact or charges that has been written for any ah. [Arabic phrase]

TRANSLATOR: [Translating] Person is accused.

DETAINEE: So, if I been accused then if you want to put facts against me also the definition for these facts. If you now read number N now what is written the *bojinka* plot. Is known many lead investigation it is not related to anything facts to be against me. So when I said computer hard drive/hard disk, same thing. All these point only one witness he can say yes or not cause he is this computer is under his possession him computer. And also specifically if he said Mohammad Atta picture been this hard drive. I don't think this should accepted. There are many 100 thousand Americans who have a lot of picture on their computer. You cannot say I find Muhammad Atta on your computer then you use this fact against you. Or you find any files in your computer to be what about it's mine, it's not my computer. If this witness, he will state that this known and here that has been ninety percent of what is written is wrong. And for Ramzi, for reporter in Jazeera, he claimed that I state this one and you know the media man. How they are fashionable. What they mean in their own way in a whole different way. They just wrote it so he say I state. But I never stated and I don't have any witnesses and witness are available here at Guantánamo. He is Detainee. He was with me. Which he been mostly in all my interview with him. Me and them, there was three person, me and Ramzi and this reporter. So if you not believe me, not believe him, believe my witness Ramzi. Then he's what he state the reporter most is false. I'm not denying that I'm not an enemy combatant about this war but I'm denying the report. It not being written in the proper way. Which is really facts and mostly just being gathered many information. General information that form in way of doing, to use in facts against me.[52]

While Khalid Sheikh Mohammed's finicky attempts to correct the tribunal's procedures had no bearing on his own guilt or innocence, they did have a great deal to do with the fate of others detained in US custody. For very much like the Mahatma again, Mohammed, while acknowledging his own guilt, altruistically asserted that the lack of procedures that marked his capture had also resulted in the capture and detention of many innocent Muslims, whom he advised the Americans to treat carefully:

DETAINEE: I want to just it is not related enemy combatant but I'm saying for you to be careful with people. That you have classified and unclassified facts. My opinion to be fair with people. Because when I say, I will not regret when I say I'm enemy combatant. I did or not I know there are other but there are many Detainees which you receive classified against them maybe, maybe not take away from me for many Detainees false witnesses. This only advice.[53]

So when we say we are enemy combatant, that right. We are. But I'm asking you again to be fair with many Detainees which are not enemy combatant. Because many of them been unjustly arrested. Many, not one or two or three. Cause the definition you which wrote even from my view is not fair. Because if I was in the first Jihad times Russia. So I have to be Russian enemy. But America supported me in this because I'm their alliances when I was fighting Russia. Same job I'm doing. I'm fighting. I was fighting there Russia now I'm fighting America.[54]

Many of these men, claimed Mohammed, had fought in Afghanistan during the first, US-supported war against the Soviets and then stayed behind, having nothing to do either with Al-Qaeda or the Taliban, while others joined any battle in the name of Islam, or anyone in power in Kabul, without any predisposition against America.[55] Even the Taliban, he pointed out, did not share Al-Qaeda's purpose and entertained no anti-American feelings until the US invasion.[56] Indeed the Taliban

---

52   Ibid., pp.11-12.

53   Ibid., p. 15.

54   Ibid., p. 22.

55   Ibid.

56   Ibid.

had even tried to assassinate Osama bin Laden, and Khalid Sheikh Mohammed relished the irony not only of having these would-be assassins detained with him in Guantánamo Bay, but also of asking for the men to be treated fairly despite his enmity for them:

So, this is why I'm asking you to be fair with Afghanis and Pakistanis and many Arabs which been in Afghanistan. Many of them been unjustly. The funny story they been Sunni government they sent some spies to assassinate UBL then we arrested them sent them to Afghanistan/Taliban. Taliban put them into prison. Americans they came and arrest them as enemy combatant. They brought them here. So, even if they are my enemy but no fair to be there with me.[57]

In a remarkable transformation, then, the man who began by proudly admitting to numberless murders and terrorist plots ended up pleading in an almost Christian way that justice be rendered others, and even his own enemies, in accordance with American principles of human rights. Whether or not he did so out of vanity, so that he could be the most notorious Al-Qaeda operative in custody, or in order to save his accomplices, it is nevertheless extraordinary that Khalid Sheikh Mohammed should have concluded his testimony at Guantánamo Bay with a plea for the human rights of strangers:

The American have human right. So, enemy combatant itself, it flexible word. So I think God knows that many who been arrested, they been unjustly arrested. Otherwise, military throughout history know very well. They don't war will never stop. War start from Adam when Cain he killed Abel until now. It's never gonna stop killing of people. This is the way of the language. American start the Revolutionary War then they starts the Mexican then Spanish War then World War One, World War Two. You read the history. You know never stopping war. This is life. But if who is enemy combatant and who is not? Finally, I finish statement. I'm asking you to be fair with other people.[58]

Throughout his statement Khalid Sheikh Mohammed referred to war as a language, and even as the common language that enemies shared with each other, one rendered universal by its very partiality. For in a world of differences it was the only common element, whose ironical role it was to bring people together even as it appeared to drive them apart. Mohammed went so far as to describe the intimacy that war

---

57   Ibid., p. 23.
58   Ibid., pp. 24-5.

wrought by comparing it to a marriage that produces corpses in place of children:

The way of the war, you know very well, any country waging war against their enemy the language of the war are killing. If a man and a woman they be together as a marriage that is up to the kids, children. But if you and me, two nations, will be together in war the others are victims. This is the way of the language.[59]

So in a startling reversal of received views on the subject of human difference, Khalid Sheikh Mohammed described conflict as the element of similarity in men's affairs, attributing difference to more peaceable forms of interaction. The way to peace, therefore, was to depart the common language of war and be true to oneself, in the way we have seen he asked America to remain true to its principles of human rights. For the intimacies of war had no end, each side being able to justify its actions by those of the other, so that the responsibility of neither could ever be determined. Mohammed used George Washington as an example of this endless intimacy, claiming that it was impossible to differentiate the hero of the American Revolution from Osama bin Laden as far as the universal language of war was concerned:

So, we derive from religious leading that we consider we and George Washington doing same thing. As consider George Washington as hero. Muslims many of them are considering Usama bin Laden. He is doing same thing. He is just fighting. He needs his independence.[60]

When I said I'm not happy that three thousand been killed in America. I feel sorry even. I don't like to kill children and the kids. Never Islam are, give me green light to kill peoples. Killing, as in the Christianity, Jews, and Islam, are prohibited. But there are exceptions of rule when you are killing people in Iraq. You said we have to do it. We don't like Saddam. But this is the way to deal with Saddam. Same thing you are saying. Same language you use, I use. When you are invading two-thirds of Mexican, you call your war manifest destiny. It up to you to call it what you want. But other side are calling you oppressors. If now George Washington. If now we were living in the Revolutionary War and George Washington he being arrested through Britain. For sure he, they would consider him enemy combatant. But American they consider him as

---

59   Ibid., p. 23.

60   Ibid., p. 22.

hero. This right the any Revolutionary War they will be as George Washington or Britain.[61]

If the heroes and villains of one nation were reversed in another, and Osama bin Laden could play the role of George Washington to America's Britain, how then might responsibility finally be determined in war? By anchoring its language to some external source of authority—though not of course to an institution like the UN that was as partial as any state. The authority referred to by Mohammed was something freely chosen and highly individual in character, a law for oneself that might or might not be shared with others, something like human rights. Not conscience, in other words, since it presupposed a common law against which to measure one's actions, but something completely external was required, for the fragmentation of a collective legal order in the global arena seems to have made individual judgements super-legalistic by devolving all the duties of jurisprudence upon them. And this indeed is what has finally happened to Islamic law in the rhetoric of militant pluralism: torn from its traditional moorings to become the source for a thoroughly individualized jurisprudence whose first and only rule is being true to oneself. Thus Khalid Sheikh Mohammed spoke in his halting and ungrammatical way about his own efforts to exit the undifferentiated realm he called the language of war by judging it according to the Sharia as a freely chosen though completely external authority:

I don't like to kill people. I feel very sorry they been killed kids in 9/11. What will I do? This is the language. Sometime I want to make great awakening between American to stop foreign policy in our land. I know American people are torturing us from seventies. [REDACTED] I know they talking about human rights. And I know it is against American Constitution, against American laws. But they said every law, they have exceptions, this is your bad luck you been part of the exception of our laws. They got have something to convince me but we are doing same language. But we are saying we have Sharia law, but we have Koran. What is enemy combatant in my language?

DETAINEE (through translator): Allah forbids you not with regards to those who fight you not for your faith nor drive you out of your homes from dealing kindly and justly with them. For Allah love those who are just. There is one more sentence. Allah only forbids you with regards to those who fight you for your faith and drive you out of your homes and support others in driving you

---

61   Ibid., p. 23.

out from turning to them for friendship and protection. It is such as turn to them in these circumstances that do wrong.

DETAINEE: So we are driving from whatever deed we do we ask about Koran or Hadith. We are not making up for us laws. When we need Fatwa from the religious we have to go back to see what they said scholar. To see what they said yes or not. Killing is prohibited in all what you call the people of the book, Jews, Judaism, Christianity, and Islam. You know the Ten Commandments very well. The Ten Commandments are shared between all of us. We are all serving one God. Then now kill you know it very well. But war language also we have language for the war. You have to kill.[62]

No less than any Muslim liberal, our militant acknowledged the shared heritage of Christians, Muslims and Jews, as well as the proscription on killing within their common tradition, only to justify his own murders as juridically approved exceptions to this law. Through a translator, Mohammed cited the Quran in support of this exception, reiterating the now standard argument by which responsibility for violence is evaded if it simply mirrors that of one's opponent. Even this invocation of a legal exception, however, falls into the mirroring practices that characterize the language of war, since it does nothing more than reflect the legal exception that is Guantánamo Bay, with its "enemy combatants" and proceedings conducted without benefit of lawyers and by the use of secret evidence. According to Mohammed, the difference between his form of legal exception, and that by which his captors worked, was that the exceptionality of Guantánamo Bay remained disconnected from any legal norm. But the validity or otherwise of Khalid Sheikh Mohammed's reasoning is irrelevant to the point at hand, which is that the pluralistic global society militants inhabit depends upon self-rule rather than the rule of others. And self-rule is being true to the path one has chosen. If it weren't a murderer mouthing them, these would be sentiments that Gandhi might have voiced.

---

62   Ibid., p. 24.

4

ARABIAN KNIGHTS

Having sided with Germany during the First World War, the Ottoman Empire was dismantled at its termination and a new geopolitical region, called the Middle East, created from its wreckage. Until recently, the constellation of Arab states and Israel that together make up the heartland of this new Middle East provided the framework for all politics in the region, but with the emergence of global networks like Al-Qaeda this is no longer the case. After all places outside the Middle East, like Afghanistan or Pakistan, are now more important to militancy in the region than Israel, insofar as they provide it with new causes, practices and vocabularies that have lost all regional reference. Such for example are the suicide bombings and sectarian killings that have become so common in Iraq following its occupation by Anglo-American forces, whose distinctive forms are all too familiar in the subcontinent. This development not only questions the very integrity of the Middle East as a geopolitical unit, it also permits Muslim militants to redefine this region's Arab character, or rather to redeploy the language of Arabness outside a Middle Eastern context.

In the midst of plots to raise the flag of war from one end of the world to another, militants like Osama bin Laden sometimes pause to contemplate the immense changes that have occurred in the geopolitics of the Middle East. In doing so they tend to invoke the Ottoman Empire, whose sultan had also claimed the title of caliph, or successor to the Prophet Muhammad's worldly authority. For Bin Laden and those he inspires attribute what they see as Islam's greatest humiliation in modern times precisely to the dismantling of the caliphate and the creation of a Middle East carved out into British and French zones of influence. By ruing the passing of what had been a Turkish empire, and the placing of its Arab territories under European jurisdiction, these men announce their break with the ideology of Arab nationalism, itself an outgrowth of the Anglo-French condominium that came to define this region following the Great War. And by holding up the caliphate as a model for the Muslim future, they assign militancy a self-consciously global project, or at least one that cannot be confined to the Middle East.

Militants invoke the caliphate in a conceptual rather than politically instrumental way, since it serves as an idea that delegitimizes an international order they consider to be the result merely of European conquest and colonization. Ayman al-Zawahiri says as much in an interview posted by a jihadist website on September 11, 2006, referring in particular to the Sykes-Picot Agreement, by which the British and French secretly planned to divide the Ottoman Empire up between them after the First World War, thus giving rise to the Middle East as we know it. Zawahiri calls this new order of nation states idolatrous, thus following the precedent of Indian Muslim thinkers from the early twentieth century, who had transformed this old theological term by applying it to the realities of modern politics:

My dear brother: The facts of international politics which they talk about stem from what they term as international legitimacy, the United Nations, and secular states which are the fruits of the malicious Sykes-Picot Agreement. All these systems have been imposed on Muslims and the Muslim nation following the fall of the Caliphate state to force it to submit to systems and organizations that violate the Islamic law and to ensure the fragmentation of the Islamic nation. This will ultimately leave the Islamic nation subordinate, humiliated, and pillaged. The time has come for us to destroy these idols and false gods that they forced us to worship instead of Allah.[1]

Although it remains a mere name among them, possessing neither theological nor political substance, the caliphate serves to globalize violent networks like Al-Qaeda as well as nonviolent ones like Hizb al-Tahrir, both of which are multinational and in fact present for the most part outside the Middle East. But this is hardly accidental, since the

---

1   "Al-Zawahiri calls on Muslims to wage 'war of jihad', reject UN resolutions" *United States Central Command* (http://www.centcom.mil/sites/uscentcom1/ What%20Extremists%20Say/Al-Zawahiri%20Calls%20on%20Muslims%20 to%20Wage%20'War%20of%20Jihad'%20,Reject%20UN%20Resolutions. aspx?PageView=Shared), p. 3.

Muslim majority beyond the Middle East has always been at the fore-front of international, and now global forms of Islam, it being only very recently that Arabs have become involved in them. So when the Otto-man Empire was finally replaced by republican Turkey it was an In-dian prince, the Nizam of Hyderabad, who cashed in on the caliphate's popularity among his South Asian coreligionists by supporting its ex-iled incumbent with a pension and marrying into his family. Perhaps Muslims outside the Middle East have taken a leading role in pan-Is-lamism because the religion's Arab antecedents and Arabic scriptures prevented it from becoming part merely of their national identity in modern times—instead forcing non-Arabs to think about their religion globally. The more recent Arab participation in Islam's globalization, then, might well indicate the fragmentation of the Middle East as a foundational category for their religious life, and thus its dispersal into the universal narrative of Islam.

The decline of Nasserism, Baathism and other forms of pan-Arabism that had once striven to integrate the region ideologically is matched today by the Middle East's economic disintegration, with the rich states of the Persian Gulf connected more to Europe and America, or India and China, than to their poorer Arab neighbours. Indeed in terms of its demography and transportation links alone, it is possible to split the Middle East in half, grouping its eastern portion with India, Pakistan and Iran rather than with the Fertile Crescent or North Africa. And this is not even to take into account the region's political disintegration, due to the presence and influence of American and European forces there. Yet it is these very forces that also keep the Middle East together by treating it as a single entity, having after all put it together in the first place. The region's globalization has also proceeded apace, with a so-called "Shiite crescent" cutting through the Middle East and lifting out of it a different kind of geography connecting non-Arab Iran, Paki-stan and Afghanistan to Saudi Arabia, Kuwait, Bahrain, Iraq, Syria and Lebanon—all countries with large Shia populations.[2]

Whether or not there exists such a thing as a Shiite crescent, sectar-ian violence in the Middle East, particularly that perpetrated by Sunni militants, takes both its rhetoric and practices directly from Pakistan,

2   For an influential statement of this position see Vali Nasr's *The Shia Revival* (New York: Norton, 2006).

where such violence has been endemic for some two decades now. Interesting about the transportation of these practices is the fact that they are replicated not in generic fashion but rather in the most particular of ways, including for instance suicide bombings in Shia mosques by militants disguised as Shiite worshippers. In other words even the forms of Middle Eastern militancy have been imported from the wider Muslim world, largely as a result of events like the anti-Soviet jihad in Afghanistan—which provided in fact the first pan-Islamic cause in which Arabs were active. I suspect it is the political and economic disintegration of the Middle East that has permitted it to be globally redefined in sectarian terms. And while the caliphate, too, is a sectarian institution, being in fact the premier form that Sunni authority has taken in the past, it provides another way of gauging the dispersal of the Middle East and of re-imagining it in non-sectarian ways. For it is the caliphate as a cosmopolitan and pluralistic entity, rather than a specifically Sunni one, that informs the global imagination of Al-Qaeda, not least by providing a new context for its Arab character, represented as this is by the words and appearance of militant icons like Osama bin Laden.

Before its contemporary popularity with Al-Qaeda and other militant networks, the caliphate had enjoyed its most sustained support outside the Ottoman Empire, particularly in British India, home to the world's largest Muslim population and the site of more than one jihad movement in the past. At the close of the First World War, Indian Muslims, who had contributed a large number of soldiers to the British army that defeated the Ottomans in the Middle East, invoked their loyalty as well as the promise to respect Islamic sanctities made by Britain's prime minister, to demand the caliphate's preservation. Indian soldiers had not taken Jerusalem, they said, to see the Ottoman Empire liquidated and infidel troops occupy the land housing Islam's holiest sanctuaries—to say nothing of Palestine itself being given over to Jewish immigration. The popular mobilization generated by this demand united Hindus and Muslims into the first and greatest mass movement of India's history—one led by Gandhi, who was therefore considered by his Hindu assassin to be the father of pan-Islamism.[3] Insofar as the

---

3   See Godse, *Why I Assassinated Mahatma Gandhi*. For an analysis of Gandhi's role in the Khilafat Movement, see Faisal Devji, "A Practice of Prejudice: Gandhi's Politics of Friendship", *Subaltern Studies*, New Delhi, 12 (2005), pp. 78-

Mahatma was killed for his supposed betrayal of Hinduism, therefore, he might even be considered a martyr for Islam.

While the Khilafat (Caliphate) Movement was motivated by a complex set of causes, it illustrates very clearly that the roots of Islam's globalization lie beyond the Middle East. Indeed it was in this movement that the inviolability of the *jazirat ul-arab* or Arabian "island" first became a political cause, well before it was summoned for similar use by Osama bin Laden, with Indian clerics writing treatises demanding the removal of infidel soldiers from the peninsula that housed the sacred cities of Mecca and Medina.[4] So it is more than appropriate that Al-Qaeda should have been founded precisely on the boundary of what was once British India, a borderland that had witnessed one of the great struggles for the caliphate, with tens of thousands of Indian Muslims passing through it without the least disorder when abandoning British territory for Islamic Afghanistan, from which some of them hoped to launch attacks upon the infidel and restore the caliph—or to establish a socialist state in the subcontinent.[5] Even eighty years ago, then, the caliphate represented Islam's modernity as much as its tradition. More traditional than the cause of the caliphate was the refuge that Afghanistan and the North West Frontier had offered Indians fighting the British since the nineteenth century, a history that Osama bin Laden and other foreign fighters have nestled into very comfortably.

The North West Frontier, which today forms the porous borderland between Pakistan and Afghanistan, was then a stronghold of the Indian National Congress, and despite being the most fully Muslim province of British India, was opposed to the creation of Pakistan as a Muslim homeland even after having been absorbed by the new state in 1947. Its Pathan population, furthermore, who are today famed for their militancy, were among the Indians most devoted to Gandhi's nonviolent ways. Their practice of civil disobedience, peacefully carried out in the face of British reprisals much more brutal than those inflicted in less sensitive

---

98.

4   See especially Abul Kalam Azad, *Maslah-e Khilafat* (Delhi: Hali Publishing House, 1961).

5   For this extraordinary emigration see Dietrich Reetz, *Hijrat: The Flight of the Faithful; A British File on the Exodus of Muslim Peasants from North India to Afghanistan in 1920* (Berlin: Verlag Das Arabische Buch, 1995).

parts of the country, has even been described as "the most heroic and extraordinary of all such episodes in the Indian nationalist movement."[6] These Pathans were led by Khan Abdul Ghaffar Khan, known as the Frontier Gandhi, whose standing among his people was demonstrated long after the end of nonviolent protest in the North West Frontier, when an unprecedented one-day ceasefire was declared between the Soviet army and the Afghan *mujahideen* on the day of his funeral in 1988, so that thousands of mourners could pay him their last respects in Jalalabad, many accompanying his body there across the Pakistan-Afghanistan border that had been temporarily opened for this purpose.[7]

How can this first movement of mass politics among the Pathans, which continued well after the Khilafat Movement and dominated political life in their homeland for nearly twenty years between 1930 and 1947, be fitted into existing narratives of religion, tribalism and warfare on the North West Frontier? Perhaps by recognizing that Gandhian nonviolence rather than bloodshed might have constituted the founding moment of popular Pathan militancy there, which would make a Hindu Mahatma as much an ancestor in the Taliban's family tree as the Muslim Prophet. Indeed Gandhi's supporters on the North West Frontier even called their practice of nonviolence a "jihad", thus transforming the modern history of this word and inadvertently giving substance to liberal Muslim efforts at reinterpreting it as a peaceable form of struggle. The fact that all this happened in a place famous since the nineteenth century for its violent tradition of jihad presents an embarrassment to those who would trace the continuous and self-contained character of such a tradition there, which might explain why the Khudai Khidmatgars or Servants of God, as Gandhi's Pathan allies were known, have systematically been written out of the history of militancy on the North West Frontier. And yet in the Pakistani elections of 2008, it was the Frontier Gandhi's organization, now called the Awami National Party, which staged a spectacular victory in the province on its old platform of nonviolence, thus demonstrating that it remains the longest surviving and most successful Gandhian movement in existence. The party's much-touted "secularism", in other words, has more to do with

---

6   Mukulika Banerjee, *The Pathan Unarmed: Opposition and Memory in the North West Frontier* (New Delhi: Oxford University Press, 2001), p. 71.

7   Ibid., p. 2.

the Mahatma and indeed with the modern history of jihad than with any idea of freedom being pushed by the West today.

Returning to Khan Abdul Ghaffar Khan's early career, we should recognize that Muslims resident in other parts of India refused to be outdone in their commitment to the caliphate by those who had migrated to Afghanistan, donating enormous sums of money as well as medicine and clothing for the Turks fighting to preserve their Anatolian homeland from European depredation. What could prefigure today's globalized Islam more than such an event? Al-Qaeda's founding fathers are fully conscious of this history, with Ayman al-Zawahiri, for example, lauding the long history of pan-Islamic zeal among Pakistani Muslims in a way that he never does for the Arabs. However he also recognizes that the mercenary role of Britain's Indian army around the world, especially in Iraq and other parts of the Middle East, has in no small way been inherited by its Pakistani successor.[8] None of this is to suggest that the Middle East has no role to play in the globalization of Islam, indeed quite the contrary, though I will argue in this chapter that it has been fragmented and dispersed throughout the Muslim world as a conceptual rather than political category, and one that takes on a new meaning in the terms of an imagined caliphate.

The Middle East that is studied and discussed by scholars and journalists in the West remains a Euro-American category defined primarily in terms of its natural resources and political instabilities, both overlaid with a patina of religiosity. The same region looks rather different when seen from places other than Washington or London, as my brief recounting of the Khilafat Movement illustrates. My point here is not that this extraordinary event occurred outside Euro-American politics, but that it created both a different history and a different geography while being internal to the politics of the great powers during the First World War. How might standard narratives of Middle Eastern history even begin to account for a mass movement, led by Gandhi no less, that was dedicated to preserving the caliphate against its Arab as well as European enemies? In fact they cannot account for it, and must margin-

---

8   "Al-Qaeda Leader Ayman Al-Zawahiri's Interview to Al-Sahab (Part II): Osama Bin Laden Still Commands the Jihad, but the Jihad is Larger than Individuals. Mujahideen Should Attack Oil Infrastructure in the Middle East", *The Middle East Media Research Institute*, TV Monitor Project, Clip No. 952, 12 July, 2005 (www.memri.org).

alise this history in order to protect the autonomy of the Middle East as a political stage upon which Americans or Europeans can play the only foreign parts.

The Turks themselves abolished the caliphate in 1924, at least partly in response to Indian attempts at internationalizing this institution beyond the jurisdiction of their newly founded state. But now that it has returned bearing an even ghostlier mien than before, the caliphate recapitulates the pre-history of Islam's globalization in events like the Khilafat Movement, which fundamentally destabilize received ideas of the Middle East as constituting some origin for global Islam, though we shall see that the region does indeed provide a conceptual focus for it. Perhaps this is why we are now faced with the unedifying spectacle of "experts" on the area trying desperately to claw militant Islam, in particular, back to the Middle East, which they can only do by concentrating on the "Arabness" of men like Osama bin Laden and ignoring his location outside the Arab world, to say nothing of the Afghans or Pakistanis who risk their lives in sheltering him, and who themselves participate so enthusiastically in global forms of militancy. Only a few voices, like that of the sociologist Olivier Roy, have so far been raised against this attempt to read global Islam primarily in Arab terms—these of course being identical with Euro-American terms.[9]

Locating militancy in the Middle East allows specialists on the region to predicate it on traditional political causes like the Israeli-Palestinian conflict, as well as to the poverty and oppression that are said to afflict the Arab world in general. But how are we to explain the Britons of Pakistani descent who are also willing to die for Palestine, without undermining this political account of militancy by their entirely vicarious identification with Palestinian suffering? Like millions of their fellow South Asians living in the Middle East, such men are often treated by academics and journalists in the West as servants there only to take instruction from their Arab masters, with the issues that animate them seen as psychological rather than political in nature.[10] Instead of relying

---

9   See Olivier Roy's *Globalised Islam* (London: Hurst, 2004), and *The Politics of Chaos in the Middle East* (London: Hurst, 2008).

10   Given that South Asian labourers, clerks and businessmen form a long-standing and indeed overwhelming demographic majority in some Persian Gulf states, the fact that scholars regularly write about Islam and Arabness in these places without any reference to them is astonishing. It would be like (though much

upon such forced distinctions as that between the psychological and political causes for militancy, or by engaging in the futile effort to measure the relative strengths of each, I propose taking the globalization of Islam seriously and looking at the way in which militancy fragments the Middle East in its quest for a global politics, doing this by stretching the term Arab beyond geography and even language to locate it within Al-Qaeda's caliphal narrative as a globalized concept.

Fantasy island

Osama bin Laden's Arabness, and particularly his provenance from the Arabian Peninsula, are crucial to his global stature as Islam's greatest rebel. No Muslim from another geographical or linguistic tradition, I would warrant, has a chance of assuming a comparable role, however spectacular his career. Of course Arabia and its language have always possessed a certain prestige in the larger Muslim world, but it is well to remember that not so long ago it was Istanbul rather than Mecca, and the Turks rather than the Arabs, who were seen by Muslims as well as Christians to represent the politics of Sunni Islam in particular. Indeed the Arab world, and the Arabian Peninsula not least, remained relatively unimportant as far as the exercise of Muslim leadership was concerned until the break-up of the Ottoman Empire in the twentieth century. It is true that the Wahhabi revolts of the nineteenth century created something of a stir throughout the Muslim world, because of their attempts to proscribe certain religious practices in the holy cities of Mecca and Medina, as well as to destroy saintly tombs and other monuments revered by the generality of pilgrims there. But this agitation for one of the earliest international Muslim causes only supported Ottoman efforts to reestablish control of the peninsula, and to protect the passage and practices there of pilgrims who were for the most part non-Arabs.

Given this history it is tempting to trace the emergence of Arabia and the Arabs as figures of Muslim leadership to the carving out of independent states in the Middle East after the First World War, and particularly to the discovery of oil in countries like Saudi Arabia, which suddenly brought them to the centre of the global economy. While the

---

worse than) dealing with Christianity among Whites in the American south without mentioning the presence and influence of Blacks upon them.

new wealth and therefore influence of these states in the greater Muslim world is undeniable, not least because of the huge migrant flows they invited from it, we should not overestimate the effect of Arab forms of Islam like Wahhabism, even with its aggressive marketing by the Saudis there. For one thing Wahhabism has never managed to reproduce itself in any significant way outside its homeland. Thus hardly any Muslim group outside the Middle East acknowledges the authority of Abd al-Wahhab himself, which is a remarkable thing given the Saudi funding that so many of them receive. Indeed the name Wahhabi is more often used as a slur to be defended against than otherwise, notwithstanding any other gestures of loyalty these groups owe their donors.

But then the Wahhabi establishment has itself been unable either intellectually or even in terms of manpower to expand its reach globally, despite the many foreign students who are trained in Saudi Arabia to spread its message abroad. This is why their global outreach programmes, like the famous *Rabitat al-Alam al-Islami* or Muslim World League, are so often staffed by sympathetic but not necessarily Wahhabi hirelings from countries like Pakistan. Even their propaganda material is sometimes taken from non-Wahhabi sources, for instance an English translation of the Quran by the Indian Shiite Abdullah Yusuf Ali, whose objectionable passages and footnotes the Saudis simply expurgated after purchasing its copyright. Militants like Ayman al-Zawahiri are themselves fully conscious of the limitations of Wahhabi and other fundamentalist movements in the greater Muslim world, however important Saudi funding may be there. Thus he comments sarcastically upon the fact that Sufis and even footballers have a far greater following among Muslims than any fundamentalist, let alone militant movement.[11]

As figures of Islam's leadership, Arabia and the Arabs have a history prior to the emergence of the Persian Gulf states as economic powers, one that continues to inform the global charisma of men like Bin Laden. This prior history is significant enough to mitigate the great resentment and even hatred that Arab wealth and the arrogance it gives rise to so regularly provoke among non-Arab Muslims both within and without the militant pale. Indeed we shall see that for many of them the term Arab by no means refers solely to a region, language or people

---

11   "Al-Zawahiri calls on Muslims to wage 'war of jihad', reject UN resolutions", p. 12.

in any narrowly ethnic sense. On the contrary Arabness has assumed a global dimension to become a category that is open in various ways for Muslim occupation more generally, something that is not true of any other "cultural" designation in the Muslim world, no matter how glorious its history. One cannot lay claim to Turkishness, for example, in the way that one can to Arabness. And of this global category Osama bin Laden is probably the best spokesman.

Based as he is outside the peninsula, and speaking as he does to a global audience, Bin Laden's frequent invocations of Arabia and Arabness cannot be seen merely as elements in some debate internal to the Middle East. In fact his deployment of the category Arab is markedly global in its separation from any ethno-linguistic particularity. To begin with this most notorious and celebrated of Arabs routinely redraws the map of the Middle East by linking it to an older cartography, of which the "Arabian island" forms only one part. Thus we have seen how Mesopotamia replaces Iraq and Khorasan replaces Afghanistan in militant rhetoric, though neither name is coterminous with the state it displaces. The Middle East, along with its constituent states, disappears altogether from this revived cartography, turning Arabness into a floating category. As for the Arabian island, which is also produced by erasing the Peninsula's political boundaries, it has meaning only within the ambit of a larger imperial order, or of today's Muslim world, and not regionally or in its own right.

We may recall here that the first modern use of this designation was made during India's Khilafat Movement, with Muslim divines allied to Gandhi laying out the island's sacrosanct character to defy the military presence of Britain and France there in the aftermath of the First World War. The Mahatma himself was not averse to inhabiting this older Islamic geography within which the Arabian island belonged, most famously in referring to India by the medieval Arabic name of Hind, which, though it continues to be used in modern Arabic, had already become archaic in Indian and European languages alike by the Mahatma's time. Using the word Hind for his treatise of 1909 titled *Hind Swaraj* or Indian Self-Rule, then, to say nothing of its common use elsewhere in slogans like "Jai Hind" or Victory to India, allowed Gandhi to peel away the British map of empire and position India within a precolonial Islamic cartography, one that included the *Jazirat ul-Arab* but not, say, Italian Somaliland or German East Africa—to say nothing of British India.

Focussing on the Arabian Peninsula as part of Islam's sacred geography rather than as part of the Middle East allows Osama bin Laden to ignore descent from the Prophet or tribal affiliation, which are supposedly important elements in traditional Arabness. Of course those who claim descent from Muhammad or his companions are to be found throughout the Muslim world, but the relative unimportance of such genealogical factors among militants is significant nevertheless, for it is linked to the explicitly formulated criticism of Arabness as an ethnic category. So Ayman al-Zawahiri, in his famous letter to Abu Musab al-Zarqawi, who was then the head of Al-Qaeda in Iraq, warns the latter to guard against the possibility of his struggle devolving into something purely Iraqi or Arab.[12] Apart from any utilitarian reasons for preventing the localization and ethnicization of Al-Qaeda's war, then, Zawahiri's warning evoked a whole history of anti-nationalist and anti-racialist feeling in modern Islamic thought, itself probably derived from a deep suspicion of European racism and nationalism. Moreover in this letter and elsewhere Zawahiri pointed to the fact that he and Bin Laden had sworn allegiance to the Taliban's Mullah Omar, even calling him by the caliphal title "prince of believers", despite the fact that he was neither an Arab nor even a proper Muslim by their lights:

Praise be to God, all the Jihadist movements are ideological enemies not only to the Iraqi Ba'th Party but to all the nationalist and secular trends whose principles conflict with the fundamentals of Islam, which is based on equality between Muslims and the bonds of faith and not on the nationalist spirit. Almighty God says: "O mankind! We created you from a single (pair) of a male and a female, and made you into nations and tribes, that ye may know each other (not that ye may despise each other). Verily the most honoured of you in the sight of Allah is (he who is) the most righteous of you." This is the point as far as the faith is concerned. As for the practice, the mujahidin everywhere—from the Philippines to Iraq—have in their ranks Muslims from all countries and races without discrimination between and Arab and a non-Arab, white or black. [...] We in Al-Qaeda organization have pledged allegiance to the com-

---

12   "Letter from Al-Zawahiri to Al-Zarqawi", *Office of the Director of National Intelligence*, 11 October 2005 (http://www.dni.gov/release_letter_101105.html), pp. 10-11.

mander of the faithful, Mulla Muhammad Omar, who is not an Arab. So by
the grace of God, we are the farthest people from the nationalist trend.[13]

[We must conduct our struggle from] the standpoint of not highlighting the
doctrinal differences which the masses do not understand, such as this one is
Matridi or this one is Ashari or this one is Salafi, and from the standpoint of
doing justice to the people, for there may be in the world a heresy or an in-
adequacy in a side which may have something to give to jihad, fighting, and
sacrifice for God. We have seen magnificent examples in the Afghan jihad, and
the prince of believers, Mullah Muhammad Omar—may God protect him—
himself is of Hanafi adherence, Matridi doctrine, but he stood in the history of
Islam with a stance rarely taken.[14]

While the caliphate had been more or less delinked from its tribal
Arab origins by the time the Ottomans adopted it in the sixteenth century, it was only in the twentieth that the institution came to be set
against modern forms of national and racial belonging. The Iranian
pan-Islamist Jamal al-Din Afghani, who identified himself as an Afghan
to avoid being dismissed as a Shiite in the nineteenth-century Sunni
world he hoped to influence, is by common consent seen as the greatest
propagator of a modern and thoroughly ecumenical caliphate, though
he was still wedded to its Ottoman form.[15] It was therefore only after
the First World War that the idea of the caliphate was truly radicalized,
with Muslim thinkers willing to redefine it not only in anti-national
or anti-racial ways, but even to reconstitute it as an elected assembly.
One of the most important of these thinkers, and one active in the
Khilafat Movement, was the cleric-turned-politician Abul Kalam Azad,
who became a close associate of Gandhi's, president of the Indian National Congress and independent India's first minister of education.
His celebrated Urdu book on the caliphate, published in the immediate
aftermath of the Great War and called *The Question of the Caliphate
and the Arabian Island*, advocated an Arabia free of infidel troops and a
non-specific or rather non-Arab caliph, and could therefore almost have
served as a primer for Bin Laden and Zawahiri.

---

13   "Al-Zawahiri calls on Muslims to wage 'war of jihad', reject UN resolutions" ,
      p. 8. Square brackets mine.

14   "Letter from Al-Zawahiri to Al-Zarqawi", p. 6.

15   For Afghani see Nikki R. Keddie, *Sayyid Jamal al-Din "al-Afghani": A Political
      Biography* (Berkeley: University of California Press, 1972).

Azad denuded the caliph of his traditional qualifications, including membership of the Prophet's tribe, wisdom and even piety, by acknowledging that none of the dynasties laying claim to the caliphate in the past had in fact possessed all of these.[16] In the absence of such personal traits the caliph was to represent a modern function—that of constituting a source of authority and focus of loyalty for the Muslim world. Azad justified this functional interpretation of the caliphate by attributing the personal qualifications that had once marked this institution to the rival Shiite concept of the imamate, which would confine the leadership of the Muslim world to a direct descendant of Muhammad.[17] Yet the caliph as Azad defined him continued to bear a close resemblance to the Shia imam, not only because he is always called an imam in *The Question of the Caliphate and the Arabian Island*, but also because his authority is made equivalent to that of God and the Prophet.[18] The Ottoman sultan, it is important to point out, possessed neither of these characteristics. Moreover like the Shia imam, Azad's caliph does not actually have to rule the world's Muslims in even the most formal of political senses but rather to give them meaning as a global community, if only by serving as their symbolic point of reference.

Abul Kalam Azad's book on the caliphate, then, was not some old-fashioned contribution to Islamic theology but an attempt to conceive of the Muslim community as a new kind of actor in the wake of the First World War. The text spiritualized the caliph's role in a very Shiite way, though it also did the opposite by reducing it to a function. In other words Azad's paradoxical mission was to spiritualize a caliphate that he had himself made into a geometrical point. Thus he described the worldwide Muslim community as a circle whose centre was the caliphate, which meant that the caliph was not an historical entity so much as a logical requirement.[19] Similar was the function of the Arabian Peninsula, which for Azad constituted the territorial centre of Islam not because it lay at the heart of the Muslim world, since it wasn't even the seat of the caliphate, but because it represented a geometrical centre

---

16   Azad, *Maslah-e Khilafat*, p. 127.

17   Ibid., pp. 91-3.

18   Ibid., pp. 34-43.

19   Ibid., pp. 31-3.

without which the very idea of an Islamic territory could not exist.[20] It was only by divesting the caliphate as well as the Arabian "island" of any ethnic, linguistic, or even geopolitical particularity, that Azad could invest them with significance for Muslims worldwide. And it is interesting to note in this respect that like Abul Kalam Azad, Osama bin Laden, too, has turned the caliphate and the Arabian Peninsula into the most abstract of entities, with the "island" taking its significance from a new global arena named by the caliphate.

If Al-Qaeda's leaders have, like their Indian forebears, emptied the Middle East of its Arabness and dispersed it within the global geography of Islam, their dealings with the Arabic language have not been any less radical. Bin Laden, for example, is famous for speaking in a beautiful if archaic style, full of Quranic cadences, that is sometimes difficult even for Arabic-speaking laymen to understand. This does not stop many of them from trying to imitate him, and we have a description of the Kuwaiti-based Pakistani Khalid Sheikh Mohammed doing just that, though rather unsuccessfully, in the interview he gave to Al-Jazeera just before being captured.[21] At first glance it might seem counter-productive for Osama bin Laden to speak a stilted Arabic when he wants to reach the largest possible audience. But this would be to presume that he is speaking primarily to an Arab audience. Let us suppose, however, that Bin Laden's language, whatever forms it takes in private life, is rendered difficult for broadcast precisely because it presupposes translation. For his words are very deliberately directed at a global rather than Arab audience, often explicitly to the British and American people or their leaders. In fact Al-Sahab, the media arm of Al-Qaeda, increasingly provides English translations and subtitles for their broadcasts, just as Bin Laden provided English translators to foreign fighters at his Afghan camps. And this is to say nothing about Al-Sahab's bilingual or made-in-English productions, such as those featuring the American convert Adam Gadahn—whose English perorations are sometimes prefaced by Zawahiri's Arabic comments.

Is it possible that Osama bin Laden can afford to speak in archaic Arabic because he relies upon its English translation? This would make

---

20   Ibid., p. 247.

21   Yosri Fouda and Nick Fielding, *Masterminds of Terror* (New York: Arcade Publishing, 2003), pp. 116-117.

English and not Arabic into the language of global Islam, which is probably true enough since it is primarily from English that Bin Laden's words are translated even into other Muslim languages like Urdu. In any case most Muslims around the world are used to hearing Arabic only in the Quranic style that Bin Laden favours and without understanding a word of it. Yet the globally broadcast Arabic used by militants cannot simply be received traditionally, as a ritual language across the Islamic world. Like a number of religious and social practices associated with it, Arabic has become instead a kind of operating code for many Muslims, a standardized technique made up of recognizable if not necessarily comprehensible words, phrases and scriptural citations. These bits of code, Olivier Roy points out in his book *Globalised Islam*, work to produce global Islam as a kind of universal technology cut off from the vagaries of living cultures and languages.

In addition to the usual quotations from the Quran or sayings of the Prophet, Osama bin Laden's Arabic in particular is larded with adulatory references to pre-Islamic Arabia, and especially to its heroes and poets, though these have for centuries been criticized by pious Muslims and indeed by the Prophet and the Quran themselves. Such references to the chivalric tradition of pagan Arabia were popular in the literary works of profane writers attached to royal courts in the past, and continue to be so among both secular and nationalist Arabs. What then does it mean for Bin Laden to associate his jihad with pre-Islamic battles and compare his martyrs to pagan warriors, especially given the execration that fundamentalist thinkers tend to reserve for this period of ignorance, or *jahiliyya*, whose evil they think survives into the present? In a certain sense it is precisely the particularity of this pagan past that defines Arabness, and not the universal narrative of Islam, which is all about Muhammad's truth departing its Arabian cradle. In other words Osama Bin Laden can only anchor his own much-trumpeted Arabness to this pre-Islamic past, which thus serves as a caesura connecting Arabia to Islam.

That there is something paradoxical about this move to the pagan past goes without saying, though it pales into insignificance beside the greater paradox of locating pre-Islamic Arabia in the mountains of the Hindu Kush. For it turns out that it is on the war-weary frontiers of the Muslim world, in places like Afghanistan, Chechnya and Somalia as much as in Iraq, that the pre-Islamic chivalry Bin Laden celebrates can find its modern manifestation. The charging horses and fiery deserts of pagan Arabia take on a new life in the battlefields of Africa and Central Asia, and perhaps even on the buses and trains of London. And so having been anchored in the pre-Islamic past, this chivalrous form of Arabness is immediately put into global circulation, as if Arabia had itself become a nomad in the world. But this is exactly what has happened, with Arabness globalized by way of sartorial, linguistic and ritual signs that evoke romantic images of virtuous knighthood, as if in a kind of Arthurian romance for the Muslim world that books like Ayman al-Zawahiri's *Knights Under the Banner of the Prophet* purposefully gesture towards. Thus also the "Arab" headscarves worn by the London bombers in their martyrdom videotapes, articles of clothing which had nothing to do with their Pakistani background. More interesting is the fact that these signs of Arabness are often mixed with sartorial elements from other Muslim traditions, not least among Arab fighters themselves in places like Afghanistan, creating a cosmopolitan Islam in this theatrical way by subverting its cultures of origin.

Empires of the mind

The globalization of Arabness as a moral category has a well-established pre-history in the Muslim world beyond the Middle East, which has for centuries now had to reconcile the Arab element in Islam with its own traditions and languages. Naturally in the period before nationalism this reconciliation had nothing to do with any culture war between Arab and non-Arab, such terms themselves being fluid and changeable, though a nationalist factor does enter the equation in modern times. Prior to the emergence of the oil-rich states of the Gulf, then, and prior even to the emergence of the Middle East, let alone the Israeli-Palestinian conflict, Arabness was defined as a conceptual category in important and influential ways outside the region. It found expression in British India, through the literary and expository work of the poet-philosopher Muhammad Iqbal, who was undoubtedly the most important and indeed the most popular Muslim thinker of twentieth-century South Asia, though his influence went well beyond the subcontinent. For I want to suggest that only by attaching itself to such histories of the imagination does globalized militancy today achieve intellectual and political traction in the larger Muslim world.

Like Azad's claims for the sanctity of the Arabian Peninsula, Iqbal's conception of Arabness as an intellectual category fell heir to a long literary history in which the word Arab had exercised the Indian imagination. In earlier times, of course, Arabia was imagined neither in ethno-linguistic nor territorial terms, but was defined rather by the cosmopolitan and, as we would say today, multinational pilgrim cities of Mecca and Medina. And because these cities had lost power very soon after the Prophet's death, with Arabia as a whole becoming a minor province within the great empires that succeeded him, they possessed little if any political importance of their own. Indeed the holy cities were treated both by Muslim rulers and their rivals as honourable places of exile, a role the peninsula continues to play even today for deposed heads of state. Naturally the sanctuary of Mecca in particular was even more important as a place of exile for dissident clerics, and it is remarkable how many of them fled there from the exactions of colonial rule eventually to return and lead resistance movements, whether violent or pacifist in nature. The Mahatma's associate Abul Kalam Azad was himself born in Mecca, and throughout his career made full use of the prestige this Arabian background lent him. Dependent though this prestige was upon Azad's use of the Arabic language, or rather an Urdu larded with Arabic locutions, there was nothing of the ethno-national in it. In fact the stereotyped character of the Bedouin, as Arabia's indigenous peoples were called, possessed mostly negative connotations in the literary culture to which Azad belonged, being associated mostly with savagery and the looting of pilgrim caravans. We owe the romantic image of the desert Arab to European influence.

By the middle of the eighteenth century this distant peninsula that was so difficult to traverse had begun to occupy a different kind of space in the imagination of India's Muslim elite. For one thing the emergence of Wahhabism as a military force that would in due course threaten the great cities of the Fertile Crescent suddenly put Arabia back on Islam's political map. Yet far more important was the fact that it provided Muslim intellectuals with an alternative political geography: Mecca and Medina could now be juxtaposed with capital cities like Istanbul or Delhi, not to foreground the former's religious status so much as to withdraw from the contracting circle of the latter's power. So Shah Waliullah of Delhi, an eighteenth-century thinker claimed as a founding father by all the subcontinent's reformers, modernist as well as fundamentalist, had in his last testament urged his descendants to adopt the Arab dress and mannerisms of his ancestors, an injunction that was much derided at the time given the peculiarity of such habits in his city of residence.[22] But in retrospect it seems clear that this instruction, with its echoes in the sartorial and linguistic "Arabness" of so many Muslims outside the Middle East today, represented a recognition of Delhi's declining power and a repudiation of its Islamic character. Well into the nineteenth century, then, Arabia and Arabness continued to define neither an ethno-linguistic nor a territorial entity but precisely the religious void created by India's political disintegration. Thus the popular Urdu writer Nazir Ahmad, in a novel promoting girls' education that was published in 1873, very typically described Arabia in the lesson on geography he imparts his female students as a place devoid of all meaning but that of Islam's revelation.[23]

In the tradition that Muhammad Iqbal inherited, therefore, Arabia occupied an increasingly important place within a pan-Islamic imagination. And while it had always been part of a larger Muslim geography in India's literary culture, by the beginning of the twentieth century the peninsula's fate was bound closely to that of the Ottoman Empire. Indeed Turkey had come to represent as important a figure in the Muslim imagination as Arabia, though for very different reasons, since unlike the latter it represented both Islam's power and its modernity. And so from the nineteenth century Indians who identified with these qualities very commonly sported the Ottoman fez as a sign of their own intellectual and political aspirations, but with the fall of the caliphate this whole world of the imagination collapsed, its modernity being replaced by the accoutrements of an Arabian purity. How did this transformation occur and what were its implications for imagining the Muslim world anew? Looking in more detail at Iqbal's conception of Arabness

---

22   Shah Waliullah, *Armughan-e Shah Waliullah,* trans. Muhammad Sarvar (Lahore: Idarah-e Thaqafat-e Islamiyya, 1971), pp. 17-18.

23   Nazir Ahmad, *Banat un-Na'ash* (Lucknow: Munshi Nawal Kishore, 1967), pp. 185-6.

should allow us to trace the outlines of Islam's globalization, not least among militants like Osama bin Laden in our own times.

Although Iqbal did not support the Khilafat Movement, which he thought was too medieval in fancy, he was certainly a pan-Islamist and one who was not averse to defining the caliphate in terms of an elected parliament. Indeed he saw the Turkish leader Mustafa Kemal Pasha, the Atatürk who had abolished this centuries-old institution, as a great Muslim figure and almost a modern caliph himself, excessive and unfortunate though his republicanism might be. And it was from this modernized idea of the caliphate, or rather of pan-Islamism, that Iqbal's idea of Arabness drew its meaning. Like many other Muslim thinkers of the period, Muhammad Iqbal set his face against the racial and national ideologies that he thought lay at the root of European colonialism and that were destructive of Christian ethics in the West as much as they would be of Muslim ones in the East. If it was Iqbal's distrust of such ideologies that accounted for his pan-Islamist vision of the caliphate, in other words, this very distrust also led him to support the Roman Catholic Church as its Christian equivalent. And so it was the Reformation's destruction of Latin Christendom that he thought had brought about the racial nationalism that lay behind liberalism, imperialism and fascism alike:

The result is a series of mutually ill-adjusted states dominated by interests not human but national. And these mutually ill-adjusted states after trampling over the morals and convictions of Christianity, are today feeling the need of a fed-erated Europe, i.e., the need of a unity which Christian church-organisation originally gave them, but which instead of reconstructing it in the light of Christ's vision of human brotherhood they considered it fit to destroy under the inspiration of Luther.[24]

Despite its Islamic particularity, therefore, the caliphate represented for Muhammad Iqbal a conceptual form with equivalents in other re-ligious traditions. Crucial here is the fact that he linked pan-Islamism with the Roman Catholic Church rather than with the Holy Roman Empire, specifying in this way its religious dimension over any merely political one. Perhaps it was the generality of its form that also allowed Iqbal to redefine the caliphate so radically, making of it a bulwark

---

24   Muhammad Iqbal, *Thoughts and Reflections of Iqbal*, edited with notes by Syed Abdul Vahid (Lahore: Sh. Muhammad Ashraf, 1992), pp. 163-4.

against the violent practices of European nationalism. This criticism of ethno-national ideology was not confined to Europe but included modern Arab as much as Indian forms of chauvinism. More importantly it also extended to what Iqbal called "Arabian imperialism", referring thus to the Arabization of Islam in the course of its early expansion. Muhammad Iqbal then sought to modernize Islam by purifying it of what he saw as the medieval tradition of Arab conquest. This was in fact his only religious reason for supporting some kind of autonomous Muslim state within India—what eventually became Pakistan. Such autonomy was required not in order to save Muslims from any Hindu or British dominion so much as to set them free from an Arabian one:

I therefore demand the formation of a consolidated Muslim state in the best interest of India and Islam. For India it means security and peace resulting from an internal balance of power; for Islam an opportunity to rid itself of the stamp that Arabian imperialism was forced to give it, to mobilize its law, its education, its culture, and to bring them into closer contact with its own original spirit and with the spirit of modern times.[25]

Today Iqbal is acclaimed as the spiritual father of Pakistan, though his criticism of Arabian imperialism has been replaced in the curiously anti-nationalist ideology of this state by the poet-philosopher's glorification of Arabness as an intellectual ideal. Muhammad Iqbal invoked this Arab ideal in two ways: first by using the word *hijazi*, an adjective referring to that part of the Arabian Peninsula called the Hijaz, which had been the Prophet's homeland. Used thus, *hijazi*, like the Arabian island as a whole, referred not to a political entity but to a set of historical ideals that were attached in the literary imagination to the region it named. These are the same ideals, comprising courage, honour, daring and the like that Osama bin Laden invokes in our own times, often also under the rubric *hijazi*, when he glorifies the chivalric spirit of pre-Islamic Arabia. The second way in which Iqbal describes this ideal is by counterposing the Arab (*arab*) to the Persian (*ajam*). The distinction between Arab and Persian is a long-standing one in the history of Islam, but for Iqbal it does not stand either for a political or an ethno-linguistic difference between two peoples. These terms refer instead to distinct philosophical ideals, with the Arab standing in for passionate

---

25   Ibid. p. 173.

action and an unyielding insistence on the letter of the law, while the Persian stood in for a contemplative life and the intellectual flexibility of compromise.

Whatever the literary precedents for the pairing of Arab and Persian in Islamic tradition, Muhammad Iqbal modernized their relationship by adding some European leavening to it. To some degree this included elements from the field of Semitic studies, and even from the ethno-linguistic classification of humanity into categories like Aryan and Semite. Given Iqbal's dislike of racial categories, however, the ethnic and national ballast of such classifications tended to be thrown overboard in his work, and their categories lent philosophical weight instead. Oswald Spengler's highly influential book *The Decline of the West* provided Muhammad Iqbal with one model of such philosophical classification, though he remained deeply critical of some aspects of it.[26] More important as a model perhaps was the nineteenth-century pairing of Athens and Jerusalem, or Hebraism and Hellenism, as Matthew Arnold put it in *Culture and Anarchy*.[27] And in fact the distinction of Arab and Persian mirrors that of Jew and Greek in almost every respect, with the formers' moral grandeur differentiated from the latter's aesthetic perfection.

Nietzche's pairing of the Apollonian and the Dionysian provided a final model for Iqbal's *ajam* and *arab*. And like Nietzche, whose Indian admirer he was, Iqbal investigated these terms not merely as names, but because their very reduction to stereotypes indicated that the Arab and the Persian, much like the Jew and the Greek, had become embodied in popular attitudes and prejudices, manifested as these were in articles of clothing, uses of language and forms of behaviour. Such categories were in this sense almost visceral in their effects and not simply ideas that flitted across minds while leaving bodies both undifferentiated and untouched.[28] Like Nietzche again, Muhammad Iqbal thought of these categories not as cultural particularities but precisely as philosophical principles that could be identified by different names over more than

---

26   See Mohammed Iqbal, The Reconstruction of religious Thought in Islam (New Delhi: Kitab Bhavan, 1990), pp. 142-45.

27   See Matthew Arnold, *Culture and Anarchy and Other Writings* (Cambridge University Press, 1999), pp. 126-137.

28   The key text here is Friedrich Nietzche, *On the Genealogy of Morality*, trans. Maudemarie Clark and Alan J. Swensen, (Indianapolis and Cambridge: Hackett Publishing, 1998).

one civilization. It is possible, in other words, to read Iqbal's Arab as an equivalent for Jew, and his Persian as an equivalent for Greek. Moreover these principles were neither autonomous nor discrete, representing instead historical traits of human dimension that always interacted with one another and sometimes even took each other's place, whether this was among a people or within a single individual. The Arab and the Persian, in other words, named the Muslim history of an intellectual relationship that stretched beyond the world of Islam, though this history possessed its own particularity. And as intellectual principles the Arab and the Persian were open to occupation, whatever the role that "actual" Arabs and Persians had played in their constitution. Thus Muhammad Iqbal sang the Arab's praises while writing in Persian.

Now if the Arab and the Persian represented principles that were in a constant state of play, then there was no question of opting for one over another in any absolute sense. Indeed this would make of them a Manichaean duality, something that Iqbal thought was un-Islamic and that he placed in the Persian world. On the contrary, the Arab and the Persian each had its virtues, and it was only right that one should dominate the other at certain historical moments. So Muhammad Iqbal's doctoral dissertation, *The Development of Metaphysics in Persia*, describes the universalism of Islam in medieval times by evaluating the Aryan contribution to this Semitic religion, something that he thought made it into a truly synthetic phenomenon.[29] And while Iqbal identified the term Aryan in this work with Persia, he also recognized India as its home, thus making *ajam* itself into a complex and expansive category more or less equivalent to the scholarly designation of Indo-European. Whatever its past glories, however, Muhammad Iqbal believed that in his own day, when so much of the Muslim world lived under European colonialism, the passionate activism and moral rigour of the Arab was required more than the contemplative aesthetic of the Persian for an Islam revived.

Here then we have a whole genealogy of Arabness outside the Middle East, one in which it is transformed into a philosophical principle that is neither autonomous nor absolute, but open to occupation and in a constant state of play with a Persia that complements rather than

---

29   See Muhammad Iqbal, *The Development of Metaphysics in Persia: A Contribution to the Study of Muslim Philosophy* (Lahore: Bazm-e Iqbal, 1959).

opposes it. And however different in origin Osama bin Laden's conception of Arabness may be, his vision converges with that of Iqbal in setting up the category Arab against ethno-nationalism to have it represent a remarkably similar set of intellectual ideals. Bin Laden's globalization of Arabness, in other words, has assimilated itself to the category's prehistory outside the Middle East, in formulations like Muhammad Iqbal's, to turn the stuff of geopolitics into a philosophical principle of great depth and complexity. But whatever its genealogy, Arabness does not possess its own meaning, instead deriving it from the larger Muslim world, precisely in contrast to entities like Persia, with which it has formed a stereotyped pairing for many centuries now. In fact for Osama bin Laden today as much as for Muhammad Iqbal yesterday, the Arab is compared, contrasted and otherwise related to elements only within the Muslim world and not to the West. For the West's peer in friendship as much as enmity is Islam or the Muslim world as a whole—just as among Middle Eastern nationalists in the past Arabness was counterposed to the West only as part of the East however defined.

The militant and the Mahatma

As part of a narrative internal to Islam but external to the Middle East, it is easy to see how Arabness can achieve meaning within the imaginative context of a caliphate. But despite its Arab beginnings as well as its long and glorious Arab history, militants today insist on linking the caliphate primarily to its last owners, the supposedly decadent Ottoman Turks who not only ended up being defeated by European powers, but with their Westernized ways are not even considered to be models of Islamic piety. Why then insist on attaching the caliphate, even as a future possibility, to the House of Osman, which had in addition to all its other faults also reduced the Arabs to servitude? Having fought for long periods against Christian powers, and having been defeated by them in living memory, the Ottoman caliphate offers militants both a cause and a model. The consequences of adopting this model, however, go well beyond such tactical reasoning. For in addition to announcing its anti-national and cosmopolitan credentials, the Ottoman model of a militant caliphate foregrounds precisely the modernity and even the secularism of this imaginary order—or at the very least its anti-fundamentalist character.

The caliphate as it is reinterpreted in contemporary Muslim thought tends to be resolutely modern in form, as we have seen, even as the precedents for its transformation are still sought in the past. Nevertheless it is evident to all those who reimagine it that no future caliphate will constitute simply a reiteration of some original model, no matter how updated in appearance. In this sense the caliphate cannot be linked back either to its earliest period under the "rightly guided" caliphs, nor to its later Ummayyad and Abbasid glories. Interesting about this recognition of historical change is that its upholders will often refuse to countenance such change when thinking about individual Muslim states. The nation state, therefore, is to be domesticated by being modelled with technical alterations upon the Prophet's dispensation in Medina, while the caliphate, perhaps because it is an indigenous and imaginary entity, can be envisioned in more transformative ways.[30] After all the language of the Islamic state is essentially defensive in nature, seeking as it does to translate the nation state into Islamic terms, as well as to regulate and limit its inroads into traditional Muslim societies.[31] And for this to happen great weight must be placed upon an original constitution. Yet when they have actually come into being, Islamic states have never in practice been able to fulfil their regulative role, and are now in the process of casting it off to become, quite self-consciously, the primary agents of change in Muslim societies.[32]

The caliphate, in other words, has always had a modern and even secular form in contemporary Muslim thought, this being the truest link it possesses with the Ottoman Empire, which was itself officially secular from the late nineteenth century.[33] Indeed the Turkish sultan only started emphasizing his caliphal authority late in the eighteenth

---

30   This is true not only of the secularist Abul Kalam Azad's *Maslah-e Khilafat*, but also of his contemporary and compatriot the fundamentalist Abul Ala Mawdudi's *Khilafat o Mulukiyyat* (New Delhi: Markazi Maktabah-e Islami Publishers, 2006).

31   For this see the work of Olivier Roy, particularly *The Failure of Political Islam*, trans. Carol Volk (Cambridge, MA: Harvard University Press, 1994).

32   Olivier Roy describes these efforts in *The Politics of Chaos in the Middle East*.

33   See for this the classic work by Niyazi Berkes, *The Development of Secularism in Turkey* (London: Hurst, 1998).

century, and claiming authority over Muslims outside his domains on the same principle as Christian powers were doing for their co-religionists in Ottoman lands. So the Arabist T. W. Arnold, who had been Muhammad Iqbal's teacher at Government College, Lahore, and who advised Britain on dealing with the Khilafatists, points out that the first such claims put forward in a diplomatic document were in the 1774 Treaty of Kuchuk Kainarji between Sultan Abdul Hamid I and the Empress Catherine II of Russia.[34] Though it had become an institution by which Muslim thinkers imagined their modernity, the caliphate was paradoxically not envisioned in completely utopian terms even after the abolition of its Ottoman form. So just like Osama bin Laden and in very similar terms too, Gandhi was adamant about defending the institution's latter-day reality, however decadent its Ottoman form might be, even going so far as to describe the First World War as a crusade against Islam and the dismantling of the caliphate as the greatest humiliation suffered by Muslims in the twentieth century:

Oppose all Turkish misrule by all means, but it is wicked to seek to efface the Turk and with him Islam from Europe under the false plea of Turkish misrule. [...] Was the late war a crusade against Islam, in which the Mussalmans of India were invited to join?[35]

I do say that the affront such as has been put upon Islam cannot be repeated for a century. Islam must rise now or 'be fallen' if not for ever, certainly for a century.[36]

The Mahatma was undoubtedly the most important propagator of the caliphate in modern times, not least because it was he rather than the much-acclaimed Afghani who managed to lead a significant religious and political movement in its favour, one with incalculable consequences for Islam in South Asia and beyond. For Gandhi the caliphate was a moral ideal but not a utopian one because it referred to a reality that, half-vanished though it might be, existed with neither name nor form in the world of European politics. Similarly for Bin Laden this institution names the otherwise nameless reality of an Islam that occupies

34 T.W. Arnold, , *The Caliphate* (Oxford: The Clarendon Press, 2000), p. 165.

35 M.K. Gandhi, "The Meaning of the Khilafat", *Young India*, 8 September 1921. Parenthesis mine.

36 M.K. Gandhi, "At the Call of the Country", *Young India*, 21 July 1920.

a global arena lacking political forms proper to itself. But the caliphate's curious realism harbours a momentous secret: that as an imaginary institution it serves to hold back another imaginary one with equally deep roots in the history of Islam. What the caliphate in all its profane reality forestalls is a messianic order based on the institution of the Mahdi in Muslim tradition. Indeed messianism is remarkable by its absence from modern narratives of the caliphate—which do not lend the institution any religious charisma—and in fact from Muslim militancy more generally. The messianic impulse, as well as the apocalypse to which it is related, is far more characteristic of contemporary Jewish and Christian movements instead.

Maybe it is the caliphate's very lack of any utopian project or religious charisma that allows it to name the global arena in all its cosmopolitan reality. Ayman al-Zawahiri's letter to Abu Musab al-Zarqawi, for instance, does more than underline the anti-national and non-Arab character of the jihad. It also expostulates with the bloodthirsty head of Al-Qaeda in Iraq to cease gratuitous attacks upon the Shia—not simply for tactical reasons, but because Zawahiri recognized that however strong sectarian passions may run in any region, and however perfidious he considered Iraq's Shiites, the world's Sunni majority limning his imaginary caliphate would not countenance such attacks.[37] So while denouncing these treacherous heretics and reserving their punishment for God, Zawahiri was careful to name them not as Shiites so much as American collaborators. It also worth noting that the more sectarian passions are stoked in parts of the Muslim world the less do Zawahiri or Bin Laden invoke them, so that in recent times we even see them referring for the first time to sacred Shiite heroes like the Imam Husayn as models of martyrdom.[38]

But the cosmopolitanism of this uncharismatic caliphate has precedents more recent than the Ottoman Empire. For the Khilafat Movement, seen by so many Indian Sunnis as comprising a religious obligation, also managed to win not only Hindu but also Shiite support—because it re-imagined the new world that emerged from the First World War in terms that differed radically from those in use among the surviving

---

37   "Letter from al-Zawahiri to al-Zarqawi", pp. 8-9.

38   "Al-Zawahiri calls on Muslims to wage 'war of jihad', reject UN resolutions", pp. 5-6.

European empires. Now while Hindus are indifferent to the religious status of the caliphate, it is for the Shia a quite illegitimate institution because the Ottomans, like the caliphs who went before, are seen as having usurped the position of their imams. Yet among the many Shia leaders who supported the Khilafat was the eminent jurist and privy councillor Syed Ameer Ali, who apart from his desire to support Muslim sentiment in India, argued that the caliphate's abolition would fragment religious as much as political authority in the Sunni world and thus leave it prey to fanaticism and violence—a rather prescient analysis and one echoed by Osama bin Laden in our own times.[39] Ameer Ali and the Aga Khan, who as the imam of a Shia subsect was himself a religious rival of the caliph, nevertheless supported the institution's Ottoman form so assiduously that it was their public letter to the Turkish prime minister urging its preservation that provided Atatürk with a reason to terminate the House of Osman. The founder of the Turkish republic thought India's interference in his country's affairs unseemly, and failed to understand how a Sunni caliphate could be defended by Shiites, for whom it was after all religiously illegitimate.

Looking back at the caliphate's abolition after some three decades, the Aga Khan, than whom no Muslim more Westernized existed, still justified India's battle for the Ottoman cause, which Indian delegates to the Peace of Versailles had been the only ones to champion at that august assembly. The Aga Khan's defence of the caliphate against Arab nationalism as much as European imperialism was conducted in terms that lent rationality to an institution whose supporters are too often dismissed as irrational today, seeing in it the potential for a Middle Eastern federation that bears comparison with the Commonwealth of Nations as it was meant to be and with the European Union as it is. Agreeing in most respects with militant advocates of the caliphate in our own times, this very "moderate" defence of a Sunni institution by one of the most prominent Shia leaders of the period deserves to be quoted at length, if only to cast light upon the curiously mixed genealogy of pan-Islamism:

---

39   See for instance "Ameer Ali's letter with the Aga Khan to His Excellency Ghazi Ismat Pasha, the Prime Minister of Turkey", in Shan Muhammad (ed.), *The Right Hon'ble Syed Ameer Ali: Political Writings* (New Delhi: Ashish Publishing House, 1989), pp. 288-290.

Muslim opposition to the break-up of the Turkish Empire had a basis—however much misunderstood it may have been—of true statesmanship and of understanding of the absorbing political realities of the Middle East. First, we felt that the separation of the Arabs from the Turks (hailed at the time as emancipation from a tyranny, although within a few years all Arab nationalists were singing a very different tune) would not lead to the emergence of a single strong Arab nation extending from Egypt to Persia and from Alexandretta to Aden and the Indian Ocean. We foresaw in large measure what actually happened; the formation of a number of small Arab nations, for many years of little more than colonial status, under British and French overlordship. We predicted that the Arabs would in fact merely be changing masters, and where these masters had been Muslim Turks they would now be Christians, or (as ultimately happened in a large part of Palestine) Jews. Even now, after the lapse of thirty years or more, the Arab states that succeeded the Ottoman Empire—though the ignominious protectorate and mandated status has been abolished—are nothing but an aggregation of small kingdoms and republics, not one of them capable of standing up alone in the face of any powerful opposition and, despite the Arab League, incapable of maintaining either individually or collectively real resistance to the influence either of Soviet Russia or the Western Democracies. Neutrality in any conflict between these two is a forlorn dream.

Consider for a moment how different matters might have been had there emerged after the First World War a federal union of Turkey, the Arab states of the Middle East, and Egypt, with a single defence force and a united foreign policy. Our instinctive Muslim faith in the idea of the continuance of Turkey as a Great Power had wisdom in it, for it would have achieved practical results, in the security and stability of the Middle East, far transcending anything that the makeshift, haphazard policies of the years since the end of the Second World War—piecemeal withdrawal of political suzerainty by Britain, piecemeal financial, economic and military aid by the United States have been able to effect. Consider the disruption and the political *malaise* which have been the lot of the Middle East in recent years; consider all the unavailing effort that has gone into the attempt to build up a Middle East Defence Organization, in any degree paralleling N.A.T.O., and ponder how easily, how honourably all this might have been avoided.[40]

How did this extraordinary alliance of religious groups come about in the Khilafat Movement? Whatever the pragmatic politics and horse-trading that occurred between the leaders of these groups, for Gandhi it

---

40   Aga Khan, *The Memoirs of the Aga Khan: World Enough and Time* (London: Cassell and Co., 1954), pp. 156-7.

was clear that as a popular movement, the Khilafat was founded upon relationships that were suprapolitical in nature. Thus the Mahatma was strongly drawn to what he called the idealistic motives of India's Sunnis, who were after all sacrificing their time, money, well-being and even freedom for a faraway cause that seemed to bear no relation to their everyday needs and concerns. According to Gandhi its lack at least of direct political or economic advantage was what made of the Khilafat Movement something truly religious. And if the Mahatma admired this religious spirit, it was because he realized that only disinterested and sacrificial movements were capable of transforming entire societies, thus creating new political possibilities in their aftermath. So it was the idealistic character of Sunni sacrifice that he thought allowed Hindus, Shiites and others to befriend them, because by doing so they were supporting a neighbour's heartfelt prejudice rather than some cause that competed with any of their own. Whether or not this support was extended to India's Sunnis for reasons of self-interest, then, the Khilafat's idealism reduced such interests to relative insignificance by subordinating them to a movement that was not itself structured according to any recognizable calculus of interests.

The movement was in fact replete with sacrifices volunteered to secure the friendship of others. Such for example were the *fatwas* issued by Muslim divines prohibiting cow-slaughter because it was a practice offensive to Hindus: religious pronouncements whose gratuitous nature the Mahatma insisted upon in order to prevent this sacrifice from turning into the basis of a political deal. And however recent the attachment of India's Muslims to the caliphate might be, dating back to the nineteenth century and thus to the period of colonial domination at its earliest, these forms of sacrifice had a history that predated both Gandhi and the Khilafat Movement. For it was in the Indian Mutiny of 1857 that such sacrifices made their first appearance, with Hindu and Muslim soldiers of the East India Company taking to arms in support of each other's very particular fears about what they saw as British attempts to destroy their caste and religious distinctions, thus turning them into an undifferentiated race of Christian slaves. So when the Company's Muslim soldiers refused to bite open the bullet cartridges that were believed to have been greased with animal fat and rose up in revolt against the British, they did so not because of any religious prohibitions of their own, but out of solidarity with those of their Hindu compatriots who constituted the bulk of the mutineers. It was for the sake of their Hindu countrymen, too, that they gave up slaughtering cows, though this was a customary practice especially during the Islamic feast of sacrifice.[41] More important about these events than their interested nature is the fact that they often ignored the language of compromise and contract to rely upon that of sacrifice alone—and in the case of cow-slaughter even upon its doubling to achieve a sacrifice of sacrifice itself. These were, in other words, gestures that invited the friendship of others by defining sacrifice as a form of hospitality.

Gandhian forms of sacrifice, therefore, possessed not only a prehistory but a violent one at that, since the Mutiny represented the most important revolt by far against European imperialism in the nineteenth century, leading to savage reprisals by the British, who emptied out entire cities of their inhabitants while indulging in massacre, loot and rapine. The Khilafat Movement was often compared by its advocates as well as detractors to the Mutiny because it constituted the most significant threat to British rule in India since 1857, but also because it brought together different religious groups not to further some common aim so much as to achieve a completely pluralistic freedom each by sacrificing its interest for another's ideal. And so like the Hindu mutineers before them, the caliphate's Hindu supporters strengthened Muslim resolve by offering up their own sacrifices as a reminder of the former's Islamic obligations. By cultivating these disinterested relationships, said the Mahatma, Indians of all faiths were cultivating their own moral capacities and therefore claiming their freedom—which they could in any case achieve not by military but only such hospitable forms of sacrifice. Whatever the truth of Gandhi's analysis, it was broadcast in pamphlet and speech to become the mantra of the Khilafat Movement, which is why he is probably the greatest and certainly the most creative modern thinker of the caliphate: a Hindu who received the adulation of Muslim divines and was credited with nothing less than the revival of Indian Islam by friends and enemies alike.

---

41   See Irfan Habib, "History from below", *Frontline*, New Delhi, June 29, 2007, pp. 11-18, as well as Salim al-Din Quraishi's *Cry for Freedom: Proclamations of Muslim Revolutionaries of 1857* (Lahore: Sang-e-Meel Publications, 1997).

Of course the Khilafat Movement finally failed, not only because the Turks abolished the institution, but even before this when Gandhi himself called it off though agitations were at their peak—because he objected to the violence that began breaking out among his followers, Hindu as well as Muslim, whom the Mahatma did not therefore think possessed the requisite spirit of sacrifice. He would rather have them volunteer to die than kill for material gain. Nevertheless Gandhi saw the movement as a successful experiment that demonstrated the possibility of what he called idealism in political life. The comparison with Al-Qaeda's advocacy of martyrdom in the service of a new caliphate needs no belabouring, since like the Indian Mutiny and the Khilafat Movement before it, the language of militant sacrifice today is pluralistic and hospitable enough to possess no common ideology. And yet the truly interesting thing about Gandhi calling off a movement which the British Empire was struggling to contain, was that he could do so without either an army or a police force and despite the disagreement of many Muslim leaders, who tried unsuccessfully to carry it forward on their own. Little did these men realize that the radical simplicity of a Hindu's logic might have more effect upon Muslims than their own complicated theology, since it was Gandhi rather than any of his Muslim partners who was acknowledged as the movement's "dictator". But this is precisely the role that the Mahatma's alter ego Osama bin Laden plays in our own day, especially when offering his enemies a truce while himself living in fear of his life.

However disenchanted Indian Muslims eventually become with him, the Mahatma laid a deep impress upon South Asian Islam by opening it out to the world in a quite novel way. Indeed Gandhi's form of religious leadership among Hindus even provided Muslim divines with a model for their own participation in political life, with some among them vying to become Muslim mahatmas.[42] So it is no accident that while Gandhi's Hindu enemies saw him as pro-Muslim, and his Muslim enemies saw him as pro-Hindu, both concurred in regretting his opening the subcontinent's political arena to Islam's religious class. And in fact the largest body of clerics in India, called the Jamiat-ul Ulama-ye Hind or Society of Indian Divines, was founded in 1919 to support Gandhi and

---

42   See for example Dietrich Reetz, *Islam in the Public Sphere: Religious Groups in India, 1900-1947* (New Delhi: Oxford University Press, 2006), p. 145.

the secular vision of the Indian National Congress during the Khilafat Movement, providing in its turn the founding model for clerical organizations belonging to different political orientations in Pakistan. If anything this reveals that Islam, whether in its peaceable or militant forms, is not self-produced but, as Muhammad Iqbal might say, a synthetic phenomenon. More than this, Gandhi's role in the Khilafat Movement and his influence upon Muslim politics subsequently tells us that Islam, even in modern times, is not defined simply by its relationship with the West but possesses a far more complex historical constitution.

This complexity was evident in the Khilafat Movement's effort to reimagine the still inchoate new world emerging from the ruin of both imperial and national states after the Great War—a world in whose creation the Indian army had played a leading role in the Middle East. The pluralistic and anti-national form taken by this effort of imagination is mirrored in militant thinking about the caliphate today, which I would argue represents an effort to re-imagine the new global arena still emerging from the ruins of the Cold War—one which possesses as yet no institutions of its own. It is therefore no accident that Osama bin Laden and his epigones should so insistently compare Islam's current predicament to the transformation it underwent after the Great War, since then as much as now it is not the Middle East so much as the Muslim world as a whole that is in the process of being redefined. Gandhi's caliphate, however, resembles Bin Laden's in more than its geographical sweep, for unlike Muslim attempts to set up caliphates elsewhere, for example in colonial Nigeria, neither of these projects is strictly speaking a territorial one. Indian Muslims therefore struggled for the caliphate as what Gandhi called an ideal rather than territorial entity, since they had no intention of becoming Ottoman subjects, while militants today refuse even to locate the caliphate territorially let alone to plan for its establishment. The Mahatma's description of the caliphate is therefore as valid now as it was then:

In my opinion, if the demands of the Muslims of India are conceded, it will not much matter whether Turkey's are satisfied or not. [...] The Khilafat is an ideal and when a man works for an ideal, he becomes irresistible. The Muslims, who represent the ideal, have behind them the opinion of the whole mass of the Indian people.[43]

---

43   M.K. Gandhi, "The Khilafat", in *Young India*, 23 March 1921. Parenthesis mine.

Unlike the imperial and internationalist vision of Jamal al-Din Afghani, or indeed of the Ottomans themselves in their promotion of pan-Islamism both before and during the First World War, the caliphate promoted by a Gandhi or a Bin Laden certainly re-imagines the Muslim world and even the global arena as I argue, but it does so in a way as removed as it can possibly be from the conventions of political life. And yet it is precisely the caliphate as a thoroughly unconventional project that has had any traction among Muslims—which suggests that its role is in fact to re-imagine the world for a politics yet to come. This is true even when such projects touch ground and assume a territorial politics. Not only the so-called "Islamic state of Iraq", therefore, but also the "caliphate state" set up in south-western India by the Mappila Revolt in 1921 take their meaning from such moments of idealism. Launched against colonial authorities as much as against Hindu landlords and moneylenders at the height of the Khilafat Movement, this violent uprising by Muslim peasants who traced their descent to Arab traders from the Yemen resulted in the establishment of a short-lived state dedicated to the pan-Islamist cause of the caliphate and not to its own sovereignty.

In the bowels of the Islamic state

The Khilafat Movement did survive Gandhi's abdication of leadership, though only in a minor note, with a number of India's Muslim leaders travelling to the Middle East to participate in discussions over the institution's possible future. These Indians remained opposed for the most part to the making of such caliphs on the cheap, especially if their claims were founded, as were those of its primarily Arab applicants, upon tribal and other genealogical forms of legitimacy. But with the hope of a revived caliphate receding, the remnants of the Khilafat Movement were eventually dedicated to the cause of Palestine, with Azad, for instance, clearly linking this cause to that of the caliphate well before the latter's abolition.[44] The end of the caliphate, in other words, resulted in the transference of pan-Islamist passions to a national cause, though one that derived its meaning not from its Arab character so much as from the defeat of the Turks. So the widespread outcry against Jewish immi-

---

44   See Azad, *Maslah-e Khilafat*, pp. 261-4.

gration to Palestine had pan-Islamic resonance precisely because it had come to inherit the conceptual tools and affective motivations of the Khilafatist cause, including the sanctity of the Arabian Island and the resistance to European imperialism. For South Asian Muslims at least, Zionism had to be opposed not in its own right, given that it was quite insignificant in their eyes, but because it was part of Europe's re-shaping of the world in the wake of the First World War, of which the passing of the caliphate became the greatest symbol. And like his Indian forebears, Osama bin Laden, too, sees Zionism and Arab nationalism in the same light, considering both the Arab states and Israel to be creations of the West implanted like weeds in the grave of the caliphate. Or as Gandhi put it in 1921, describing a "holy war" between Jews and Christians on the one side and Muslims on the other nearly three decades before the creation of Israel and seven decades before the emergence of Bin Laden:

Britain has made promises to the Zionists. [...] The Jews, it is contended, must remain a homeless wandering race unless they have obtained possession of Palestine. I do not propose to examine the soundness or otherwise of the doctrine underlying the proposition. All I contend is that they cannot possess Palestine through a trick or a moral breach. Palestine was not a stake in the war. The British Government could not dare have asked a single Muslim soldier to wrest control of Palestine from fellow-Muslims and give it to the Jews. Palestine, as a place of Jewish worship, is a sentiment to be respected, and the Jews would have a just cause of complaint against Musulman idealists if they were to prevent Jews from offering worship as freely as themselves. [...] By no canon of ethics or war, therefore, can Palestine be given to the Jews as a result of the war. Either Zionists must revise their ideal about Palestine, or, if Judaism permits the arbitrament of war, engage in a 'holy war' with the Muslims of the world with the Christians throwing in their influence on their side.[45]

The nation-state came to embody Islamic aspirations as well as Muslim politics only with the dismantling of the Ottoman Empire and the reconstitution of an international order following the First World War.[46] In this sense it served as a consolation prize for the loss of the caliphate as a way of thinking about Islamic authority beyond political borders, though we have seen, with respect to the Indian and later

---

45   M.K. Gandhi, "The Khilafat". Parentheses mine.

46   For a discussion of the transformation in Muslim politics wrought by the caliphate's abolition see Bobby Sayyid's *A Fundamental Fear: Eurocentrism and the Emergence of Islamism* (London and New York: Zed Book, 1997).

Pakistani support of the Palestinian cause well before the establishment of Israel, that Muslim national movements too were often defined in pan-Islamic terms whose popularity dated back to the Khilafat Movement. Now the quest for a Muslim version of the nation state, I have said, represents a fundamentally negative enterprise, its proponents grappling with the task of translating this state into Islamic terms while at the same time limiting the reach of its institutions within traditional Muslim society. However visions of the caliphate continued to proliferate even in its heyday during the Cold War, with great thinkers of the Islamic state like the Pakistani Abul Ala Mawdudi, the Egyptian Sayyid Qutb and even the Shiite Ruhollah Khomeini of Iran all feeling the need to deal with this institution, though it be only as an historical and future ideal.

Mawdudi, for example, began his book *Caliphate and Monarchy*, first published in 1966, by defining this institution as the stewardship of a divine trust. This definition explicitly set the caliphate against any concept of state sovereignty, which was something Mawdudi thought belonged to God alone.[47] And while the distrust of dictatorial as much as popular intervention in the affairs of society is evident in this attempt to curb the sovereign power of states by placing it under religious guidance, Mawdudi's criticism of the idea of sovereignty went much further. Recognizing its theological origins and character, he pointed out that sovereignty was a dangerous concept because it represented the divinization of power even in the secular West. Quoting from standard European definitions of sovereignty in another work, Mawdudi showed that its absolute and untrammelled nature, however hedged by conditions and limited to emergencies it might be, nevertheless exposed the tyrannical foundations as well as possibilities of the modern state. Not stopping at this analysis worthy of Carl Schmitt, he went on to claim that the real problem with sovereignty was not power but the lack of it, since not even the most powerful and ruthless of dictators could match up to its formal definition. And it was this inability to express itself fully that inevitably made sovereign power violent and abusive. The modern state, in other words, depended upon God insofar as it required a theo-

---

47   Mawdudi, *Khilafat o Mulukiyyat*, pp. 18-39.

logical concept of sovereignty, but became tyrannical the moment it tried to exercise this sovereignty in its own name.[48]

The founder of the Jamaat-e Islami, now a global fundamentalist organization, was dedicated to displacing sovereignty altogether by handing it over to God and turning politics into a merely administrative matter. While he was happy to describe as theocratic the Islamic state created by this abnegation of sovereignty, then, Mawdudi's political ideal actually excludes theocracy from the state by proscribing its exercise of divine power. But whether or not this procedure enjoyed any success even at a theoretical level, it does have the virtue of explicating Mawdudi's purpose in limiting the realm of politics within the modern state. For whether the caliph is to be an individual or a parliament, he is selected by the Muslim community to act as the steward of a sacred trust.[49] By focussing on the caliph's guardianship role, then, Mawdudi tried to shift politics from its instrumental character by dealing with it precisely as a divine trust. And despite the many differences between them, this definition of politics as a trust was characteristic of Gandhi's thought as well. So perhaps it was no accident that Mawdudi should in his younger days and at the height of the Khilafat Movement have written a book, proscribed by British authorities, that sang the Mahatma's praises. Indeed the Jamaat-e Islami still bears Gandhi's impress, particularly in its call for Muslims to nonviolently withdraw their cooperation from what Mawdudi defined as the tyrannical and infidel order of secular nationalism.

Now Mawdudi's vision of the caliphate differed very little from his vision of an Islamic state, whose president possessed the same duties as a caliph, though without his title or eminence. And this meant that Mawdudi modelled his Islamic state upon the caliphate, though of course the reverse is also true, since the caliphate was in fact predicated upon the existence of a modern state. What purpose then did the caliphate serve? On the one hand it functioned as a universal ideal, something like the Communist International, which made of actual states only its provisional and limited forms. But on the other hand Mawdudi's caliphate addressed the general problem of sectarian difference within the Muslim

---

48   Sayyid Abul Ala Mawdudi, *First Principles of the Islamic State*, trans. Khurshid Ahmad (Lahore: Islamic Publications, 1960), pp. 16-26.

49   Mawdudi, *Khilafat*, pp. 51-65.

world—just as his work on the Islamic state addressed the specific one of religious differences between its Muslim and non-Muslim citizens. It was over the question of the caliphate, after all, that sectarian differences were said to have arisen within Islam in the first place, and particularly the difference between Shia and Sunni claims to the succession of Muhammad. In addition to setting the stage for the now customary rejection of racial or national privilege in both its European and Arab forms, in other words, the caliphate provided Mawdudi with the ground from which to address the plurality of the Muslim world.

Mawdudi's task in *Caliphate and Monarchy* was to show that the emergence of sectarian differences followed a certain historical logic and could not be reduced to plots and conspiracies against Islam. And this logic Mawdudi found in the transformation of what he considered the democratic caliphate of earlier times into a dynastic institution. In other words Mawdudi attributed sectarian differences to the caliphate's corruption, which he in turn attributed to the entirely legitimate attempts by Muhammad's companions to deal with the new problems that faced them after his death.[50] Rather than blame Shia malevolence for Islam's fragmentation, which he thought was to give them too much say in the course of Muslim history, Mawdudi derived it from the sometimes mistaken but always inadvertent actions of the Prophet's successors in battling political exigencies whose logic eventually led to the replacement of the caliphate by a monarchy.[51] This setback nevertheless brought its own virtues with it, making for a division of powers where Muslim divines separated from the state protected Islam while Muslim kings separated from religious authority fitfully protected its domains.[52] Mawdudi's theory of the caliphate was thus very clearly an effort to think about Muslim plurality on a global scale. No wonder he was accused by so many of his detractors for being pro-Shia.[53]

In addition to its theoretical afterlife in the writing of men like Mawdudi, the caliphate continued to influence Islamic states in more material ways. Pakistan, which was the first state founded for Muslims as well as being the world's first Islamic republic, provides us with a good

---

50   Ibid., pp. 87-122.

51   Ibid., pp. 129-166.

52   Ibid., pp. 167-180.

53   For his response to these accusations see ibid., pp. 243-286.

example of this. Though created by men who had repudiated both Gandhi and pan-Islamism, Pakistan has never been able to constitute itself as a nation-state but must always reach out to the wider Muslim world for self-definition. For it is Islam rather than any historical, linguistic, or even territorial bond that constitutes Pakistani citizenship—these latter elements in fact depriving the country of integrity by linking it back to India. But this means that the Islamic Republic of Pakistan can only be defined as a nation-state by virtue of its non-Muslim citizens, who are therefore the only true Pakistanis because the only ones whose citizenship is defined by territory, language and the like. And indeed Muslim or rather Sunni Pakistan continues to be agitated by pan-Islamic causes that descend in a single file from India, which is to say from the Mahatma's first popular experiment in suprapolitics.

Yet the caliphate by no means represents some traditional way of doing politics or of ordering the world that has willy-nilly survived in modern times to subvert the nation-state. I have tried to show with reference to the Khilafat Movement that the contrary is rather the case, since the caliphate was very little invoked in South Asia before the twentieth century, with Muslim dynasties in precolonial times not granting the religious claims of the House of Osman even ritual recognition. So while a Muslim ruler like Tipu Sultan in the nineteenth century sought to gain caliphal investiture, as well as French assistance, in his fight against the British during the 1830s, these acts can be seen as attempts to size up the worldwide contours of British dominance both conceptually and strategically. The Mutineers of 1857, however, paid the caliphate little heed, though they did place credence in rumours that the Persians and Egyptians were dispatching armies in their support. In fact the Ottomans had been persuaded by the British to issue an edict urging India's Muslims to remain loyal to the East India Company, though to no perceptible effect. Whatever its religious status or past glory, then, the caliphate is a thoroughly modern ideal, something that Gandhi himself acknowledged when supporting Muslim efforts to re-imagine a new world in its name. And after an interregnum of eighty years, this ideal today enjoys the support of Osama bin Laden, for whom it serves to re-imagine the new global arena that has emerged in the Cold War's wake with neither a name nor a politics of its own.

5

GWOT

Despite the massive amount of force deployed in its service the quickly baptized Global War on Terror was not in fact a military operation. Even the phrase "war on terror", after all, had a civilian rather than military genealogy in American history, deriving as it did from the metaphorical use of military action in slogans like the "war on drugs" of the 1980s, which was also marked by the international use of armed force despite falling short of war in both its political and juridical senses. Many of the legal provisions in this War on Terror, moreover, especially the preventive or preemptive ones, were derived precisely from the metaphorical wars waged before it.[1]

Enemies of the old fashioned kind are notable by their absence from the War on Terror, which moved so quickly from Al-Qaeda to the Taliban to Saddam Hussein and beyond, as if to demonstrate the constantly shifting shape of enmity in this new kind of conflict, one that dispenses even with the ideological movement as its antagonist. Whether operating within a domestic or international arena, the old-fashioned terrorist had possessed a criminal rather than military status, one that was marked by a degree of legal precision. It was the War on Terror that blurred the terrorist's criminal status without at the same time lending him any military distinction, so that it became unclear what kind of enemy he represented.

Given the absence of an enemy in the War on Terror, it is not surprising that the United States should conduct it by ignoring so many

---

1   Robert M. Chesney and Jack L. Goldsmith, "Terrorism and the Convergence of Criminal and Military Detention Models", *Wake Forest Legal Studies Research Paper Series*, no. 1055501, November 2007, pp. 14-15.

of the traditional laws of war, from issuing formal declarations to refraining from torture and assassination. But it could hardly do otherwise, since America's military might is so disproportionate in extent compared to that of any other power as to render the US incapable of waging a traditional war anyway, which is to say one fought at its full technological capacity against a foe who presents the country any kind of military challenge. Indeed the United States can no longer wage war, only mount enormously costly and destructive spectacles of deterrence or revenge—whether or not these secure it any geopolitical advantage.[2] In other words the War on Terror is more a police than a military operation, though we shall see that its form of policing departs from the norms of criminology to become a conflict occurring outside the inherited institutions of our political life. For if deterrence is a feature of criminal rather than military law, revenge is an aspect of criminality that exists outside the law itself. After all one of the classical functions of a legal order is to bring private revenge to an end by substituting public justice for it. In turning to vengeance as a rhetorical and would-be political device, which it must do because enemies like Afghanistan and Iraq cannot by any stretch of the imagination pose it a military let alone an existential challenge, America does not simply violate the rule of law by unilateral actions ranging from air strikes to torture or indefinite detention, it also returns to the sphere of private life governed by moral rather than juridical precepts.[3]

None of this happens automatically, by reason of US power alone, but requires the participation of a particular kind of foe—one who is neither an enemy in the military sense nor a criminal in the civilian one, but instead someone who evades the terms and categories of traditional politics altogether. And while a great deal has been written about the way in which Al-Qaeda's organizational and ideological novelty have made it into such an enemy, too much of this material is concerned either with narrow technological issues or broad historical ones to be analytically useful. In Carl Schmitt's *Theory of the Partisan*, however, we

---

2   Alain Badiou, "On September 11 2001: Philosophy and the 'War Against Terrorism'", in *Polemics*, trans. Steve Corcoran (London: Verso, 2006), pp. 26-29.

3   Alain Badiou points out how revenge as a motive puts American actions in a pre-legal if not illegal framework. See "Fragments of a Public Journal on the American War against Iraq", ibid., pp. 50-4.

possess perhaps the most sophisticated analysis of irregular warfare, one that provides us with an ideal framework in which to plot the trajectory of global terrorism today. Written at the height of the Cold War in 1962, Schmitt's essay makes two preliminary points. Its first is that the partisan or non-state fighter emerges alongside the nation-state's army as its particular product, first coming to light with the Spanish guerrilla during the Napoleonic wars.[4] The second point is that this state and its regular army can only combat the partisan by adopting his methods wholly or in part, which puts their integrity and very constitution at risk if the threat of irregular warfare is very great, as was the case with the French in Algeria or the Americans in Vietnam.[5]

The intimate threat partisans posed a regular army, claims Schmitt, could be marginalized and even ignored in military theory throughout the nineteenth century and much of the twentieth. It was only once irregular warfare began to aim at the destruction of a given social order, rather than focussing on its mere defence on the one hand or conquest on the other, that the partisan became a key figure of global history.[6] Because he is intent on transforming his own society as much as destroying that of any invader, the partisan is by definition a revolutionary figure, whose first great representative was therefore Lenin and whose most radical innovator Mao.[7] According to Schmitt this figure arises out of the brutal civil and colonial wars of the last two centuries, not the rule-bound and interstate conflicts characteristic of modern European history.[8] Lenin's great innovation was to raise the partisan's struggle from its territorial particularity to make a universal category of it—for tactical considerations apart, class war dismisses the juridical distinctions of interstate conflict to conceive of itself as a global civil war.[9] Against this radically universal posture Bolshevism's liberal opponents could only react by declaring their own global struggle in favour of capitalism, democracy and human rights. And this universalism slowly

4   Carl Schmitt, *Théorie du Partisan*, trans. Marie-Louise Steinhauser (Paris: Flammarion, 1992), p. 208.

5   Ibid., p. 279.

6   Ibid., p. 280.

7   Ibid., p. 286.

8   Ibid., p. 213.

9   Ibid., p. 302.

but surely ended up depriving partisans everywhere of what Schmitt calls their telluric or patriotic form, with the processes of technological and political abstraction finally divesting these irregular combatants even of the defensive stand that had marked their initial struggles as guerrillas.[10]

It is easy to see how Lenin's magnification of the partisan struggle into a global civil war might provide a precedent for Osama bin Laden, though Al-Qaeda has gone much further than the Soviets did in freeing their party from the state. Schmitt does make the point, however, that despite its embodiment in the Soviet Union, the communist party moved decisively beyond the political rationality of the state, which it had made into nothing less then an instrument for the greater cause of a global civil war. That this move beyond the state's political rationality was not merely rhetorical is demonstrated in the fact, writes Schmitt, that what we call the "total state" of communist or fascist vintage was in either case managed by the party structure as distinct from that of the state itself.[11] At the theoretical level, of course, communism is explicitly dedicated to the "withering away" of the state as a bourgeois institution, and Lenin devoted his chief work to explicating how this condition might come about. But even the Nazis ended up working for the destruction of Germany as a state to further the cause of an international fascism free from territorial confines, whose models, according to Hannah Arendt, were provided by communism on the one hand and, on the other, by international Jewry as represented in the anti-Semite's imagination.[12]

If certain elements in the communist or fascist parties of the past aimed to destroy the state form, those who go under the name of Al-Qaeda have destroyed the party form itself, as if recognizing it to be an institution too closely connected with the state and its particular rationality. Like all the partisans before them, today's militants also achieve political meaning by a more or less clandestine and mutually instrumental relationship with "friendly" states or parties, which prevent them from sinking to a merely criminal status, as the anarchists whom

---

10   Ibid., p. 282.

11   Ibid., p. 218.

12   See Hannah Arendt, "The Seeds of a Fascist International" in *Essays in Understanding, 1930-1954* (New York: Harcourt Brace and Co., 1994), pp. 140-50.

they otherwise resemble so closely did in the nineteenth century.[13] But unlike their predecessors the terrorist networks of our day have undermined this relationship by abandoning the party form and therefore detaching themselves from political rationality in its institutional sense. Their meaning, in other words, is increasingly derived from the future of politics in a global arena rather than from its institutionally parochial present, and it is because they are aligned with this future that global networks like Al-Qaeda, which otherwise possess negligible human and financial resources, can threaten the political rationality of powerful states. Al-Qaeda is dangerous, in other words, because of the threatening future it inaugurates and not by reason of its own strength.

I will argue in this chapter that the emergence of Al-Qaeda as a new kind of enemy has resulted in the paradoxical de-militarization of the war waged against it. Central to my discussion are the American government's creation of new juridical enclaves to hold terrorist suspects in places like Guantánamo Bay, as well as the much-publicized incidents of abuse at the Abu Ghraib detention centre in 2004, which provide us with examples of how the War on Terror has increasingly become a quasi-criminal rather than a military operation. My larger point will be to suggest that this war is more and more conducted according to the civilian practices of private life, which disrupt military hierarchies by their networked form. I will suggest moreover that such networks, which possess both pacifist and militant forms, push suprapolitical considerations forward as bridges to a new politics for the global society they represent.

Criminalizing the enemy

The transformation of war into a species of policing, and therefore its de-militarization is something that has been widely recognized, not least within the US armed forces themselves. In 2004, for instance, the "Final report of the independent panel to review Department of Defense detention operations" dealt with the incidents of prisoner abuse at Abu Ghraib precisely by placing them in this context. It argued that the emergence of global terrorism and its "asymmetric warfare" made the "orthodox lexicon of war," like state sovereignty, national borders, uni-

13   For this see Schmitt, p. 284.

formed combatants, declarations of war and even war itself irrelevant, for today "the power to wage war can rest in the hands of a few dozen highly motivated people with cell phones and access to the Internet."[14]

Furthermore "the smallness and wide dispersal of these enemy assets make it problematic to focus on signal and imagery intelligence as we did in the Cold War, Desert Storm and the first phase of Operation Iraqi Freedom. The ability of terrorists and insurgents to blend into the civilian population further decreases their vulnerability to signal and imagery intelligence. Thus, information gained from human sources, whether by spying or interrogation, is essential in narrowing the field upon which other intelligence gathering resources may be applied."[15] With the increasing importance of human intelligence, then, or what in military jargon is called HUMINT, the practice of modern war has been dragged down from its technical heights to the messy level of interpersonal relations in which the enemy's humanity, as well as one's own, becomes crucial whether or not it is recognized as such.

So it was that a place like Abu Ghraib was transformed into something it was never meant to be, an interrogation centre that was part of a new form of warfare in which "the distinction between front and rear becomes more fluid."[16] Which is to say the novelty of the Global War on Terror was represented at the prison by the virtual collapse of distinctions between internal and external enemies, as well as between front and rear lines. So quite apart from the ineptitude exhibited by all concerned with the prison, as well as the infractions committed by some among its staff, the abuse at Abu Ghraib was important because it threw light upon the new role assumed by military detention, which was no longer to process front-line suspects quickly for distribution to judicial bodies in the rear, but rather to hold them for extended periods in order to extract urgent or "actionable" information that might prevent future acts of terror, a function which is effectively one of policing because it turns enemy actions into criminal ones.

Extracting information from prisoners of war is of course no new thing, but to do so in the theatre of war by intertwining and even con-

---

14   See *The Abu Ghraib Investigations*, ed. Steven Strasser (New York: Public Affairs, 2004), p. 27.

15   Ibid.

16   Ibid., p. 28.

fusing the jurisdiction of the army and the CIA appears to be a departure from standard practice. The very presence of the CIA at the prison signalled the introduction there of rules outside traditional military logic as well as jurisdiction. So a facility like Abu Ghraib lost its traditional function of providing one service in the linear logic of military deployment, something like an old-fashioned factory line, to become a multitasking node within a nonlinear or network logic. The criminalization of the enemy within military jurisdiction did not result simply from a mirroring of civilian practices, but rather from the dispersal and recombination of both these categories in radically new ways. And indeed there has been an increasing convergence in the US between criminal and military law over the past few decades, in which the latter is brought ever closer to civilian norms, even though its own jurisdiction may be expanding all the while. In other words the creation of new military enclaves such as Guantánamo Bay, themselves linked to civilian models like tax shelters and residences that exist beyond the reach of domestic law, is paralleled by their continuous movement towards criminal norms, which means that the problem is one of convergence between these spheres rather than the opposite.[17]

It was this very criminalization of enemy actions that had led to the partial suspension of the Geneva Conventions, which included the president approving in principle the use of what these Conventions defined as torture for Al-Qaeda and Taliban detainees in Afghanistan and at Guantánamo Bay in Cuba. It was because such detainees did not seem to fall under the formal, public and state-centred categories listed by the Geneva Conventions that they could be described as unlawful combatants, enemy combatants or unprivileged belligerents. The debate generated by these developments has focussed on the fact that such new enemies appear to possess no legal status at all, being defined neither as soldiers nor as civilians, neither as foreign subjects nor as domestic ones. This was exactly the concern expressed by the International Committee of the Red Cross as well as by the US Supreme Court, since the government did not even have a negative definition for such combatants, i.e. those who could not fall into their ranks.[18]

---

17   For this see Chesney and Goldsmith, "Terrorism and the Convergence of Criminal and Military Detention Models".

18   Stasser, pp. 88-9.

What the debate overlooked is the fact that suspending any juridical definition for the enemy shifted him from the public status of foreigner and soldier to the private one of domestic and civilian ambiguity. Because this enemy had no legal status under international as much as domestic statute, in other words, he existed underneath the law rather than under it. And since even a criminal enjoys rights because he possesses juridical status, this new enemy was not classed as a criminal, but only as someone like a criminal who could at best be defined in the traditional parlance of law as a pirate, that is to say an outcaste on the high seas belonging to no jurisdiction and thus possessing no rights. And what this did was to transform the landscape of war into one of civilian and therefore of moral life, because removed from the legal fiction of the high seas this enemy was now increasingly given his due not by right but as a gift or favour. Treated thus he became a human being rather than a prisoner of war properly defined, which meant that his captors, too, were suddenly and not without irony defined merely as human beings and not as soldiers subject to a set of positive regulations.

Opponents of the Global War on Terror have seen in the US administration's manoeuvres to deprive Al-Qaeda detainees of legal process nothing but an ill-concealed attempt to evade judicial and indeed public review of repugnant actions like torture that it has sanctioned for them. While these critics are right in thinking that the American constitution's jurisdiction and even the balance of powers it institutes between the different branches of government are threatened by such moves, their fundamentally conservative anxiety to restore the *status quo ante* in these matters blinds them to the novelty of a situation in which the old rules make less and less sense. In some ways it is irrelevant whether the use of torture and the creation of extralegal enclaves in places like Guantánamo Bay was necessary to recover intelligence and prosecute the War on Terror, assuming all those detained for this purpose were genuine terrorists rather than petty criminals or hapless bystanders. For even if the answer to this question turns out to be a negative one, the Bush administration's establishment of jurisdictions and practices outside the reach of civil as much as military law followed a different logic. Whatever its eventual fate, this expansion of the political field into unknown territory signalled the state's ungainly effort to occupy the new global arena uncovered in the most spectacular fashion by Al-Qaeda.

Armed with portable technologies of communication and destruction, Osama bin Laden and those he inspires have divested themselves of both the organizational and ideological forms of the old party, whether communist, fascist or fundamentalist. They have also revolutionized the nature of war by dispensing with armies and battlefields, and more crucially by ceasing to pose their enemies any military or existential challenge. And yet the destructive power of these global networks, together with the internal transformation and destruction of the societies in which they operate, makes of them a distinctly political rather than merely criminal threat. But since there is no traditional way in which Al-Qaeda can be engaged either politically or militarily, the US is forced to do so by partially dismantling its own political and military structures, though at enormous cost to itself, especially when compared with the severely limited numbers and resources of its enemies. The Global War on Terror, then, can be seen as an attempt to bring contemporary militancy into the political field, but only by expanding this latter to the point of turning it into its opposite. Thus the paradox of the US struggling to occupy a global arena that Al-Qaeda has infiltrated by transforming it into a quasi-criminal and even civilian space.

The laws of war inherited from Europe's interstate conflicts are based precisely upon renouncing the enemy's criminalization by making hostility a relative matter and thus absolute enmity impossible.[19] But the game-like character of war under these rules, which derive from the age of dynastic conflict, is exactly what partisans have always rejected in their role as representatives of modern conflicts like class or colonial wars.[20] Nevertheless these laws or at least the principles underlying them have consistently been restored after each great military transformation. Thus after the Napoleonic Wars in the early nineteenth century the Congress of Vienna reinforced legal distinctions between peace and war, combatant and non-combatant, enemy and criminal that survived until the end of the First World War.[21] This despite the fact that the introduction of military service had by that point effectively made all

---

19 Schmitt, p. 300.

20 Ibid., p. 299.

21 Ibid., pp. 211-12.

conflicts into people's wars, thus obscuring many of these distinctions and bringing the partisan to the fore as someone who could no longer be dealt with as a marginal figure to be defined as if he were a variation of the regular soldier.[22] Similarly after the Second World War, the partisan was recognized by the Geneva Conventions as the civilian member of a resistance movement of the kind that fought Nazi rule in Europe, though the introduction of atomic weapons had already transformed him into the global combatant of a conflict occurring below the status of war at its full technological capacity.[23]

By expanding the political field through the sanctioning of extra-legal jurisdictions and practices, therefore, the Global War on Terror has ghettoized the traditional laws of war, thus turning its enemy into a quasi-criminal figure. And while it was the emergence of networked forms of global militancy that provided the occasion for this limitation, the changing nature of conventional war had turned these laws into antiques a long time ago. Thus Carl Schmitt pointed out as early as the 1960s that the stipulations by which legal combatants could be recognized, such as by carrying arms openly or bearing insignia, had been rendered meaningless by nocturnal raids and long-distance or aerial bombardment.[24] Equally meaningless is the distinction between civilian and military targets in the conditions of a modern war, which is invariably fought in civilian areas.[25] By recognizing the new military landscape confronting the United States the limits placed by the Bush administration on the laws of war had the contradictory effect of limiting the military character of war itself in appearing to criminalize the enemy, yet not quite managing to do so.

Morals and the military

Though the ambiguous legal status of militants in the Global War on Terror may be compared to that enjoyed by pirates on the high seas in times past, the more apt precedent from territorial American history might well be the position of slaves, who also existed underneath the law

---

22   Ibid., p. 213.

23   Ibid., p. 227.

24   Ibid., p. 229.

25   Ibid., p. 230.

governing free men as much as criminals, becoming therefore merely human beings along with their masters.[26] For what could be more human than social relations governed by moral practices rather than by juridical ones based on the idea of contract? After all the legal rights enjoyed by slaves were based not on the contract of citizenship but rather on the kind of humanitarian obligations that were due to animals as well. In the American context slavery as a moral relationship arising from the absence of contractual duties has taken on a paradigmatic name, that of Uncle Tom. Even at its source, Harriet Beecher Stowe's abolitionist novel *Uncle Tom's Cabin*, the relationship of Uncle Tom and his master is portrayed as a moral one. Indeed it is the slave's demonstration of this morality that allows Stowe to call for his emancipation.

All this is made plain by the presidential memorandum of February 7, 2002, which suspends certain articles of the Geneva Conventions while simultaneously emphasizing the need to adhere to their principles. "As a matter of policy," the president declared, "United States Armed Forces shall continue to treat detainees humanely and, to the extent appropriate and consistent with military necessity, in a manner consistent with the principles of Geneva."[27] In other words these formerly juridical duties of military experience have been turned into the ethical prescriptions of an ambiguously civil life, becoming discretionary and therefore gift-like. The place evacuated by the language of the law is occupied by the vocabulary of morality precisely because there exist neither legal obligations nor even a clear doctrine regarding the treatment of detainees. Given this, it is not I suspect incidental that the "Final report of the independent panel to review Department of Defense detention operations" should recommend that all "personnel who may be engaged in detention operations, from point of capture to final disposition, should participate in a professional ethics program that would equip them with a sharp moral compass for guidance in situations often riven with conflicting moral obligations."[28] Indeed the

---

26   I am thankful to Uday Singh Mehta for bringing this link to my notice. For a comparison of slave codes, criminal law and the legal reasoning governing the War on Terror, see Joan Dayan, "Cruel and unusual: the end of the eighth amendment" in the *Boston Review*, October-November 2004.

27   Strasser, p. 30.

28   Ibid., p. 99.

report not only recognizes the moral context within which human intelligence or HUMINT operations often occur, it recommends that soldiers who break this discretionary morality by torturing prisoners to extract information in some version of a "ticking time-bomb" scenario should in an equally discretionary way turn themselves in for punishment afterwards:

A morally consistent approach to the problem would be to recognize there are occasions when violating norms is understandable but not necessarily correct—that is, we can recognize that a good person might, in good faith, violate standards. In principle, someone who, facing such a dilemma, committed abuse should be required to offer his actions up for review and judgement by a competent authority. An excellent example is the case of a 4th Infantry Division battalion commander who permitted his men to beat a detainee whom he had good reason to believe had information about future attacks against his unit. When the beating failed to produce the desired results, the commander fired his weapon near the detainee's head. The technique was successful and the lives of US servicemen were likely saved. However, his actions clearly violated the Geneva Conventions and he reported his actions knowing he would be prosecuted by the army. He was punished in moderation and allowed to retire.[29]

Whatever the validity of the "ticking time-bomb" theory, or of torture's effectiveness, the report contends that it turns the soldier dealing with HUMINT into a moral actor, even and especially after he sees fit to break the legal code that defines his profession. Instead of reading the recommendations of the independent panel either as a lot of eyewash, or as routine ways of addressing routine military problems, I see them expressing a genuine attempt to deal with a novel situation—one which includes the troubling insertion into military life of an ambiguously civilian space of moral rather than juridical existence. "Some individuals," states the report, "seized the opportunity provided by this environment to give vent to latent sadistic urges. Moreover, many well-intentioned professionals, attempting to resolve the inherent moral conflict between using harsh techniques to gain information to save lives and treating detainees humanely, found themselves on uncharted ethical ground, with frequently changing guidance from above."[30]

---

29   Mark Danner, *Torture and Truth: America, Abu Ghraib, and the War on Terror* (New York: New York Review of Books, 2004), p. 401.

30   Ibid., p. 25.

As if to support this position, the "Investigation of the Abu Ghraib Detention Facility and 205th Military Intelligence Brigade" even quotes Staff Sergeant Ivan L. Frederick II, a soldier accused of the most egregious abuse, telling colleagues who rescued one of his victims, "I want to thank you guys, because up until a week or two ago, I was a good Christian."[31] Similarly Specialist Charles A. Graner Jr., who had been a prison guard in civilian life and was accused of even more heinous abuse, is reported to have responded to a colleague's questioning of his behaviour by saying, "The Christian in me says it's wrong, but the corrections officer in me says, 'I love to make a grown man piss himself.'"[32] These comments were made well before any photographs had surfaced from Abu Ghraib or any investigations launched, and they illustrate for us the exclusively moral and civilian context in which such incidents occurred, since nothing about the army or military culture was even mentioned by the two men.

Indeed the men and women accused of abuse at Abu Ghraib all described their photographs as documentary evidence of the army's complicity in crime, or however unlikely it may seem, as proof to use against the army in case it betrayed them. While such statements are to be expected from those who have already been accused of wrongdoing, some of the soldiers invoked these justifications well *before* they were discovered, with men like Sergeant Hydrue Joyner keeping an illicit log of the "phantom" or unregistered prisoners interrogated by Military Intelligence just in case "They might be trying to come after me."[33] In other words the civilian and moral arena in which these soldiers acted was made to stand in opposition to military regulations and authority, both of which were disbelieved and distrusted. Of course such attempts to "document" the army's crimes were sacrificial insofar as they were at the same time a record of the soldiers' guilt, however these men and women might try to convince themselves that they were bystanders in crimes permitted by the military, or even coerced to participate in them though doing so only with a view to exposing the injustice of which

31   Ibid., pp. 167-8.

32   Ibid., p. 215.

33   Philip Gourevitch and Errol Morris, *Standard Operating Procedure: A War Story* (London: Picador, 2008), p. 96.

they partook.[34] Whatever the case, these soldiers saw themselves as occupying a different kind of space than that prescribed by the army.

The emergence of such new spaces within the cultural and institutional life of the armed forces is neither accidental nor unplanned, for the prison we have been looking at outside Baghdad marked one site in which the eminently private, civilian and even moral vision for the military proposed by the US Secretary of Defense, Donald Rumsfeld, achieved its crude beginnings:

We must transform not only our armed forces but also the Defense Department that serves them—by encouraging a culture of creativity and intelligent risk-taking. We must promote a more entrepreneurial approach: one that encourages people to be proactive, not reactive, and to behave less like bureaucrats and more like venture capitalists; one that does not wait for threats to emerge and be "validated" but rather anticipates them before they appear and develops new capacities to dissuade and deter them.[35]

Both the Armed Forces and the State Department had opposed the president's suspension of certain articles in the Geneva Conventions, arguing not only that these were sufficient to deal with the enemy threat, but also that "to conclude otherwise would be inconsistent with past practice and policy, jeopardize the United States armed forces personnel, and undermine the United States military culture which is based on a strict adherence to the laws of war."[36] Apart from the repercussions of this suspension in terms of international law as well as of international reputation, which were primarily the concerns of the State Department, the military was concerned with the fragmentation of its own culture that such partial suspensions of juridical uniformity represented. And indeed a whole new world of private or civilian practice soon hove into view, or rather out of view, within the armed forces. For example interrogation techniques as well as moral liberties that had been permissible in Afghanistan and Guantánamo Bay, where the relevant articles of the Geneva Conventions had been suspended, were introduced into Iraq, where they were still in force, through "a store of common lore

---

34   See for instance Gourevitch and Morris, p. 201.

35   Donald H. Rumsfeld, "Transforming the military", *Foreign Affairs*, vol. 81, no. 3. May/June 2002, p. 24.

36   Strasser, p. 30.

and practice within the interrogator community circulating through Guantánamo, Afghanistan and elsewhere."[37]

The juridical fragmentation and privatization of military life was compounded by its institutional fragmentation and privatization, given the presence of private contractors or the CIA at a facility like Abu Ghraib, all working under different rules. Naturally the absence of legal or doctrinal uniformity, and the sheer multiplicity of guidance, information and authority present, created areas of confusion, negligence and criminal opportunity in the prison.[38] All this would be avoidable once a doctrine governing relations between these various elements was formulated and enforced. What seems to be unavoidable even under the most serene of conditions is the military's cultural and institutional fragmentation, signalled most disturbingly not by the infiltration of private contractors and the CIA into its domain, but by the spread of private or civilian practices among its own troops. And this is not a matter merely of temporary exigencies having to do with the particularities of time, place or resources, but apparently marks a new paradigm of war that has emerged since the attacks of 9/11. It is in this light that the deference accorded at Abu Ghraib to non-commissioned officers who had civilian correctional backgrounds becomes significant.[39] For no matter how accidental or temporary it might have been, such deferral points to the private, civilian and even moral nature of new military practices— which, paradoxically, end up treating foreign enemies like but not as domestic criminals.

A community of spectators

The emergence of the American soldier as a photographer, one who carries a digital camera everywhere, might well play a role in the transformation of the military by way of its infiltration from private and civilian life. These soldiers are as likely to photograph the Commander in Chief on tour, which presents a disconcerting breach in the serried ranks when seen on television, as they are to photograph some instance of abuse. In both cases the act of photography breaks up the public

---

37   Ibid. pp. 34-5.
38   Ibid. pp. 73-4.
39   Ibid. p. 81.

and collective identity of the military by introducing within it a strictly private and even civilian desire, since these pictures transform public and professional events into personal ones. One wonders, for example, whether the soldiers at Abu Ghraib had intended to use their cameras as tourists in the friendly Baghdad they expected to encounter, and if the photographs of abuse they took served also as tourist memorabilia. And indeed some of these images were claimed by the soldiers to be souvenirs, while others were meant to offer forensic proof of the army's complicity in crime, for instance the series of photographs in which Specialist Sabrina Harman and Staff Seargent Frederick uncovered and recorded the wounds of a "phantom" prisoner who had been murdered during his interrogation by an unnamed government agency.[40] But in fact it was difficult to untangle the soldiers' tourist from their torture photographs, with Sabrina Harman flashing the same thumbs up sign she had picked up from the Iraqi children she used to play with, both at archaeological sites and the "hard site" where prisoners were abused in Abu Ghraib.[41]

Those in the United States who exculpated the soldiers at Abu Ghraib by comparing their actions to hazing rituals at college campuses were not wrong, in the sense that both situations entail the creation of communities that are moral because based on trust, being in addition part of civilian and private life. Indeed the active participation of women in such incidents of abuse underscores the fact that we are not dealing here with some traditional military "boys club" or even of "male bonding" behaviour. On the contrary it was precisely the presence of women that made this abuse possible especially in its sexual form. Not only was the presence of American women crucial in attempts to sexually humiliate male detainees, female soldiers also allowed their male counterparts the chance to express their sexual fantasies simply by being there. In this sense the abuse of detainees represented only one end of a continuum where military regulations were routinely flouted by civilian desires. Thus a lot of photographs were taken of these soldiers breaking army rules by the keeping of pets, pornography and alcohol, while Charles Graner, in an equally forbidden adulterous relationship with

---

40   Gourevitch and Morris, p. 180.

41   Ibid., p. 75.

Private First Class Lyndie England, liked to take pictures of them having sex, or of her exposing herself beside a sleeping colleague.[42]

I would even argue that the routine and explicit invocation of homosexuality during these incidents, in threats of sodomy as well as in the posing of prisoners to simulate images from American gay culture, including orgies, fellatio and the "circle jerk" or group masturbation, were made possible by these women. It was their presence as voyeurs, participants and sexual objects that permitted these homosexual fantasies safely to occur as staged spectacles, and as it were rehearsals of the anxious debates over "gays in the army" that had assumed such public form during the Clinton presidency. So when Specialist Joseph M. Darby, who ended up reporting the abuse at Abu Ghraib to military authorities, first saw images of naked Iraqis forming a pyramid, he laughed, mistaking them for American soldiers engaged in particularly kinky horseplay.[43] The presence of women at Abu Ghraib also invokes the earlier debate over mixed-sex units in the armed forces, if only to show how counterproductive such mixing can be, since as Darby pointed out, soldiers in mixed sex units invariably paired off in adulterous and other illegal unions.[44]

The inverted multiculturalism that apparently made soldiers degrade inmates in specifically "cultural" ways like stripping before women or each other is also something imported from civilian life—though it serves as a red herring here, disguising the soldiers' own sexual desire in the acting out of standard pornographic roles, which they were more than familiar with, being avid consumers of pornography in defiance of army regulations. It is as if these men and women required the sexual complicity or participation of their victims, even therefore commanding them to masturbate. This form of intimacy, in which American soldiers participated by exposing their own sexual acts to the eyes and ears of Iraqi prisoners, defines Abu Ghraib as a site of moral practice. For like the relationship of master and slave, that between soldier and prisoner gained its intimacy by losing all regulation.

If slavery sometimes created bonds of passion as much as loyalty between master and servant, intimacy among captors and captives in the

---

42   Ibid., pp. 134-5.

43   Ibid., p. 232.

44   Ibid., p. 242.

War on Terror is also a phenomenon deserving the name of morality, since it can also lead to a relationship of mutual respect. This is the kind of relationship that we see in places like the US prison at Guantánamo Bay, as well as in the military bases scattered over Afghanistan and Iraq, some of whose soldiers have converted to Islam at the hands of their captives. A more familiar example of this relationship is provided by the so-called Stockholm syndrome, which refers to the sympathy that hostages often develop for their kidnappers. Oddly these captors are rarely if ever said to participate in the syndrome, being credited only with the sort of imposture and subterfuge that is characteristic of a theatrical villain. Yet in Abu Ghraib the intimacy between jailor and prisoner often took on the character of mutual identification, such as when Sergeant Javal Davis hurled himself onto a heap of naked detainees before stamping upon their fingers and toes with his boots.[45] That unexpected leap into the midst of his victims Davis described as a demonstration of the sentiment "We're here sucking it up just like you".[46] If this act of identification seems unlikely, here is another example from Davis's treatment of his prisoners:

"I got me a detainee who speaks English. I said, 'Tell them everything I'm saying. You all live in a cell. I live in a cell. You all are eating bad food. I'm eating bad food, too. You all want to go home. Hell, I want to know when I'm going home, too. I don't even know when I'm going home. You all are locked up. I'm locked up, too. You all can't see your family. I can't see my family.' From that point they started to relate with me."[47]

Imparting a sexual edge to this sense of identification, Davis would strip to his waist in front of the detainees and work out, then release and offer cigarettes to any of them who could beat the number of his push-ups or pull-ups. He also learnt passable Arabic and organized prayer hours for the men, all of which they seemed to appreciate.[48] And Javal Davis was not the only one to be torturer and friend at the same time. Sabrina Harman, too, assuaged her anxiety about the abuse she participated in by playing with imprisoned children and offering painkillers

---

45   Ibid., p. 188.

46   Ibid., p. 189.

47   Ibid., p. 103.

48   Ibid.

to the adults.[49] Sometimes the identification even went the other way, such as when two men, who were accused of raping a teenage boy, were punished by the soldiers to the uproarious approval of the other prisoners, despite the fact that the accused were meted out the same abuse their fellow detainees suffered day after day.[50]

Commanding prisoners to masturbate at Abu Ghraib, therefore, might well have served as a method to force into being an intimacy that the facility's lack of regulation invited. What does it mean for an inmate to be aroused by such procedures—if indeed any were? The consent given to his treatment by the prisoner's putative arousal works like the videotaped confessions of those who have been captured and executed by insurgents in Iraq. Indeed the circulation of digital photographs and video clips by US military personnel simultaneously with those of Al-Qaeda and other militants, sometimes on the same websites, like www. ogrish.com, is highly significant. Not only does one set of images often provoke and comment upon the other, each brings into being a secret community by its circulation. The resilience of this community is such that even after being forbidden by military authorities to do so, suspects in the Abu Ghraib incidents, according to the "AR 15-6 Investigation of the Abu Ghraib Detention Facility and 205th Military Intelligence Brigade," continued conducting email campaigns "soliciting support from others involved in the investigation," [51]or "giving interviews to the media, and passing the questions being asked by investigators to others via a website." [52]And this only fragments and multiplies the war's global audience, for the benefit of which so many of its battles are in fact fought.

The problem posed by asymmetric warfare to conventional deployments of force is described succinctly in the "Final report of the independent panel to review Department of Defense detention operations," which states that asymmetric warfare "can be viewed as attempts to circumvent or undermine a superior, conventional strength, while exploiting its weaknesses using methods the superior force can neither

---

49   Ibid., p. 116.

50   Ibid., p. 152.

51   Danner, p. 557.

52   Ibid., p. 561.

defeat nor resort to itself."[53] While this definition recognizes the structural impasse posed by the kind of militancy that goes under the name Al-Qaeda, whose organization, mobility and aims no longer bear much comparison to those of guerrilla or terrorist groups in the past, it does not consider the ways in which such asymmetrical warfare has changed the armed forces itself.

But does not the collapsing of military distinctions between the external and internal enemy, or the front and rear line, mirror the global jihad's own collapse of the distinction between the near and far enemy, or the military and civilian one? Does not the juridical, cultural and institutional fragmentation of the US armed forces mirror that of Al-Qaeda, whose franchised character and identity as a brand name they have also adopted by the inclusion of outside contractors? And does not diverting military life into private, civilian and even moral channels mirror a similar diversion in the lives of Islam's holy warriors? In addition to pointing out numerous lapses in leadership, procedure, accountability and discipline at Abu Ghraib, for instance, the "Article 15-6 Investigation of the 800th Military Police Brigade" of 2004 makes the following comments on the appearance and relations among US personnel there:

In general, US civilian contract personnel (Titan Corporation, CACI, etc...), third country nationals, and local contractors do not appear to be properly supervised within the detention facility at Abu Ghraib. During our on-site inspection, they wandered about with too much unsupervised free access in the detainee area. Having civilians in various outfits (civilian and DCUs) in and about the detainee area causes confusion and may have contributed to the difficulties in the accountability process and with detecting escapes.[54]

Finally, because of past associations and familiarity of Soldiers within the Brigade, it appears that friendship often took precedence over appropriate leader and subordinate relationships.[55]

There was no clear uniform standard for any MP soldiers assigned detention duties. Despite the fact that hundreds of former Iraqi soldiers and officers were detainees, MP personnel were allowed to wear civilian clothes in the FOB after

---

53   Strasser, pp. 26-7.
54   Danner, p. 302.
55   Ibid., p. 313.

duty hours while carrying weapons. [...] Some soldiers wrote poems and other sayings on their helmets and soft caps.[56]

Saluting of officers was sporadic and not enforced. LTC Robert P. Walters, Jr., Commander of the 165th Military Intelligence Battalion (Tactical Exploitation), testified that the saluting policy was enforced by COL Pappas for all MI personnel, and that BG Karpinski approached COL Pappas to reverse the saluting policy back to a non-saluting policy as previously existed.[57]

However dependent such incidents were upon individual and structural failures particular to the prison outside Baghdad, it is clear from all the reports I have cited that the particularity of Abu Ghraib was itself dependent upon more general factors, such as the waging of war by non-state actors and the consequent importance of HUMINT within it, that characterize the Global War on Terror as a whole. Interpreting the prison incidents quoted above in the context of these general factors allows us to compare the US personnel responsible for abuse with the enemy or unprivileged combatants they fight. For are not the latter deprived of prisoner of war status, and thus released from some of the provisions of the Geneva Accords, precisely because they do not follow military discipline, are not uniformed and do not themselves recognize the Geneva Conventions? These at least are the arguments put forward by the Assistant Attorney General of the United States in a memo to President Bush's counsel Alberto R. Gonzales on February 7, 2002, when discussing the legal status of Taliban and Al-Qaeda fighters with respect to article 4 of the Third Geneva Convention Relative to the Treatment of Prisoners of War or GPW:

DoD's facts suggest that to the extent the Taliban militia was organized at all, it consisted of a loose array of individuals who had shifting loyalties among various Taliban and al Qaeda figures. According to DoD, the Taliban lacked the kind of organization characteristic of the military. The fact that at any given time during the conflict the Taliban were organized into some structured organization does not answer whether the Taliban leaders were responsible for their subordinates within the meaning of GPW. [...]

---

56   Ibid., p. 316. Parenthesis mine.

57   Ibid., p. 318.

Second, there is no indication that the Taliban militia wore any distinctive uniform or other insignia that served as a "fixed distinctive sign recognizable at a distance." [...]

[...]

Third, the Taliban militia carried arms openly. This fact, however, is of little significance because many people in Afghanistan carry arms openly. [...] Thus, the Taliban carried their arms openly, as GPW requires military groups to do, but this did not serve to distinguish the Taliban from the rest of the population. [...]

Finally, there is no indication that the Taliban militia understood, considered themselves bound by, or indeed were even aware of, the Geneva Conventions or any other body of law. Indeed, it is fundamental that the Taliban followed their own version of Islamic law and regularly engaged in practices that flouted fundamental international legal principles.[58]

In other words, an individual cannot be a POW, even if a member of an armed force, unless forces also are: (a) "commanded by a person responsible for his subordinates"; (b) "hav[e] a fixed distinctive sign recognizable at a distance"; (c) "carry[ ] arms openly"; and (d) "conduct[ ] their operations in accordance with the laws and customs of war."[59]

The Assistant Attorney General's lengthy memorandum describes Taliban and Al-Qaeda fighters as enemy or unprivileged combatants in terms that can very easily be applied to American forces themselves, both structurally in their infiltration by civilian personnel and practices, including the denial of prisoner of war status to their enemies, as well as in the specific circumstances of places like Abu Ghraib or Guantánamo Bay. My purpose in drawing this comparison is not to point out the hypocrisy of US policy in the War on Terror, this being the accusation brought against the administration by militants as well as pacifists, but precisely in order to agree with its premises. Whatever its intentions in doing so, the Bush administration leapt well ahead of its critics in recognizing the sheer novelty of the situation that faced it in the very first days after 9/11. This administration was also quite correct to see how the globalization of militancy has, as Alberto R. Gonzales put it in

---

58   Ibid. pp. 98-9.

59   Ibid. p. 99. All parentheses in original.

a memo to the President on January 25, 2002, made "obsolete Geneva's strict limitations on questioning of enemy prisoners and renders quaint some of its provisions requiring that captured enemy be afforded such things as commissary privileges, scrip (i.e., advances of monthly pay), athletic uniforms, and scientific instruments."[60]

What the Administration did not take into account, despite its Defence Secretary's glorification of a civilian and venture capitalist model of warfare, was the breakdown of American juridical and military forms themselves as a consequence of the War on Terror. Having accounted for the new world looming up before it by destroying the lineaments of the old, the United States remains unable to replace these with anything resembling a new order. One consequence of this is the de-militarization of the War on Terror, which, though partial in nature, is highly significant nevertheless. It provides an important example of the interface between two organizational forms, the hierarchy and the network, that now coexist at almost every level of social life. Significant about this interface is that it allows the network form to consolidate itself while infiltrating its hierarchical enemy. That the reverse does not occur is crucial, whether or not a particular network, Al-Qaeda or its clones in this instance, is eventually demolished. For in the meantime hierarchy has become a kind of monster made up of itself and its opposite.

History in a de-militarized zone

I have been arguing so far that the immensity of American power together with the globalization of militancy has changed the face of war by pushing it beyond the inherited institutions of our political life. A paradoxical consequence of this change has been the de-militarization of war and its adoption of civilian forms both moral and organizational. Though deriving from its expansion into the extralegal reaches of a new global arena, this transformation of war does possess certain historical precedents. To begin with the communist conception of a global civil war had already moved conflict beyond the juridical boundaries of an international order to make of the enemy an absolute rather than relative category. This more or less theoretical abandonment of the laws of war, however, was lent a truly global reality with the development of

---

60   Ibid., p. 84.

atomic weapons, the possibility of whose use forces nuclear powers to declare their enemies inhuman at the moral level even before annihilating them at the physical one.[61] For the atom bomb by its very nature does away with the chivalric relations set up between enemies in the laws of war, within which each sees the other as a version of himself and thus turns conflict into a game by setting limits to its destructiveness.

Weapons of mass destruction render the traditional laws of war irrelevant by the sheer capacity of their violence, which cannot distinguish between combatant and non-combatant or indeed any of the other categories listed by the Geneva Conventions. Whether or not the possibility of using atomic weapons even arises in a given conflict, then, their very existence, let alone the possibility of their deployment, has already pushed war outside the realm of the law. And the now commonplace talk of dirty bombs and tactical nuclear strikes does nothing more than generalise this new reality by criminalizing the enemy in the most thoroughgoing way. But we needn't rely upon the status of nuclear conflict, defining as it does the extreme limit of war, to point out how this latter has moved beyond its traditional legal form. For a number of conventional military operations also allow us to make the same argument. So during the Second World War the Allies had moved decisively beyond the laws of war not only by their acts of blockade, firebombing and finally the use of atom bombs, but equally by their theories of collective responsibility and unconditional surrender, which like many of this war's innovations were drawn from the more unregulated practices of colonial conflict outside Europe.[62] Writing in 1957 to oppose Oxford University granting an honorary degree to President Truman, the philosopher Elizabeth Anscombe provides us with perhaps the most succinct description of this new situation:

For some time before the war broke out, and more intensely afterwards, there was propaganda in this country on the subject of the "indivisibility" of modern war. The civilian population, we were told, is really as much combatant as the fighting forces. The military strength of a nation includes its whole economic and social strength. Therefore the distinction between the people engaged in prosecuting the war and the population at large is unreal. There is no such

---

61   Schmitt, p. 304.

62   Hannah Arendt makes this argument in *The Origins of Totalitarianism* (San Diego: Harcourt Brace and Co., 1973).

thing as a non-participator; you cannot buy a postage stamp or any taxed article, or grow a potato or cook a meal, without contributing to the "war effort".
War indeed is a "ghastly evil", but once it has broken out no one can "contract
out" of it. "Wrong" indeed must be being done if war is waged but you cannot
help being involved in it. There was a doctrine of "collective responsibility"
with a lugubriously elevated moral tone about it. The upshot was that it was
senseless to draw any line between legitimate and illegitimate objects of attack.
Thus the court chaplains of the democracy. I am not sure how children and the
aged fitted into this story: probably they cheered the soldiers and munitions
workers up.[63]

Apart from bearing a striking similarity to the kind of rhetoric used
by Al-Qaeda in justifying attacks like those of 9/11, Anscombe's description of allied propaganda during the war is illuminating because
it points out that modern conflict does not merely flout traditional law
in practice but takes conceptual leave of it as well. However genuine
the attempts to reinstate and reform these laws after each great conflict, therefore, their jurisdiction is increasingly circumscribed, as if war
conducted by such rules is shrinking back to the originally European
boundaries it occupied not so long ago. Could it be that the relatively
unregulated colonial or civil war has emerged as conflict's new form
across the world today, replacing the interstate wars of European history
with its far more global countenance? Such a conclusion is given credence by the fact that with the exception of minor conflicts, all attempts
to wage purely conventional war today seem doomed to failure, so that
it is even possible to say that the more easily a conventional war like that
in Afghanistan or Iraq is won, the more difficult is its unconventional
aftermath likely to be.

Elizabeth Anscombe did not confine her criticism of modern warfare to its breaches of the legal order. Unlike critics of the Global War
on Terror in our own day, who seem obsessed by what they see as the
militarization of everyday life, she was more concerned with the way in
which everyday life de-militarized war when this was conducted outside
juridical norms. Thus in an essay from 1961 Anscombe argued that
pacifism had as much to do with the abandonment of moral scruples
about killing the innocent as any other factor during the Second World

---

63   G. E. M. Anscombe, "Mr. Truman's Degree" in *Religion and Politics: Collected
      Philosophical Papers*, vol. 3 (Minneapolis: University of Minnesota Press: 1981),
      p. 63.

War, and this precisely because it criminalized killing as such by refusing to draw any significant distinction between its legitimate and illegitimate uses:

Now pacifism teaches people to make no distinction between the shedding of innocent blood and the shedding of any human blood. And in this way pacifism has corrupted enormous numbers of people who will not act according to its tenets. They become convinced that a number of things are wicked which are not; hence seeing no way of avoiding wickedness, they set no limits to it.[64]

The boldness of this argument lies in the fact that it so clearly recognizes the family resemblance, and even the causal relationship, between humanitarian action and military procedures—with these latter taking on a civilian aspect once released from the traditional language of law. The criminalization of the enemy achieved by setting aside a received juridical order, in other words, results in humanitarianism as much as it does in the dehumanizing violence of absolute enmity. Having noted its passing beyond the narrow confines of legal distinction, for instance that between guilt and innocence, Anscombe tried to introduce new distinctions within warlike practice. She did so by reference to a specifically religious rationality rather than to a political one having to do with the state. And if this turn to Catholic philosophy betrayed her realization that war had surpassed its old political limits, Anscombe's citing of St Thomas Aquinas bears more than a fleeting resemblance to Osama bin Laden's citation of the Prophet Muhammad. Both figures are invoked for exactly the same reason: to occupy a new global arena and account for new global practices that are not represented by institutions of their own.

Religious doctrine does not provide the only vehicle by which a global arena lying beyond the reach of law may be traversed, and Bin Laden himself is not averse to doing so by using subtler means of locomotion. Such are the repeated offers to his enemy of a global truce, which, given Al-Qaeda's lack of an institutional foundation, can only be based on the kind of trust that approaches faith, however reasonable or unreasonable its conditions might be. But who can say if engaging a figurehead like Osama bin Laden, even if only in the arena of media coverage, might not achieve a properly political result? After all it is precisely Bin

---

64   G. E. M. Anscombe, "War and Murder", in Ibid., p. 57.

Laden's soundbytes in this arena that give shape to militant ideas and practices the world over. And so whether or not such an engagement is possible, the institutionally attenuated truce that has become such a feature of Al-Qaeda's rhetoric represents the closest thing to a political gesture in its arsenal of murderous acts. Yet we have seen that it is a truce without institutional context, one that depends upon public declarations in the media rather than negotiations in private for its effect. With all its paradoxes, however, I believe that this extraordinarily novel gesture forms a narrow bridge to the globe's political future. I want to end this chapter, then, with a brief consideration of how Al-Qaeda's bizarre offers of a truce to its enemies constitutes an element in some politics still to be born.

In his *Theory of the Partisan* Carl Schmitt argues that with the rise to prominence of the irregular combatant warfare takes on a different logic because it is progressively separated from the realm of domestic or international law as this is traditionally conceived. Rather than partaking of the political rationality of a state, in other words, warlike actions among both regular and irregular combatants are now increasingly defined by the logic of risk, which possesses another rationality altogether.[65] For however dedicated they might be to the cause of a state, actions based on the calculation of risk remain free from its legal order, which alone imparts rationality to politics. Both the technologies of regular combat, claims Schmitt, and their irregular deployment by the partisan, mean that this lawless situation is becoming the norm in modern wars. And indeed it is not difficult to see how militants today conduct themselves according to a logic of risk that ends up infecting even their conventionally organized enemies, as I hope my description of the incidents at Abu Ghraib goes some way towards demonstrating.

But the calculus of risks does have a juridical incarnation, which in times of war takes the form of assurances. Being elements of commercial law in their origin, assurances have been used in wartime to allay the risks taken by traders, including those breaking embargoes or dealing in contraband, and all without reference to any common jurisdiction.[66] Instead of allaying the risk to life that is in any case run by soldiers, partisans and civilians during war, assurances allay the risk to trade in

---

65   Schmitt, p. 231.

66   Ibid., pp. 232-3.

conditions marked by the absence of law.[67] Assurances, however, have also become instrumental in the establishment of relations between militants and the state, often representing the sole political relationship between enemies who face each other outside the laws of war. As such assurances can either serve as a bridge to the kind of political rationality we have traditionally known, or to the unknown rationality of politics in a new global arena. Now the truce that those who go under the name of Al-Qaeda so frequently invoke constitutes precisely an assurance in this double sense. And my guess is that it forms a bridge to the future of politics itself in a global arena, not least because such a truce happens to be the only monument left standing in a battlefield strewn with the ruins of our political institutions.

---

[67]   Ibid., p. 234.

6

INSULTING THE PROPHET

Violence is not the only form by which Islam becomes global, and in a fine book on the subject, Olivier Roy points out that it is not even the dominant form that this globalization takes.[1] But then militancy is not itself a uniform phenomenon, with Al-Qaeda's jihad routinely overshadowed by other causes that enjoy far more popularity than it does in the Muslim world. Such are the periodic protests that sweep the globe in response to some real or perceived insult, generally leveled by someone in the West, against the Prophet Muhammad. Not only are these protests autonomous of Al-Qaeda, whose globalization of Islam is predated by their own, they also tend to reject its language of jihad in the most overwhelming way.

Despite appearances these global events by no means represent the fanatical fringe of an otherwise familiar politics of protest, that is to say they do not represent a politics of interest. Muslims protesting what they consider to be insults to Muhammad's person are not interested in proposing some alternative vision for the world. Rather than making an argument or backing some cause, we shall see that these men and women protest so as to exhibit their suffering and call for its recognition. Their only demand is that such recognition be followed by a symbolic withdrawal of the hurtful insult. No claims are made for compensation and few for retribution, since the threats and violence of the protesters are intended, at least rhetorically, to compel only the global recognition of their suffering, and lead therefore to the removal of its entirely sym-

---

1   See Roy, *Globalised Islam.*

bolic cause—whether this be a book, a set of images or some comments in a speech.

In other words protest here is not about some popular interest staking its claim to political life, but instead represents the offer of a stark moral choice to the world by a display of Muslim suffering. I am not of course denying that interest politics are integral to these protests in local settings, only contending that as global events they are necessarily disinterested, since such world-encompassing phenomena possess a unity of their own and can by no means be defined simply as the sum total of local politics. This is why such protests are concerned more with the creation of a global Muslim constituency than with the offensive actions of non-Muslims, working according to an internal dynamic that is rarely affected by the reaction of outsiders. Drawing inspiration from each other as much as from the would-be insult that is apparently their cause, these protests sweep the globe according to an internal calendar and rhythm. Such events are suprapolitical, as Karl Jaspers might say, because their abandonment of politics in its traditional form is matched by the adoption of sacrificial practices that go beyond the mere exhibition of Muslim suffering to deliberately produce it. Thus the routine spectacle of injury and even death among so many protestors, from the Rushdie Affair of 1988 to the papal controversy of 2006, transforms protest itself into a practice of sacrifice.

It is worth noting the difference between these protests and those of pacifists or anti-globalization activists, especially because the latter have so clearly demonstrated their political failure, despite marshalling unprecedented numbers globally, as in the anti-war demonstrations that preceded the invasion of Iraq in 2002. Writing about the direct ancestor of today's anti-war movement, which is to say the pacifism of the Cold War, Jaspers attributes its failure to the rejection of sacrifice as a suprapolitical fact in favor of mere demands, judgment and theory.[2] To this riskless politics of fear he counterposes Gandhi's practice of nonviolence, whose sacrifice made a politics of fearlessness possible, in no matter how temporary a form. For unlike such pacifists the Mahatma's actions were dictated not by the fear of death, but by a truth for which, as Gandhi so frequently proclaimed, he was willing to tolerate a million

---

2   Jaspers, *The Future of Mankind*, p. 40.

lives voluntarily sacrificed. And if the politics of protest that character-izes global pacifism today continues in the footsteps of its Cold War progenitor, I hope to show that the suprapolitical element of Gandhian sacrifice has been inherited in a perverse and barely recognizable form by Muslim protests over insults to their Prophet. These latter have indeed globalized the Mahatma's sacrificial practices in the name of Islam.

Burning books

The massive protests occasioned in 1988 by the publication of Salman Rushdie's novel, *The Satanic Verses*, arguably provided the non-Muslim world with its first demonstration of Islam's globalization. This differed from an international Islam in that more than any such incident in the past, the protests over Rushdie's novel referred neither to a particular interest being threatened, nor to a particular cause being fought. Rather their apparently idealistic concern with the Prophet Muhammad's por-trayal meant that these protests were defined in terms of equal relevance for Muslims everywhere. More than pilgrimage, holy war or the kind of pan-Islamism that would mobilize Muslims internationally in support of Bosnians or Kashmiris or Chechens, in other words, the Rushdie Affair was global because it concentrated Muslim attention on an issue completely detached from persons and places.

Of course protests against *The Satanic Verses* did have particular meaning at every point in their trajectory, from Bradford to Srinagar, Islamabad, Tehran and beyond. But what made these events global was their lack of fixed location, geographic and political, a phenomenon rendered possible in large part by the unprecedented media exposure within which they occurred, such events being made available instan-taneously and repeatedly in the virtual space of television. Given the highly publicized refusal by Muslims to read *The Satanic Verses* or deal with issues like its author's freedom of expression and interpretation, it is even possible to say that Muhammad's portrayal became the site of a global debate for which Rushdie was himself incidental.

Early protests against the novel used it almost randomly as a kind of weapon at hand. A weapon, for example, that allowed Muslims in Bradford to find a voice that could be heard outside the cloisters of state-funded race relations programs, in this way ironically fulfilling the novel's attempt to give British Asians their own voice. Or one that allowed Indian Muslims to agitate against the bigotry of Hindu nationalists, who delighted in the novel, by asking for a ban on the book. In this pre-global phase of the Rushdie Affair, when *The Satanic Verses* represented British or Indian bigots in almost random fashion, the rest of the Muslim world remained unfazed. Even the Ayatollah Khomeini dismissed the novel as yet another petty irritant in the eye of Islam. But somehow, with the media blitz in Britain and riots in the Indian subcontinent, the Rushdie Affair was catapulted, again randomly, into a global event.

My point here is twofold: that the author and his novel were incidental to the Rushdie Affair, and that randomness was essential to its globalization. So attempts by certain Muslim groups to stage a repeat performance of this event, in concert with sections of the media in Europe and America, have not been successful. For instance efforts to make the Bangladeshi author Taslima Nasreen into another Rushdie seem to have been believed only by her and Rushdie himself. One imagines the local Islamists and global media that promoted Nasreen for this role being concerned more with their advertising and sales than with her freedom of expression or anything else. But then for many Muslims the real subject of the Rushdie Affair was not Salman Rushdie but the Prophet Muhammad. It was the interpretation of his life and work that constituted the stuff of their debate, which I believe was so passionate because it radicalized the portrayal of Muhammad in a more thoroughgoing fashion than did *The Satanic Verses* itself.

The title of Rushdie's novel refers to an obscure event in the life of the Prophet, a case of satanic interpolation in the revelation he was vouchsafed, which ostensibly puts both Muhammad's integrity and that of this revelation in doubt. Yet Muslim reaction to the novel, including the Ayatollah Khomeini's *fatwa* against it, did not deal with any of the theological issues raised by the book. It consisted instead of objections to Rushdie's unflattering portrayal of the Prophet as leader, friend and family man, in the process putting aside a whole polemical tradition that would demonstrate Muhammad's veracity by textual interpretation and theological reasoning. Muslim reaction to the novel was not concerned with demonstrations of veracity, only those of offence and injury.[3] This is particularly true for the Shia branch of Islam, to which Khomeini belonged, since it refuses to acknowledge the occurrence, and so the theological status, of the historical incident named in the title of *The Satanic Verses*.

The Prophet was not a properly religious figure in this debate but rather a model of civic virtue, in keeping with the long-standing efforts of Muslims to conceive a new social order by rethinking the idea of citizenship on the model of Muhammad's Medina. The Prophet's properly religious position was even undermined by this debate, in which he no longer related to his followers by way of miracles, saintly figures, sacred texts or even theological reasoning, but simply by representing a civic ideal. And Muhammad as the model citizen of a virtual state becomes the sign of a new social order in part because he is deprived of any real particularity, having been transformed simply into the ideal of this order. A virtual order that is both everywhere and nowhere, like an after-image of the historical state. Naturally I am exaggerating the distinction between the old Prophet and the new, but only so as to point out the implications of liberating Muhammad from the chains of theological reasoning and mystical emanation that had once bound him to believers. The chief such implication is that the Prophet comes to represent a certain kind of civic ideal calling for a very different sort of allegiance from his followers.

Such an image of the Prophet Muhammad began to emerge during the nineteenth century in places like British India, where influential movements were working to reform or purify Islam. The latter, whether liberal or fundamentalist, attacked what they saw as superstitious belief in mysteries and miracles of all kinds. Distancing the Prophet from these superstitions, they held him up as a great historical figure and a model of civic virtue. But the more Muhammad was stripped of miraculous attributes, the more vulnerable he became to insult and attack, for he was, after all, only human. It was the Prophet's humanity that required the protection of his followers and made him so dear to them. This explains why a diminution of the Prophet's religious status during this period

---

3   There were a few exceptions to this rule, among the most interesting of which was an analysis of *The Satanic Verses* by Iran's minister of culture. See Sayyid Ataullah Mohajerani, *Naqd-e Tuteyeh-e Ayat-e Shaytani* (Tehran: Entesharat-e Ettela'at, 1378).

was matched by a corresponding elevation of his status as a figure of love and reverence. Thus both liberals and fundamentalists in the nineteenth century began to disapprove of the European usage "Muhammadan" for them, decrying this supposed attempt to make Muslims out to be like Christians, the worshippers of their Prophet. Yet at the same time they spilt more ink on glorifying Muhammad and writing biographies of him then perhaps all the Muslims who had gone before. And if insulting the Prophet had been a grave enough offence for the Muslims of earlier times, it became a far more volatile issue now that Muhammad had become in some sense the ward of his community.

Back to the future

In the nineteenth century, however, the Prophet was not yet a global figure, in the sense that he did not bring together Muslims in the same way as he did during the Rushdie Affair. How has the political order that served to define Muhammad as a model of civic virtue during the nineteenth century changed in the twentieth century and beyond? What role does the Prophet Muhammad play in this process? Sixteen years after the Rushdie Affair, insulting depictions of the Prophet provided occasion for another grand manifestation of Islam's globalization, in which the answers to all these questions became evident.

In September 2005 the Danish newspaper *Jyllands-Posten* published a number of caricatures on the subject of Islam, Muslims and the Prophet Muhammad. It had solicited these as part of a competition in which cartoonists were asked to address the supposed fear that Danes and other Europeans felt in depicting Islam critically. In response to the publication Muslims in Denmark protested against some of the cartoons, especially that portraying Muhammad as a terrorist, with one group of protestors actively trying to gain the support of Muslim leaders in the Middle East. The series of diplomatic and other representations made by Muslims to the Danish government during this period all resulted in the latter invoking the liberal principle of freedom of expression in defence of *Jyllands-Posten*'s right to print such material.

By the end of the year this obscure event had snowballed into a global controversy, with Muslims the world over protesting, often violently, against Danish and other Western interests in countries from Indonesia to Lebanon. In their nonviolent aspect these demonstrations included a widespread boycott of Danish goods that was unprecedented in its extent. Such events kept the cartoon controversy at the centre of global attention for many weeks, even pushing news from the war in Iraq off the front pages. But despite the extraordinary passions unleashed among the protestors as much as among their opponents, Muslim demonstrations had completely dissipated by March 2006, leaving in their wake a state of universal confusion about what the crisis had all been about.

Both controversies, that of 1988 and of 2006, revolved around the portrayal of Islam's Prophet, and both were discussed in the West as threats to freedom of expression. Now the debate on freedom of expression goes back to the origins of liberalism—or rather to the origins of the nation-state that is its political body. Sadly the terms of this debate also go back to the beginnings of liberalism, and are unable to encompass the radical novelty of the challenge that confronts it. Unlike the weight of tradition that loads down such debate, the illiberal character of Muslim protest is astonishingly modern in form. After all freedom of expression only has juridical meaning within old-fashioned national states, because it protects the speech of one section of citizens against another, and even against the state itself. Muslim protests, on the other hand, have meaning in an absolutely new global context.

The cartoon protests, like those over Rushdie's novel, were remarkably dispersed geographically, and unconcerned for the most part with the rights of states or the responsibilities of citizenship. If this unconcern were due only to ignorance or irrationality among them, such protesting Muslims might eventually be educated to become the good citizens of a liberal democracy. Unfortunately this was not the case. Muslim protests, which moved so far beyond the bounds of state and citizenship, were informed by the new rationality of a global arena. Within this arena freedom of expression's more restricted realm had been rendered irrelevant. For at the global level there is no common citizenship and no government to make freedom of expression meaningful even as an expression. Liberalism was being challenged here not by its past but by its future.

Muslim protesters did not represent some religious tradition that needs to be schooled in the lessons of modern citizenship. Rather their protests brought into being a hyper-modern global community whose connections occur by way of mass media alone. From the Philippines to Niger, these men and women communicated with each other only indirectly, neither by plan nor organization, but through the media itself. And just as during the Rushdie Affair of 1988, most Muslims in 2006 were hurt not by the offending item, a book read or an image seen, but by its global circulation as a media report. Yet it was this very circulation of the offending item as news that also allowed Muslims to represent themselves as a global community in, through and as the news. Moreover they could only do so by way of English as a global language. It is no accident that the cartoon controversy took the Muslim world by storm only when it was reported on the BBC and CNN, for English and not Arabic is the source language of global Islam.

In this hyper-modern community traditional distinctions of belief and practice have ceased to be relevant, as indeed has religion itself in an old-fashioned sense. For the generic Muslim protester who was displayed on television screens across the world could not be marked by any specifically theological concern. Indeed only the first global controversy surrounding the Prophet involved a specifically theological issue, the charge of apostasy levelled at Salman Rushdie, but even this was marginal when compared to the secular rhetoric of Muslim hurt. And if in the Rushdie Affair the explicitly religious issue of the "satanic verses" was never taken up as a cause for offence even in the Ayatollah Khomeini's *fatwa*, Muslims protesting nearly twenty years later also made nothing of Islam's supposed proscription of the Prophet's image. In any case there is a long if contested history of Muslims depicting their Prophet. Such images continue to proliferate among Shiites, for example, without in any way dampening the outcry over the cartoons in Baghdad or Tehran.

These theological concerns are in fact interesting only to the old-style defenders of liberal democracy, who think of challenges to its freedoms in terms that are a few centuries out of date. That it should be a religious group demonstrating its globalization here was in any case consonant with liberalism's past. The nation state, after all, was founded to subdue religion, seen as the only entity capable of providing an alternative foundation for political life. So it is only natural if today Islam seems to confront the liberal state with its own founding myth, having become the Frankenstein's monster of its history. Liberal democracy appears doomed to repeat its own past by the way in which it prefigures its enemies—always understood as offering politics alternative foundations like that of religion. If not religion, then anarchism, fascism or some other historical rival of the liberal state comes to occupy this role in the long-running drama of its founding. But this is not true of global Islam, which should be defined in terms of liberalism's future instead of its past.

As in the Rushdie Affair, the Prophet insulted by these Danish cartoons is not a religious figure of any traditional sort. In 1988 it was Muhammad as husband and family man who stood impugned in the eyes of protesters. Many protesters in the new century continued to express their hurt by comparing the Prophet to members of their "family", hardly a religious role for him to play and one of dubious orthodoxy in any case. This is language that belongs more in the Christian than the Muslim tradition. In fact Muhammad as father, husband and family man has become a role model of the most modern kind, one representing the ideal Muslim not as the citizen or even the leader of a state, as he did for yesterday's fundamentalists, including even the Ayatollah Khomeini, but as a properly global figure instead. And the Prophet as a global figure manifests himself in domestic rather than public ways. It is his very particularity as father, husband and family man that has been universalized beyond the language of state and citizenship, giving Muhammad a mythic countenance as part of a global family.

Muslim protests over the caricatures of Muhammad published in the Danish newspaper *Jyllands-Posten* did not pose any threat to the freedom of expression in liberal democracies. They presented a challenge to old-fashioned liberalism as a political form that is being made parochial within a new global arena. Theoretically, after all, liberalism has no presence outside the nation state, which is why the international order these states operate in has never itself been liberal. Indeed such an order is not even meant to operate in a liberal way, since this would render the liberalism of its constituent units irrelevant. Whether we look to the theorists of liberalism or at the international order itself, all we see are general prescriptions for peace and particular compacts between states. In many respects the international arena remains a state of nature for liberal theory, which can only conceive of it otherwise by invoking the idea of a universal state.

However suspicious they may be of the universal state as an idea, liberals have in the past depended upon it to imagine as well as create an international order. The idea of a universal state is deeply embedded within organizations like the United Nations, which operates according to the analogy that states in an international order are like individuals in a national one. But what happens when individuals and groups themselves, rather than the nations and states that would represent them, come to occupy a space that is no longer international but global? Liberalism's historical unwillingness as well as inability to manage the global arena in its own terms leaves the latter open to challenge from without. But this challenge by no means spells the doom of nation states, forcing them rather into new shapes that put liberalism's traditional premises and foundations into question. What could be more indicative of this than the erosion of civil liberties in such states as part of the Global War on Terror? Liberal democracies today are increasingly shot through with new global vectors, running the gamut from immigrants to multinational corporations. Islam provides only one, though perhaps the most interesting one, of these vectors.

All of this means that the reality of liberal politics today far outstrips its theoretical carapace, with nation states not receding in the face of globalization so much as assuming new roles within its more expansive arena. For instance weaker states are coerced by more powerful ones into supporting their claim to be the agents of human security globally, if only in the militarized form of humanitarian interventions and peace-keeping operations. What does this indicate if not the state's armed appropriation of roles that were not so long ago reserved for non-governmental organizations? Important about the state's new role is that it subordinates the language of liberal citizenship to the biological security of human beings, in whose name alone can the traditional liberties of the citizen be taken away. But this is nothing more than a description of what is widely called neoliberalism, a global political form based upon the management of lives rather than the guarantee of freedoms that do not necessarily coincide with the former.[4]

---

4   Michel Foucault is the great theorist of this form of "biopolitics". See his *"Society Must be Defended": Lectures at the Collège de France, 1975-1976*, trans. David Macey (New York: Picador, 2003).

Muslim protest then represents only one of the incarnations taken by humanity in its emergence as the primary subject of politics. Islam's globalization is possible because it is anchored neither in an institutionalized religious authority like a church, nor in an institutionalized political authority like a state. Indeed it is the continuing fragmentation and thus democratization of authority in the world of Islam that might account for the militancy of its globalization. What did the global protests over a few Danish cartoons demonstrate if not the splintering of Islamic authority, since these expressions of Muslim outrage were rarely organized by any seminary or political party, to say nothing of any state?

In fact it was the media that allowed Muslims to organize themselves as a global community without political institutions, since their protests as seen on television inspired and even competed with each other. The media therefore functioned like a gigantic mirror, permitting Muslims to recognize themselves as a global community without any institutional form. Indeed it was this global community whose support states, parties and other political bodies in the Muslim world rushed to claim by joining in the cartoons fray. But in the absence of any significant religious or political authority in today's Muslim world, it is precisely unseen figures like Al-Qaeda or the Danish cartoons that have the ability to mobilize Muslims globally, though of course in different and even opposing ways. For example the cartoon protests by and large eschewed the rhetoric of holy war, though they did invoke the same themes of hurt and respect as Al-Qaeda does.

Islam no longer serves merely to voice reactions against colonialism or democracy, capitalism or modernity, but increasingly sets the terms for politics globally. So the unexpected escalation of the cartoon controversy moved it well ahead of any demonstrations over Iraq, Afghanistan or Guantánamo Bay. Of course these and other, more local issues certainly informed Muslim anger. But they did so by providing global Islam an opportunity to manifest itself in the most arcane and therefore autonomous way: through a set of caricatures. By chancing in seemingly arbitrary fashion upon the Danish cartoons as a cause, Muslim protesters were only proving global Islam to be relatively unhampered by the political traditions proper to old-fashioned liberalism. Like other global movements, from environmentalism to pacifism, the Muslim one we are looking at is free to map its own trajectory and will not follow the dictates of someone else's idea of political rationality.

It was left for yesterday's liberals to puzzle over the meaning of this movement, coming up with explanations for it like American imperialism, economic exploitation or Third World dictatorship. Meanwhile the protesters themselves, who must have been more than familiar with such shibboleths, were content to ignore them altogether. The Danish cartoons did not simply disguise the political or economic causes of Muslim anger in religious terms, for we have seen that their anger had little or no religious substance. Rather they allowed Muslims to set the terms for global politics precisely by fixing on an issue that national states are unable to address. Yet this very issue, of personal hurt, insult and offence, is more than familiar to liberal democracy. It is as if Muslim protesters were hesitantly feeling around the global arena they had occupied by extending to it the familiar practices of the nation state, though outside its geographical and juridical boundaries. Their recourse to legal language and categories, like calling for states to ban offensive publications, also illustrates the paradoxical way in which Muslims inhabited the global arena, for such calls became meaningless the moment they were made outside state borders. Insofar as they were global subjects, then, Muslims and their Prophet were offended because they had been denuded of the protection that states and citizenship have to offer. Their hurt was nakedly felt and nakedly expressed, existing outside the cosseted debate on freedom of expression.

It is because global Islam comes to us from the future that it exposes so clearly the historical limits of liberal democracy. Such limits are evident in the circular definition that has marked liberalism from its founding days: only those will be tolerated who are themselves tolerant. Such a definition deprives tolerance of any moral content by making it completely dependent on the behaviour of others. Tolerance therefore becomes a process of exclusion in which it is always the other person who is being judged. Even at its most agreeable, however, the definition is severely limited, because its circularity works only within the bounds of a national state. It is unable to deal with real differences at all and certainly not with difference at a global level. As important as it undoubtedly is, we should remember that liberal tolerance was never meant to replace every other ethics in a civil society, but is instead a procedural and legalistic form specific to the functioning of the nation state. And yet this state has today become only one of the actors jostling for space on a planetary stage.

There are many other kinds of tolerance possible, including the Christian one called charity, which would convert others or foster good relations with them by forbearance and example. But moral rather than legal definitions of tolerance, like the Christian one, tended not to be invoked in this controversy, with commentators abandoning the claims of civil society altogether to become ventriloquists for the state. Yet it is surely within civil society that the problem lies, and statesmen from Gandhi to Mandela have in the recent past mobilized precisely such nonlegal conceptions of tolerance to effect great social transformations. For tolerance can have no moral content if it exists only as the legal provision of mutual indifference. Indeed this kind of respect is not even amenable to legislation, which only recognizes it in the act of proscription. It occurs outside the law as a moral principle, and can be grasped only by sinking below the negative universality of liberal tolerance, tied as it is to the state's neutrality and indifference, to reach the positive if particular tolerance of Hindus, Christians or indeed atheists. The paradox of this particularity is that it is far more expansive than the universality of liberal tolerance, because it cannot be confined within the borders of a nation state.

It was this particularity of respect, and even the positive tolerance of Christian charity, that so many Muslim protesters had been demanding, in no matter how frightening a manner. Their fulsome expressions of hurt, after all, were not derived from the cartoons in any direct way, since these remained unseen for the most part, but from the absence of respect for Muslim feeling. Unlike the photographs of American soldiers abusing Iraqi prisoners at Abu Ghraib, these images had not been globally circulated to spur Muslim anger. Like Rushdie's novel before them the cartoons were in fact not supposed to be seen at all, which explains popular actions against newspapers in the Muslim world that did try to incite protests by printing them. Indeed the rumour of disrespect has proven a greater incitement to protest than any evidence of desecration. Thus the violent protests of 2005 in some parts of the Muslim world over unconfirmed media reports that American soldiers in Afghanistan had flushed pages of the Quran down toilets. The hurt experienced by such acts has to do not with their materiality so much as with the disrespect that such materiality only brings to light.

That a few invisible caricatures should cause more offence globally than large numbers of photographs depicting torture in the most real way is an important fact, and one that has little to do with the outrage of any specifically religious feeling. Given the invisibility of the cartoons in the Muslim world, there was no real outrage to religious feeling there but only the report of European disrespect. In other words the materiality of the images themselves had nothing to do with the protests they inspired, only the apparent injury done to Muslim feeling by the report of their circulation, which made the experience of hurt one of hearing rather than of sight. It was not the public act of blasphemy or desecration that was seen to be criminal, in legalistic terms, but rather the private contempt it betrayed. More than an offence experienced, therefore, Muslims were protesting the violation of a moral principle. This was the naked because nonjuridical principle of respect within a global civil society made possible by media, markets and migration.

Yet the initial demand by Danish Muslims to have their own prejudices protected did not threaten freedom of expression in any way. Nor did Muslims in Denmark or elsewhere in Europe and North America make their demands in a criminally violent manner. Such demands are in fact made all the time in liberal democracies, whose boundaries of free expression are therefore constantly shifting. From state secrets to racial discrimination, libel and copyright to sexual harassment, proscriptions on expression are being put in place by the very defenders of its freedom. Indeed today's Global War on Terror has led to the most concerted reduction of such freedom in decades, all in the name of the biological security of a global humanity.

In the meantime Muslims are inventing new forms of moral and political practice for a global arena. Such were the remarkable boycotts of Danish goods in many parts of the Islamic world. However unfair or unjust they might have been, these peaceful and individualized boycotts of unprecedented extent were, like the controversial cartoons, perfectly legal and even democratic. Indeed they derived from a tradition of nonstate or civil society boycotts that include the movement to divest from apartheid-era South Africa. Both these boycotts operated through transnational capitalism to create a global politics outside the cognizance of states. We have already moved a step beyond the banning and burning of the Rushdie Affair here.

More important, however, is the fact that this global mobilization of Muslims should have represented itself neither in the old language of imperialism and oppression, nor indeed in that of resistance and jihad. Instead it took its rhetoric from the arsenal of liberalism itself, merely extending categories like democracy and civil society into a global arena. But this extension also transforms such categories, which seem finally to have achieved the universality that liberalism historically invested them with, if only outside the nation-state and its legal forms. What resulted from these protests and boycotts, then, was not simply damage to the Danish economy, but rather a complete reversal of the primal scene of liberal freedom as it was staged by *Jyllands-Posten*.

The scenario envisioned by *Jyllands-Posten* was of a poor immigrant minority being "tested" for its tolerance by an entrenched and wealthy majority. But isn't the classical doctrine of liberal tolerance meant to protect minorities from majorities and not the other way around? Having gone on to fulfil the newspaper's prediction by failing its test, this wretched minority could then be accused of threatening the majority's liberal constitution. I will not go into the unpleasant task of speculating about the newspaper's motives in creating its own news by scooping itself in this way, nor ask about the rise in its sales afterwards. The denouement was a sudden implosion of the paper's national audience into a global Muslim one, within which the unfortunate Danish majority unexpectedly became a minority. Did these boycotts, then, signal the slow movement of democratic practices from a national to a global arena—one in which there exist as yet no institutions to anchor them?

Longing for Christianity

On September 12, 2006, a day after the fifth anniversary of the 9/11 attacks was commemorated around the world, Pope Benedict the Sixteenth spoke about the relationship of faith and reason to an audience of academics at Regensburg University. The Pontiff began his argument by citing a medieval text disparaging the Prophet Muhammad as someone who had brought to the world "things only evil and inhuman, such as his command to spread by the sword the faith he preached".[5] The Pope did not explicitly condone these words, which for him illustrated one way in which the relationship of violence and religion had been thought about in the past. And it is worth noting that the words were quoted from a volume edited by an eminent Arab priest who had translated the Quran and was a champion of Christian-Muslim understanding. For Benedict XVI the importance of the words he was quoting lay in the fact that the Byzantine emperor who spoke them condemned such violence because it was unreasonable. What followed was a wide-ranging meditation upon the role of reason in religion whose depths I will not attempt to sound, being concerned here by the views of those Muslims who protested the speech, not least in order to uphold their own ideas of Christian virtue and papal dignity.

Whatever his intention in mentioning the Prophet and his revelation, the Pope's citation of this medieval text was broadcast around the world in the form of a soundbyte, thus provoking an almost immediate reaction, violent in places, among Muslims who called for Benedict XVI to apologise for the hurt his words had caused them. And while the Vatican was quick to issue retractions and clarifications that assuaged some of Muhammad's followers, many others pronounced their dissatisfaction at these guarded and diplomatic statements, with a few even calling for the Pontiff's abdication or conversion to Islam. The controversy allowed Muslims across the world to mount yet another spectacle of their religion's globalization, although the statements, demonstrations and acts of violence fuelling it did not match the scale of those protesting the Danish caricatures of Islam's founder earlier that year. But the fact that they should have occurred so soon afterwards, and so much more rapidly, is telling given that nearly twenty years separated the cartoon controversy from the first spectacle of Islam's globalization, which had as its cause protests over the publication of the aforementioned *The Satanic Verses*.

When authors like Rushdie or the Pope are made responsible for the offensive portrayals of Muhammad circulated in the media, they are attacked not as individuals but as the media-enhanced representatives of

---

5   "Papal address at University of Regensburg: Three Stages in the Program of De-Hellenization", *Zenit News Agency—The World Seen From Rome* (http://www.zenit.org/english/visualizza.phtml?sid=94748).

abstractions like the West, Christendom or Zionism. Unlike those who criticize them, in other words, Muslim protesters are concerned not with the individual intentions behind these media statements but with their global dissemination as collective products of the West, Christendom, etc. They are entirely taken up by the attempt to anchor these geographically dispersed and institutionally unmoored abstractions by holding specific persons accountable for them. And it is this specification of culpability that makes Muslim protest a form of address rather than interpretation. While their critics let "militants" or "extremists" remain abstractions by speaking of them indirectly and in the third person, the protesters addressed specific persons in the most direct way, and demanded equally specific responses of them. Such addresses were indeed the only invitations to dialogue to emerge from these controversies.

As with the previous spectacles of Islam's globalization, demonstrations against the Pope's words had secular rather than religious meaning, because they were occasioned only by the "hurt" caused to Muslim feeling and made no claims about the truth of Muhammad's revelation. By recognizing this hurt and responding to it in as secular a manner, the Pope undercut his own speech on the relationship of faith and reason at Regensburg University by showing how difficult it is to use religious language outside sectarian borders. On the other hand the more violently Muslims protested, the less secular their hurt became, since its expression now damaged the very image of Muhammad's character that his followers sought to defend. In other words by damaging their own cause these Muslims took leave of secular reason without adopting a particularly religious reasoning in the process. Maybe this is how the relationship of faith and reason that Benedict XVI had addressed at Regensburg University manifests itself outside the academic institutions of European democracies.

More interesting about the secularization of Muslim protest was its overwhelming rejection of the language of law. Whether marked as sacred or profane, the vocabulary of legal transgression and punishment was left unpronounced, and there were no important *fatwas* issued as in the Rushdie affair. It is also significant that jihad, which the Pontiff had referred to in his speech, was not by and large declared against him, thus illustrating the multiple ways in which Muslim protest is manifested globally. As with the Danish cartoon controversy, Muslim anger at the Pope's comments did not follow the Al-Qaeda line, and in fact put it quite in the shade by setting another kind of agenda for Islam's globalization. After all, the Pope was asked for an apology so that forgiveness might be extended him. However coercive in its violence, this Muslim demand can be taken as an invitation to the kind of dialogue that Benedict XVI called for in his speech, and it was indeed seized upon as an opportunity by the Pope himself as well as a number of Muslim leaders.

At the very moment that Christian and Muslim leaders determined to engage in a dialogue, however, it became evident that such a thing was no longer possible in a global arena. How could dialogue, in its traditional form, hope to interrupt the fractious and fragmented exchanges of this controversy without itself becoming a media spectacle? In any case the Pope had nobody to talk to, since there exists no ecclesiastical authority in Islam. The only thing that Benedict XVI could do was speak to a more or less random selection of Muslim representatives, the first of whom were the ambassadors of Muslim countries to the Vatican. Yet these men were sometimes themselves Christian, and unlikely to be religious leaders in any case. As representatives of the international order, furthermore, they were incapable of managing the global community within which the controversy had occurred. It was because they had all realized the impossibility of dialogue in this new arena that the meetings convened and statements issued by these leaders assumed a distinctly theatrical countenance. Indeed the controversy ended by providing both "moderate" and "extremist" Muslims with a lot of free advertising, very little of which had anything to do with dialogue. For at the end of the day the only exchange possible in the controversy's global arena was that between repentance and absolution.

Contrition and forgiveness are of course religious acts, which is why their entirely secular deployment in this controversy becomes significant. If it was not before God but Muslims worldwide that the Pope was meant to repent, and not from God but these Muslims that he was to receive forgiveness, then nothing separates such contrition from that which had recently been expressed by the Hollywood actor Mel Gibson, amidst much media attention, for anti-Semitic remarks he had made. Yet there is a difference here that goes beyond the fact of Muslim violence, which is that religious categories provide perhaps the only vocabulary for dialogue in a global arena whose lack of political institutions stands in contradiction to humanity's increasing interdependency. How else was the head of the world's largest religious organization to communicate with Muslims belonging to many organizations or none at all? Certainly not by way of international institutions like the United Nations, which exists only to give voice to its member states.

If Muslim anger appeared to be so raw, this is because it voiced a global presence that remains as yet unmediated by any institution or authority. And if Muslim hurt appeared so intensely felt, this is because it expressed disappointment at the supposed lapse of a religious leader who had otherwise enjoyed considerable respect in the world of Islam. Indeed given the absence of a priestly hierarchy in Islam, and the invisibility of iconic Muslim figures like Osama bin Laden, Benedict XVI may even have represented his missing equivalent in the Islamic tradition, by standing in for this nonexistent figure in the curious respect paid him by Muslims. If not the Pope himself, then certainly his title evokes for many Muslims as well as Hindus and others a specifically Christian aura of otherworldliness and sanctity, one that leads them to expect a different kind of language from him. This is why Benedict's alleged lapse into what seemed to be common prejudice was so shocking for Muslims who, as it were, accidentally overheard the Pope speak of their Prophet, since he did not choose to address them while doing so. The Pontiff's initial refusal to recognize that Muslims might be part of his audience was unlikely to have been malicious in its intent, for it is still possible in the West to pretend that the world is not in fact interconnected in such a way as to give even the most arcane utterance a global audience. This had also been Salman Rushdie's mistake.

While the Pope called for a global dialogue in Regensburg, he nevertheless addressed this call to a parochial audience, as if it was their duty alone to spread this new gospel among those, Christian as well as Muslim, who were assumed incapable of initiating it. And so it took the strong and unexpected Muslim reaction to his speech to make the Pope's wish a reality. That such a reaction had not even been afforded the far more demonized figure of the American president George W. Bush, despite his much-resented talk of a crusade in the immediate aftermath of 9/11, bears testimony to the specificity of Muslim disappointment in Benedict XVI. It is as if the protesters were acknowledging, with sadness as much as anger, that the Pope, too, had to be included in the ranks of those who would defame their religion. What is extraordinary is that Muslims should have expected anything different, given the steady diet they are fed by the militants among them of Christianity's crusading spirit. So it is in fact a hopeful sign that Muslims did not expect a description of Islam's violence from the head of a church that has contributed the words Crusade and Inquisition to our vocabulary.

Presiding as he does over an immense and venerable apostolic hierarchy, the Pope possesses the kind of reputation and respect among the world's peoples, and especially among those who are not themselves Christians, that other religious leaders can only dream of. And however unrealistic or even absurd the expectations spawned by such respect, they have informed the world's reactions to Rome's doings for a considerable length of time. Writing in the wake of the Second World War, for example, Hannah Arendt commented on the Vatican's silence at the doings of Nazi Germany, a state with which Rome had a concordat.[6] Breaking this silence, claimed Arendt, may have done little to effect the course of war or even the behaviour of German Catholics, silence therefore being one way in which the Vatican hid its impotence from the sight of the world.[7] And unlike those who would find the Church as a whole culpable of collaborating with fascism, Arendt not only pointed to the priests who risked and lost their lives defending its victims, she also made it clear that the Vatican's behaviour in no way differed from any other state when it came to protesting the extermination of the Jews.[8] But this precisely was Rome's greatest betrayal, to behave in a secular rather than a religious way by placing political considerations over religious ones, a betrayal that Arendt claimed lost the Church an opportunity to renew its own mission, as much as that of religion in general, for a humanity sorely in need of it.[9]

It is this very betrayal of what they saw as the Church's mission that Muslims were protesting in 2006, just as they had done before in celebrated instances like the Ayatollah Khomeini's address to Pope John

---

6   Hannah Arendt, "The Deputy: Guilt by Silence?" in *Responsibility and Judgement* (New York: Schocken Books, 2003), pp. 214-226.

7   Ibid., p.218.

8   Ibid., p. 217.

9   Ibid., p. 225.

Paul II, who in 1979 tried to mediate between Iran and the USA and have American hostages in Tehran released. The Pontiff had been asked by President Carter to mediate in this matter precisely because of the respect he enjoyed among Muslims, something the Ayatollah acknowledged in his response, saying that people expected more from a religious leader of the Pope's eminence than from a politician like the American president. While appreciating John Paul's concern for the fate of US embassy staff whom the Iranians accused of being spies, Khomeini wondered if any Pope had ever offered to intercede on behalf of those oppressed by dictators like the Shah:

The ears of thirty-five million Iranians, who suffered for fifty years beneath the yoke of imperialism and repression [...] as well as the ears of millions of oppressed people throughout the world, have constantly been straining to hear some expression of sympathy on the part of the Pope, or at least some indication of paternal concern for the state of the oppressed, coupled with an admonishment of the tyrants and oppressors, or a desire to mediate between the oppressed peoples and those superpowers that profess to be Christian. But our ears have never heard any such expression of sympathy or concern.[10]

Incorporating Hannah Arendt's indictment of the Vatican's secularism, Khomeini's comments add to it the disappointment of Muslim expectations, which, the Ayatollah warned the Pope, will tarnish the name of Christianity. By posing as a friend solicitous of the Church's spiritual mission, Khomeini allowed himself to become more Catholic than the Pope, even offering to join the latter in a common religious endeavour at the end of his address:

Please convey my greetings to the Pope and tell him that he and I both, as men of religion, have a responsibility to give moral counsel. We ask that he assist our weak people by giving all the superpowers fatherly advice or by summoning them to account for their deeds.[11]

However disingenuous such a statement, it demonstrates that the Ayatollah's dialogue with the Pope was premised upon his identification with Christianity. It was also one premised upon the recognition that Muslims entertained certain hopes of the Church. Indeed the rhetorical

---

10   "Address to Monsignor Bugnini, Papal Nuncio" in *Islam and Revolution: Writings and Declarations of Imam Khomeini*, vol. 1, translated and annotated by Hamid Algar (Berkeley: Mizan Press, 1981), p. 278. Parenthesis mine.

11   Ibid., p. 285.

effect of Khomeini's address is premised entirely upon the very real hope that even unbaptized populations have of the world's largest religious organization. It is the disappointment of this expectation that also gives rhetorical force to Muslim dissatisfaction with the speedy retractions and clarifications that proceeded from the Vatican in response to their protests. For what appeared to dissatisfy these protesters were precisely the secular remnants in the Pontiff's carefully couched apologies. Yet if for all their rage, protesting Muslims had the audacity to expect Christian humility of the Pope, this in no way contradicted Benedict's own audacity in asserting the role of faith within a secular dispensation. Such indeed was the import of his speech at Regensburg University.

While a great deal has already been written about the complex role that Islam and its Prophet play in the Pontiff's now notorious address, to say nothing of the position that Jews and Protestants also occupy in it, what has so far gone unremarked is the Pope's use of violence as a criterion to decide upon the truth of religion. On the surface this is an extraordinary argument for Benedict XVI to make, not only because it goes against centuries of Catholic tradition, but also because it is secular to the core. During the Inquisition violence had been justified by describing it as an act of love, since the Church was committed to saving the souls of its victims and not their bodies. Whatever else it might have been, such reasoning was religious rather than secular, because it prized the soul's salvation over the body's comfort. To abjure violence for the sake of the body is to adopt a secular form of reasoning, even if the soul's salvation remains the final goal. Nonviolence can therefore provide the criterion of religious truth only if it is separated from the reasoning of secular betterment. And this is a promise the Church does indeed possess in doctrines like the sanctity of life—though to be fulfilled it needs to be extended from abortion and euthanasia to the death penalty and perhaps even war itself.

The point of this controversy was not that Muslims had misunderstood the Pope, that Benedict XVI had misunderstood the Prophet, or that either party had acted out of hatred and prejudice. However true or false any of these points may be, the controversy's great irony was that the Pontiff's Muslim protesters should have engaged so fully his argument. They did so not by illustrating what happens when faith and reason are separated, but rather by demonstrating how difficult it is for anyone, including the Pope himself, to transcend the language of secularism. This indeed is the crisis of religion to whose resolution Benedict XVI had dedicated his papacy. It is telling in this respect that the leader of a venerable church, the world's largest religious organization, should broach the subject of religion's crisis by referring to Christianity's old rival Islam, which by posing as the very embodiment of faith's fervency has pushed Christianity in a secular direction and so into crisis. Whatever his intent in doing so, the Pope's invocation of Muhammad was remarkable for the importance it accorded the Prophet, as if it was from the fire of Islam's faith alone that Christianity could now light its own lamp, though only to look upon its own crisis of faith. For it was to describe the crisis of Christian faith that Benedict XVI delivered his speech at Regensburg, something he could only do by invoking the name of Muhammad.

Has not Islam taken control of the language of faith on a global scale, by posing as faith's most fervent exemplar in the sacrificial spectacles of its globalization? And was not this position held, not so long ago, by the Roman Catholic Church, which gloried in the mystery of doctrines that surpassed reason? Yet today these mysteries, of transubstantiation and consubstantialism, to say nothing of saintly miracles and papal infallibility, have fallen beneath the fervid star of Islam in Catholicism's very homeland. Even more interesting is the fact that Muslim fanaticism has provided a home for precisely the vices that were for centuries seen as character traits of the Roman church. Was it not Catholicism that was accused by Protestants as well as secularists of being a worldwide movement dedicated to subverting the freedom of nation states? And were not its adherents said to profess loyalty to a foreign leader who gave religious sanction to the breaking of all agreements with those he deemed heretics and apostates, up to and including approving their assassination?

While Western commentators on the controversy tended to neglect these strange parallels, those in the Muslim world were well aware of them, to the degree that Ayman al-Zawahiri hastened to add Al-Qaeda's voice to a dispute not of its making by pointing out that Roman Catholicism might even hold the copyright on the kind of faith that surpassed reason, referring in particular to its doctrines of original sin, incarnation, the trinity and papal infallibility.[12] But it is precisely this situation that makes the kind of dialogue Benedict XVI called for at all possible, if only by showing us how intertwined these religions are with each other as well as with secularism. This dialogue can even be seen occurring in the extraordinary importance that the Pontiff's address accorded the Prophet and his revelation, as well as in the corresponding importance that Muslims accorded the speech at Regensburg. But given that it is occurring among large masses of people in an uneven global arena lacking any institutions of its own, it would be foolish to expect such dialogue to be conducted in parliamentary or academic fashion. Indeed the Pope himself has made it very clear that he attaches little value to interfaith dialogue of this kind.

In his address at Regensburg University the Pontiff described Europe as Christianity's spiritual homeland, though he knows that most Christians, and indeed Catholics, live outside this partial continent. By explicitly forsaking the desire to return to Christianity's Asian origins, and even to "the God of Abraham and Isaac", Benedict XVI could not have been so crude as to reject his religion's Jewish heritage. Like the reference to Muhammad, this reference to Abraham's sacrifice of Isaac was literally and metaphorically "put in quotation marks" by being cited from another text, in this case that of a Protestant theologian, thus allowing the Pope to distance himself from its radical implications. It seems clear, nevertheless, that Benedict XVI rejected the violent sacrifice demanded by a transcendent God for the immanence of one who sacrificed Himself for mankind. God's incarnation in Jesus, therefore, means finishing with the religion of violence, whose transcendent God has been sacrificed to man and may now be found manifested in the church as well as in the papacy itself. This is certainly a striking argument to make, though it does not at any point leave the closed circle of Roman Catholic doctrine, which means that the only form of dialogue it initiates is a proselytizing one.

Yet by criticizing Muslim and Protestant attempts to recover the moral transcendence of Judaism's heritage, as signified in the story of

---

12   "Ayman Al-Zawahiri reacts to Bush, Pope; urges Muslims to support muja-
      hidin" *United States Central Command* (http://www.centcom.mil/sites/uscent-
      com1/What%20Extremists%20Say/Ayman%20Al-Zawahiri%20Reacts%20
      to%20Bush,%20Pope;%20Urges%20Muslims%20to%20Support%20Muja-
      hidin.aspx?PageView=Shared).

Abraham's willingness to sacrifice his son at the command of an un-known God, the Pontiff was also asking Christian Europe to remain true to its own past. And this Hellenistic past, the Pope well knew, was common to Judaism and Islam as much as it was to Christianity. Indeed this largely pagan heritage could be possessed by none of these religions because it was external to all three, and even to Europe itself within its current geographical boundaries. Might the Pontiff's speech be heard as an invitation for Europe to contribute her own history to the dialogue of faith and reason, one in which all Europeans, however defined, could participate? Perhaps this is too charitable a reading, but whatever the case, his boldness in turning to Europe's pagan past requires more at-tention than has been given the Pontiff's address even by his staunchest supporters. In yet another irony, then, the only people to acknowledge the Pope's radical agenda and even take it seriously were its Muslim detractors, whom Benedict XVI had to thank for the unprecedented interest that his speech evoked among Roman Catholics themselves, though it was clear that they were neither to be aroused nor united in the Pope's name as Muslims were in that of their Prophet. The impo-tence concealed by the Vatican's silence at the doings of Nazi Germany was here made evident to all, even if dressed up in the garb of tolerance and civilization.

Was it then the secularism of his own flock that prompted the Pon-tiff to retract his denial of Abraham's sacrifice by invoking this very Prophet in responding to Muslim protest? Mentioning Abraham as the common ancestor of Arabs and Jews, as well as the common patriarch of all three monotheisms, Benedict XVI lapsed back into one of the great clichés of interfaith dialogue, whose latitudinarian ways he pro-fesses to dislike. Moreover the God of the so-called Abrahamic religions is precisely the God of Abraham and Isaac, whose sacrificial transcend-ence the Pope had already rejected. Far from constituting the benign community of interfaith dialogue, in other words, the kinship of the three monotheisms is based on Abraham's violation and sacrifice of kin-ship itself. For if anything, the story of Abraham and Isaac tells us that there is no violence greater than that of kinship, and that violence is itself a form of kinship in the physical and emotional intimacy it makes possible between enemies. The task of interfaith dialogue, as the Pope himself might agree, is not merely to recognize kinship but instead to deal with its violent consequences. In any case the Abrahamic kinship of monotheistic religions is of less historical importance for Islam than it is for Judaism and Christianity. While Europe and the Middle East might well have functioned as monotheistic cloisters, the vast bulk of the Muslim world has historically bordered not Jewish or Christian societies but Hindu, Buddhist and Zoroastrian ones. For the overwhelming majority of Muslims, therefore, Christians and Jews were mythical kin who have only achieved some reality through colonialism and migration.

The universal interconnectedness that globalization engenders means that the dialogue called for by the Pope has already begun. But despite the fact that it has the whole world as its stage, this dialogue possesses no space of its own, for being global in dimension it can be conducted neither in the seminary nor the *madrassa*, to say nothing of the university. This is also a dialogue that finds no place in the national and international politics of our time. So it occurs on the street and in the media, in demonstrations and soundbytes rather than in treatises and contracts. It is easy to find examples of such dialogue outside Europe, where this controversy had received some of its most acute analysis. Indian and Pakistani Muslims, for example, were prominent in the global protests against the Pope. And while both countries have a long record of contributing to international Islamic causes, this is by no means a uniform phenomenon. Pakistani Muslims, for instance, entered the Danish cartoon protests very late in the day, and certainly much after their Indian neighbours had lost interest in it. On the other hand the latter have never joined the global jihad movements that preoccupy Pakistani militants in any significant way. Both countries have a history of anti-Christian feeling, though in India it is Hindu militants who are involved in attacks on this minority. In both countries, moreover, it is Protestant Evangelicals in rural areas, both missionaries and converts, who come under fire, and not the long-established Catholic communities who live in urban settings.

Missionary activity and licentiousness are generally the causes, actual or ostensible, of prejudice or violence against Christians in India and Pakistan, though even on these grounds they are targeted far less than other religious groups, mostly Muslims of one sort or another. In the immediate aftermath of the Danish cartoon protests, Catholics around the world, but especially in India and Pakistan, began their own much more peaceable demonstrations against the showing of a Hollywood film called *The Da Vinci Code*, which retold Christian history by claiming that Jesus and Mary Magdalene had married and produced a line of descendants who survive to this day. The villain of the piece is the Roman Catholic Church, which according the film has spent more than two millennia tracking down and killing Christ's descendants.

These Catholic demonstrations were clearly and explicitly inspired by Muslim protests over the Danish cartoons, in a startling illustration of how Islam has come to occupy the language of faith globally. Like Muslim as well as Hindu protests in the subcontinent, Catholic demonstrations expressed themselves using the secular vocabulary of hurt, making no claims to the religious veracity of their feelings. What is more, these demonstrations were joined by numbers of Muslims in both countries, with prominent Muslim clerics rallying their followers to support a cause they saw as being foreign to themselves. This support, in other words, was premised not on the fact that Muslims, too, were offended by the film's portrayal of Jesus, who is one of Islam's prophets, but on their sympathy for the hurt felt by their Christians compatriots. This form of support is not at all unusual in the subcontinent, despite the routine forms of religious violence to be found there, for whether they are granted it or not, such empathy is just as routinely invoked by Hindu or Muslim groups making their own demands. These demands are voiced in moral rather than juridical terms, being widely understood and appreciated as such.

While the Muslims who supported Catholic protesters in India and Pakistan, often against their own governments, did so for a complex set of reasons that might have included the assertion as much as the abnegation of self-interest, it is also true that in doing so they participated in a dialogue with their Christian neighbours. One part of this dialogue was to show that unlike many Christians in the West, who had refused to acknowledge Muslim hurt during the cartoon controversy, they were entirely capable of sympathizing with the followers of other religions. In the end the offending film was banned in Pakistan as well as in several Indian states, without, it seems, endangering freedom of speech more generally. Abstract rights were sacrificed to concrete feelings in a way that was constitutionally troubling while being principled at the same time.

Indeed moral considerations were paramount in the film's banning, since Christians in the subcontinent are a minority so small as to be incapable of compelling their governments to do anything by putting pressure upon them. In other words it is precisely the relative insignificance of Christians in India and Pakistan that made these countries' capitulation to their demands so significant. For banning or censoring *The Da Vinci Code* was clearly an act of principle rather than the result of pressure, and as such it worked to redeem the far more controversial concessions that Pakistan and India make to more important religious groups like Hindus or Muslims. However good or bad such concessions may be on constitutional grounds, those made to Christians in particular permit social life in the subcontinent to be marked by an explicitly moral instead of a merely juridical character. And this is only possible because of the presence of minorities in these societies.

None of this meant, of course, that Christians and Muslims during the *Da Vinci Code* controversy had suddenly become allies or even friends, only that a kind of dialogue made up of media statements and spectacles had been set in motion between them. So when the Pope became a target for Muslim ire, Catholics in India and Pakistan had to tread very carefully. However they responded in exactly the way that was demanded of them, though I do not mean by this that Roman Catholics apologised to Muslims out of fear. In India at least, where there is no history of Muslim-Christian violence, the Pontiff's flock announced its determination to endure the consequences of the controversy with fortitude, blaming neither Pope nor Prophet for their travails. Did not this expression of Christian spirit illustrate in the most striking way the unity of faith and reason that Benedict XVI had called for?

An Impossible Dialogue

If the unprecedented global protests over insulting depictions of the Prophet in a book, newspaper or a papal speech tell us anything, it is that Muslims can act in concert without following a leader or sharing an ideology. While such demonstrations might possess a local politics in other words, they are shaped by global movements that lack traditional political meaning, not least by sidelining leaders and institutions for popular action in the name of a worldwide Muslim community as seen on television. The same holds true for Muslim support of global militancy, whose televised icons are capable of attracting a following without the help of local institutions or leaders. The new global arena that such movements bring to light, then, presents a threat to politics conventionally conceived. This is a threat that Muslim liberals are trying to address by promoting the cause of dialogue and debate on a global scale, the most recent manifestation of which was the letter sent on 13 October 2007 in the name of 138 Muslim "scholars, clerics and intellectuals" to "the leaders of all the world's churches, and indeed to Christians everywhere."[13]

By engaging in this effort, though, Muslim liberals also risk moving beyond the political structures of liberalism, chief among them the nation state and its representative institutions. There is nevertheless a great deal of funding available for such efforts today, mostly from Western governments interested in promoting "moderate" Islam internationally, and it is not difficult to mount a critique of the way in which Muslim liberals are enticed into supporting the particular projects of such states by accepting this funding. As it turns out, both the letters sent by this group were written under the auspices of the Royal Aal-al Bayt Institute for Islamic Thought in Amman, whose patron happened to be the "moderate" and pro-Western King of Jordan. But even at their most genuine such state-funded projects tend to be counter-productive in the long run, having in the past done little more than create dependent and thoroughly compromised Muslim elites in Asia and Africa whose liberalism never became a living factor in their societies. I do not however intend to pursue this easy line of criticism here, focusing instead on the more general difficulties of dialogue and so on the limits of liberalism itself in a global arena lacking political institutions of its own.

In the first few years after 9/11 Muslim liberals were able to mount only defensive manoeuvres, presenting themselves as voices of moderation in the media while at the same time protesting the anti-Muslim tone that had come to mark so much public debate and government action in the West. But while the organizations they founded have had an undeniable importance in protecting the rights of Muslims living in Europe and America, the efforts of these liberals to advocate religious moderation ap-

13   "A Common Word Between Us and You", *The Official Website of A Common Word,* (http://www.acommonword.com/index.php?lang=en&page=option1).

pear to have had little effect on those who were not already moderate to begin with. In any case despite their prodigious output of apologetic writings, Muslim liberals and their supporters possessed no global presence equivalent even to the most mediocre of militants. Naturally their lack of influence does not mean that most of the world's Muslims are opposed to the liberals among them, only that these moderates have been unable to assume any position of leadership globally.

But recently some among the moderates have launched a more proactive media campaign that brings together the scattered energies of Muslim liberals in a collective enterprise. Such for example was the open letter that an array of thirty-eight Muslim politicians, clerics and intellectuals from around the world wrote the Pope while global protests were occurring in response to his Regensburg address.[14] The letter moved beyond a standard and reactive defence of Islam to instruct Benedict XVI about the necessity of tolerance and understanding for the common good. More important, however, was its attempt to achieve a global presence by neglecting the nation state and its representative institutions, in which I also include international organizations, to address the head of a church that both is and is not part of a liberal order. The Muslim letter, in other words, sought to make a global intervention by addressing itself to Christendom as a whole.

A year later more Muslim notables, including many among the letter's signatories, issued the second epistle, now addressed not only to the Pope but the heads of all the major churches. This was a letter of invitation, asking Christians and Muslims to come together by recognizing that both their scriptures preached the love of God and of the neighbour. As open letters released to the media, of course, these communications were aimed at public opinion around the world as much as they were directed to the eminences addressed. Indeed the Pope and other churchmen to whom these letters were sent served as their media of dissemination to a global audience. Such epistles of moderation therefore play the same role as Osama bin Laden's letters and proclamations to the West, which are sometimes also signed by a variety of militant Muslim leaders.

---

14   "Open Letter to His Holiness Pope Benedict XVI" *Islamica Magazine* (http:// www.islamicamagazine.com/letter/).

Unlike Bin Laden's proclamations, however, the epistles of moderation eschew all political debate by disingenuously casting the difficulties of Christian-Muslim relations in a purely religious light. Moreover they envisage a religious confrontation between Christianity and Islam that is far more extensive than anything Al-Qaeda would countenance, since it makes Christians all over the world, and not simply those from certain Western countries, into the potential enemies of Islam, ignoring the fact that the majority of the world's Christians do not live in the West and are not therefore party to some epic confrontation with Muslims. But I suspect this expansiveness of address was meant only to disguise the letter's small significance by allowing it to mount the parody of a global event. Consider, for instance, the following passage from the letter of 2007 apparently addressed to every Christian leader its Muslim authors could find:

Finding common ground between Muslims and Christians is not simply a matter for polite ecumenical dialogue between selected religious leaders. Christianity and Islam are the largest and second largest religions in the world and in history. Christians and Muslims reportedly make up over a third and over a fifth of humanity respectively. Together they make up more than 55% of the world's population, making the relationship between these two religious communities the most important factor in contributing to meaningful peace around the world. If Muslims and Christians are not at peace, the world cannot be at peace. With the terrible weaponry of the modern world; with Muslims and Christians intertwined everywhere as never before, no side can unilaterally win a conflict between more than half of the world's inhabitants. Thus our common future is at stake. The very survival of the world itself is perhaps at stake.[15]

Unlike the first epistle its second incarnation did not arrive as a reaction to some violent demonstration of Muslim offence, though it certainly staked its claims upon the possibility of such violence in the future. In this sense both letters represented a kind of negative force, depending as they did on militant Islam for the strength of their arguments, which if anything stress the dangers of militancy in a far more apocalyptic tone than the militants do themselves. Of course liberalism everywhere gestures towards the supposed horrors of an alternative political order in order to justify itself, but in the West these days it usually does so with power on its side.

---

15   *The Official Website of A Common Word.*

Muslim liberals, on the other hand, not only possess little power in their own right, they have also been unable thus far to stage the spectacular acts of sacrifice that mobilize people for a cause—acts of the kind that militants are so adept at performing. These sacrificial acts need not even be violent to be effective, as Gandhi and after him Martin Luther King and Nelson Mandela demonstrated so well through the entire course of the twentieth century. Perhaps liberals are incapable of staging such spectacles given their devotion to protecting interests rather than sacrificing them, which is why liberalism has always come to power on the back of far more radical movements dedicated to religion, revolution or revenge.

Muslim liberals, too, would like to come to power on the back of radical Islam, but they have never managed to ride the tiger of jihad and so must reach out to the West for a helping hand. But this immediately puts them in the position of their colonial ancestors, consummate middlemen who occupied a kind of no-man's land between the Christian masters and Muslim subjects of European empires by claiming to represent each to the other. Indeed the arguments of these Muslim liberals are drawn without exception from the lexicon of their nineteenth-century predecessors, down to every single scriptural citation they deploy. Such arguments do not therefore constitute any part of a dialogue but are rather the ghostly reiterations of a conversation between men long dead.

Like the spectres they imitate, the signatories of these letters, themselves a random assortment of government-appointed clerics, out of favour politicians, exiled intellectuals, university professors, aspiring spokesmen for Islam, converts and immigrants in the West appear to be religious entrepreneurs trying to squeeze out a share of influence for themselves by representing Muslims and Christians to one another. With a few exceptions, including the Secretaries General of the Jamiat ul-Ulama-ye Hind and the Al-Khoei International Foundation, these men (and a few women) do not in fact represent any significant Muslim population, for despite their sectarian, territorial and professional diversity, they include neither a single religious leader of any stature nor a single political one. Their representative character, in other words, is constituted by the sheer diversity of these individuals, who are therefore "representative men" in the colonial sense of this term. All of which means that a response from the Pope is the only way of legitimizing this ragtag group by lending it some kind of representative character as an interlocutor of the Holy See.

Yet it is not at all clear what kind of dialogue is possible between these Christian leaders and their self-proclaimed Muslim counterparts, assuming for the moment the latter's legitimacy. For one thing Islam's lack of a church and therefore of dogma strictly speaking means that there can be no equivalence even between Christian and Muslim divines, let alone between the Pope and a group of "representative Muslims" who are likely to disagree with each other on more subjects concerning Islam than they disagree with Benedict XVI. In any case the absence of an institutional structure and so of dogmatic authority among them means that these men and women cannot in fact talk about the same subjects in the same way as the churchmen they address. Moreover these Christian leaders can be addressed at all only because they happen to be churchmen.

Could our group of Muslims address Buddhists, Hindus or even Jews in the same manner? Who would they address apart from some group of religious entrepreneurs like themselves? Indeed different Muslim sects cannot even address each other in the way their representatives do the Pope, whose dogmatic authority as head of the Roman church is what finally lends his interlocutors their coherence. Lacking such a structure of authority, Islam is much closer to the world's other religions than it is to Christianity, which is in fact the great exception among these faiths. But this makes the similarities that the letters so frequently invoke between the two largest monotheisms both true and false, since in some fundamental ways Islam is closer to Hinduism (say in its lack of a church organization and hierarchy) than it is to Christianity.

Like so many things about them, the desire of Muslim liberals to make common cause with Christians has a colonial history, one in which the moderates of the nineteenth century sought to form a partnership with their European masters, generally against some other group of fellow subjects. Whether it was greed for power or the fear of rivals that motivated them, these men stressed their religious kinship with colonial rulers to connive with them in the suppression of opposing religious, sectarian, ethnic and other parties. And while the signatories to the letters we are considering are not so crude as to voice their dislike of any particular community, not even that of the militants, their words breathe the same spirit of exclusivity as any edict of ostracism.

These epistles would construct an exclusive relationship between Christians and Muslims in particular, and between Christians, Muslims and Jews in general, by displacing the possibility of a violence that marked them in the past onto some other body of traitors and quislings to the "Abrahamic" faiths. The only problem with this quest for a monotheists' alliance is that it goes against the geographical and demographic reality of the world's religions, with Hindus and Buddhists being much more likely neighbours for Muslims than Christians and Jews. In other words the quest for a special relationship with Christianity or Judaism is an explicitly Occidental one, in which attention is shifted from the geographical and demographic realities of Islam to focus on its adherents only insofar as they come into contact with Christians and Jews in Europe, North America and the Levant.

Given that the second epistle of moderation speaks so glowingly about loving one's neighbour, it seems strange that the Muslims' actual neighbours are forgotten for the only ones who count: Christians for the most part, and Jews out of courtesy, but only because both are meant to share the injunction of loving their neighbours. Yet surely loving one's neighbour has nothing to do with whether or not this neighbour shares such an injunction, indeed rather the contrary if we take the Gospels for our guide. In the haste to create an exclusive relationship with Christians in particular, their would-be Muslim interlocutors have even forgotten that among the verses of peace and amity they quote so liberally from the Quran are many that refer to pagans and polytheists as much as they do to any monotheistic faith. But pagans and polytheists are of course consigned to the flames by our moderates while Islam is lifted out of its own much more pluralistic past to enter into the paradise of monotheist uniformity.

By ignoring the rich and contentious history of Muslim relations with Zoroastrians, Buddhists or Hindus, these letters also reduce the forms and varieties of religious interaction in the Islamic world to a monotheistic point, in fact narrowing it simply to the similarities between Judaism, Christianity and Islam. And all of this is based on the presumption that the recognition of similarity necessarily leads to friendship and respect, whereas the opposite might well be true, as it certainly is in the histories of violent conflict between Muslims, Christians and Jews, to say nothing of Catholics and Protestants or Shias and Sunnis. This exclusive focus on monotheistic similarities leads to one conclusion, the rejection of religious diversity and the consequent adoption of a Christian model for faith in general. Perhaps this is why the second epistle attributes a completely Christian locution to Islam: the love of God and of the neighbour.

The Christianization of the world's religions proceeds apace, precluding the mutual respect among them that is due only to the recognition of fundamental difference and disagreement. For with similarity there comes disputation and the narcissism of minor differences. So the letter to Benedict XVI in 2006 rejected the claim that Islam was spread by the sword, and attributed the greater part of its conversions to missionary activity.[16] But before their encounter with Christian missionaries in the nineteenth century, Muslims had little notion of organized proselytism, as indeed they would not without the institution of a church, which means that conversions to Islam occurred in the absence of a mission as much as of a sword. Both epistles of moderation are narcissistic in this way, for instance by pointing to minor differences between Christianity and Islam while at the same time adopting the most Protestant views of scripture. So the Quran is approached directly and without mediation as if it were a transparent and self-evident text accessible to all, which goes completely against its traditional reading in the Muslim world.

Furthermore the holy book is interpreted as literally as any American evangelist might interpret his Bible, to the extent that the Christians and Jews it mentions are described in the letters as if they were merely the ancestors of today's religious communities, which is to say historical and sociological groups rather than the exemplary figures and juridical categories of traditional thought. In the 1920s, however, Muslim divines in India saw nothing odd in forming an alliance of Hindus and Muslims under Gandhi's leadership by invoking the Quran's description of a pact between Jews and Muslims under the Prophet's leadership. These clerics, in other words, did not see the Jews mentioned in the Quran as an historical or sociological community with contemporary descendants, but instead as nothing more than exemplary figures who could stand in for Hindus and provide the juridical precedent for a pact between Muslims and polytheists.[17] It is this kind of thinking that the monotheistic intimacies longed for by Muslim liberals puts an end to.

---

16   "Open Letter to His Holiness Pope Benedict XVI", p. 3.

17   See, for example, Maulana Hussain Ahmad Madani, *Composite Nationalism and Islam (Muttahida Qaumiyyat aur Islam)*, trans. Mohammed Anwer Hussain and Hasan Imam (New Delhi: Manohar, 2005).

Luckily Islam is not what Muslim liberals would have it be, and for this we have to thank their intellectual vapidity. Militants, on the other hand, are far more creative in their religious thinking and much more imaginative about their means of propagating it. Insofar as violence represents one of these means, of course, the intellectual adventurousness of militant Muslims poses a serious problem for their liberal counterparts, however transient such violence might be. Yet I am convinced that these militants will have done more to revolutionize Islam in the long run than any collection of Muslim liberals, no matter how diverse and representative they happen to be. For by operating in a global arena without political leaders or institutions of its own, these men reveal to us a vision of the future. By comparison all the moderates have to offer is a past endlessly recycled—but the past not of seventh-century Arabia so much as of nineteenth-century Europe.

The Islam of militancy and offence occupies a global arena in which it acts without being an actor. That is to say militancy exists as a global agent by virtue of sacrifices that are amplified in the media and mirrored around the world without the benefit of political leadership and institutions, since even Osama bin Laden exists for his Muslim admirers as nothing more than a media icon. Whatever their local causes or consequences, therefore, such acts represent the democratization of sovereignty in a global arena lacking sovereign power of its own. This sovereignty is exercised by individuals of all descriptions through the ostentatious sacrifice of their own lives as well as the lives of others in the name of a community and a cause that remain invisible everywhere but on television. What is the future of sovereignty in such a global arena? How might it be attached to a set of institutions and a form of politics that does not as yet exist there? Why has religion come to provide the only vocabulary we have to describe this new world? Such are the questions that militancy poses and will in all likelihood proceed to answer. About these questions the moderates have nothing to say.

7

IN THE BELLIES OF GREEN BIRDS

"WE LOVE DEATH THE WAY YOU LOVE LIFE."[1] These words were uttered by Shehzad Tanweer, one of the London suicide bombers, in a video released on the first anniversary of the attacks in July 2006. Other terrorists have gone further in claiming to love death more than their enemies do life, but whatever its form this striking locution appears calculated to challenge the primacy given to life in contemporary definitions of humanity. Although such a primacy has roots in the Christian sanctification of life, it is fundamentally modern in its overwhelming reference to the present, since the kind of humanity that is defined by humanism, humanitarianism and human rights tends to be strictly positive and contemporary in nature, eschewing any notion of an afterlife for instance. We are not in other words dealing with a metaphysical conception of humanity that includes both the dead and the unborn, or a philosophical conception that would treat it as a regulative ideal, but rather with humanity as a global fact amenable to technical manipulation and administrative measures.

However by erasing the past as much as the future from its definition and confining humanity, future generations included, to a purely empirical existence, we end up making it much more vulnerable to attack. Humanity thus becomes the eternal victim of history, always teetering on the brink of an apocalypse, whether of an atomic, environmental or even terrorist kind. It was the threat of nuclear war that first transformed humanity into a planetary fact, whose empirical existence alone made

---

1   "American Al-Qaeda Operative Adam Gadahn, Al-Qaeda Deputy Al-Zawahiri, and London Bomber Shehzad Tanweer in New Al-Sahab/Al-Qaeda Film Marking the First Anniversary of the 7/7 London Bombings", p. 2.

it capable of becoming an historical victim—and therefore potentially an historical actor as well. So the proliferation of fantasies about alien invasions and mutant infiltrations during this period only underlined humanity's vulnerability in the age of the atom bomb and the moon landing. Indeed these fantasies often rendered the earth into a kind of prison for the human race, a home under siege from hostile forces, or even a dead planet that a few lucky individuals bearing the future of their race might escape in a spaceship. Humanity thus assumes its mortal reality in popular imagination only within a war of the worlds.

The primacy given to life in the definition of a planetary humanity makes it prey to every kind of fear and anxiety. Moreover the militant negation of life as humanity's defining feature provokes all these fears and anxieties by putting it into question as a category familiar to us from the language of humanitarianism and human rights. What the hysteria over militant Islam's "death cult" or "nihilism" entails, then, is an attempt to redraw humanity's borders around the love of life in such a way as to deprive those who would love death of their status as human beings. So the novelty of the legal measures put into place in America and Britain to imprison people accused of being potential terrorists, if only because of the things they say or read, lies in their assumption that such people are automatons who can be set off on a murderous rampage by the least provocation, and who are more dangerous than wild animals because they do not value their own lives.[2] These men indeed resemble Hollywood's robots in the imagination of their enemies—killing machines set off by some invisible switch like bit part Terminators. Yet in placing so much emphasis on the love of life that they profess to find the love of death incomprehensible, the humanists of our time divorce their conception of humanity from Christianity more than they separate it from Islam, since the love of death is arguably more familiar in the former than the latter.[3]

In any case life has not always provided the definition or even the ideal of humanity, so that in Roman antiquity, for example, there were many circumstances in which life was not considered worth living. And

---

2 See for this Judith Butler, *Precarious Life: The Powers of Mourning and Violence* (London: Verso, 2004).

3 For this see Talal Asad, *On Suicide Bombing* (New York: Columbia University Press, 2007).

in these circumstances suicide was not only accepted but also seen as a noble act manifesting the quintessence of all that is human. I do not mean to equate Muslim terrorists with Roman suicides, only to claim that, confined to life humanity becomes a much narrower category than it ever was in the past. For even as a global fact the human race can be and is indeed divided into a hierarchy of those more or less human than others, whether by moral, legal or medical criteria, since the inhuman always lurks behind any empirical definition of humanity as its shadow. It is even possible to claim that the more civilized a people is, the more stringent will its criteria for humanity be, and therefore the more likely will it be to condemn others to the status of the inhuman.[4] Of this no better example can be given than the impassioned debates among modern humanists on militant Islam's evil and inhuman nature. By contrast the militants themselves entertain no ideas of the West's evil or inhuman character, however they may loathe and despise its representatives.

The Christian concept of evil is not one that exists in the rhetoric of militancy, and certainly not as a kind of external force, its place being taken by the Muslim's own sin in refusing to sacrifice himself for humanity. And since this humanity is not conceived of merely in terms of life as an empirical fact, being half in love with easeful death, it cannot become a category of exclusion but includes both friends and enemies within its embrace. Is this why Islam's terrorists always insist on referring to their enemies in the most familiar of ways, to the extent of joking about their hatred of each other? The paradox of loving death more than others love life is that in doing so the militant ends up rejecting humanity's status of victim together with the evil that produces it, since dying for him no longer figures as the negation of all that is human. Indeed terrorist accounts of martyrdom invariably describe the militant's corpse as being far more beautiful than his living body ever was, becoming in this way more human than the human being it had once belonged to, and even exuding a perfume that made it seem more lifelike than its own life. In the section that follows I will look at how Al-Qaeda's rejection of a politics of life allows its followers to enjoy the most intimate relations with their enemies.

4   This is an argument made by Carl Schmitt in *The Concept of the Political*, p. 54.

The militant as ventriloquist

After a three-year intermission in his media appearances, Osama bin Laden made a successful comeback as a small-screen star shortly before the sixth anniversary of the 9/11 attacks. No irony is intended in this description of a man who is after all nothing more than a celebrity, deprived as he is of any control over the devotees he inspires, and himself a fugitive with neither financial nor military resources to command. While Bin Laden's influence no doubt derives from his warlike past, his power has today become suprapolitical in character, though it also is a kind of power peculiar to the age of mass media. Indeed his Muslim admirers apart, Osama bin Laden's celebrity status is also acknowledged by his detractors, who attend so closely to his appearance that media commentators seemed to be obsessed by the dyed or even false beard sported in a videotape by the world's most wanted man. He might as well have been an MTV star.

As a celebrity Bin Laden is part of the West he criticizes, remaining firmly inside it despite all attempts to elaborate upon his foreign provenance or exotic beliefs. And of this insider's role Osama bin Laden himself is fully aware, not least because his attacks on the United States in particular are given voice in this videotape through the lips of dissenting figures like Noam Chomsky and Michael Scheuer.[5] While not himself a socialist or a liberal, in other words, Bin Laden adopts the anti-capitalist or anti-establishment stance of such people to voice his opposition to the West. His own critique of the West is therefore an immanent or internal one, but more than that it is a form of ventriloquism in which the prince of terrorists speaks through one or more dummies rather than in his own name. In itself this adoption of ready-made positions is not strange, marking in fact the language of most politicians in Europe and America, but in the case of Osama bin Laden it illustrates additionally the fact that he possesses no position outside the world of his enemies. This is why he can so easily identify with the plight of American soldiers in Iraq, whom he compares with their Muslim victims in the following

---

5   Jeffrey Imm, "SITE Transcript and Video Link to Bin Laden Video (Updated)", *Counterterrorism Blog* (http://counterterrorismblog.org/2007/09/obl_transcript.php), pp. 4, 7.

passage referring in particular to the large number of Blacks serving in the US armed forces:

If they leave their barracks, the mines devour them, and if they refuse to leave, rulings are passed against them. Thus, the only options left in front of them are to commit suicide or cry, both of which are from the severest of afflictions. So is there anything more men can do after crying and killing themselves to make you respond to them? They are doing that out of the severity of the humiliation, fear and terror which they are suffering. It is severer than what the slaves used to suffer at your hands centuries ago, and it is as if some of them have gone from one slavery to another slavery more severe and harmful, even if it be in the fancy dress of the Defense Department's financial enticements. So do you feel the greatness of their sufferings?[6]

It is because he speaks through a disparate set of dummies without occupying a position of his own that Bin Laden can be said to turn internal or immanent critique into a form of terrorism, since all he does is to deploy one kind of argument against another in a battle which none is meant to survive. It is a form of rhetorical suicide bombing in which the Muslim critic is destroyed alongside his infidel enemy, given that the Islamic element in Bin Laden's argumentation serves as a false externality, having become the sounding box for Marxism, Third Worldism and God knows what else. Of course this rhetoric is heavily ironic, but more important than its insincerity is the fact that irony here is only possible as a form of self-deprecation, given that it deprives Bin Laden of any position external to that of his enemies. Yet the internality of such a position to the US or the West means that Osama bin Laden can address these enemies in the most intimate, familiar and direct of ways, often mentioning them by name and always claiming to understand their motives perfectly. Indeed Al-Qaeda's founding father goes so far as to confess sharing many of the interests of his capitalist or neoconservative foes, at one point even joking about sharing their hypocritical innocence as much as their guilt for shedding Muslim blood:

This innocence of yours is like my innocence of the blood of your sons on the 11th—were I to claim such a thing.[7]

---

6   Ibid., p. 7.

7   Ibid., p. 4.

By contrast the way in which the West engages Al-Qaeda is strikingly different, with Bin Laden invariably seen as being irredeemably alien, rarely if ever addressed by his enemies, and usually described as sharing nothing at all with them. And yet what could be more familiar to political life in the West than the spectacle of a leader being fed bits of information and summaries of important books by his research assistants, the very procedures that allow Bin Laden to quote Noam Chomsky or assail capitalism? However the crumbling of a position that is truly external to the world of his foes results not only in the fragmentation of Osama bin Laden's critique, but in the dissolution, as well, of any alternative world-view he might hold. In addition to lacking a unified ideology or even a utopia, therefore, Al-Qaeda ends up promoting a perverse and paradoxical pluralism instead. So its founding fathers routinely ask their opponents not to convert to Islam so much as remain true to themselves—or rather to their own ideal of human rights. If anything Islam is conceived only as the fulfilment of this ideal, thus making conversion into an act of self-fulfilment:

And with your earnest reading about Islam from its pristine sources, you will arrive at an important truth, which is that the religion of all the Prophets (peace and blessings of Allah be upon them) is one, and that its essence is submission to the orders of Allah alone in all aspects of life, even if their Shariahs (Laws) differ.[8]

But conversion is by no means the sole option that Bin Laden and his friends offer the West, dwelling rather upon the possibility of a harmonious coexistence in which Christians, Muslims, Jews and others can be faithful to their own ideals. Disingenuous though it might be, this pluralistic vision forms a fundamental element in Al-Qaeda's rhetorical logic, and is lavishly illustrated in this videotape by invocations of the protection that Muslims extended to Jews fleeing the Inquisition, as well as by the words of praise that are heaped upon Jesus and Mary in the Quran.[9] Indeed Osama bin Laden states that intolerance of genocidal proportions is a characteristic of the West, mentioning as examples the Holocaust and the use of atomic weapons in Japan.[10] Interesting about

---

8   Ibid., p. 8.

9   Ibid., pp. 2-3 and p. 8.

10   Ibid., pp. 3-4.

these illustrations of Muslim pluralism is the fact that they are drawn directly from the apologetic literature of liberal or "moderate" Islam, whose quest for an accommodation with the West goes back to the beginnings of colonial rule in the nineteenth century. And this appropriation of a rival Muslim tradition constitutes yet another instance of Bin Laden's ventriloquism—which is to say his unwillingness or inability to adopt a position external to the world he fights, resulting therefore in an attempt to destroy this world from the inside.

Unlike his previous attacks on the malice and hypocrisy of American or British warmongers, Osama bin Laden's comeback videotape focuses primarily on the failure of the very pacifists and socialists he so approvingly cites. Despite their unprecedented global demonstrations against the war in Iraq, for example, or their electoral rout of administrations like the one in Washington, Bin Laden points out that the war's opponents have remained politically impotent. It is their inability to change the course of events that leads him to blame the interests upon which liberal society is founded, and the corporate interests of modern capitalism in particular, for what he considers to be the failure of democracy. If demonstrations, opinion polls, elections and other constitutional methods of registering disapproval are ineffective in changing government policy, though they may well change the party in power, this is because the democratic system itself is based on an accommodation of interests rather than on the simple representation of popular will, of the sort favoured by fascism or communism for instance:

And I tell you: after the failure of your representatives in the Democratic Party to implement your desire to stop the war, you can still carry anti-war placards and spread out in the streets of major cities, then go back to your homes, but that will be of no use and will lead to the prolonging of the war.[11]

As proof of this argument Osama bin Laden points to the Vietnam War, which was brought to a close not by public disapproval, however overwhelming, so much as by military defeat and a realignment of corporate interests in the US. He gauges the failure of American popular opinion during the Vietnam War by the fact that its termination did not result in justice being done—neither for its Vietnamese nor even its American victims. And because no government officials were brought

---

11   Ibid., p. 5.

to justice over Vietnam, Bin Laden claims that the interests these men represented could simply lie dormant, mentioning the American Vice-President Dick Cheney and the Secretary of Defence Donald Rumsfeld as good examples of Vietnam-era officials returning to their old habits in Iraq.[12] Conspiratorial though this account may be, it disdains the moral absolutism of similar theories on both Left and Right, presupposing as these do the existence of a sharp dividing-line between friend and enemy. After all Osama bin Laden is not averse to claiming a community of interest even with his worst enemies, capitalists and neoconservatives in this case:

Since the 11th, many of America's policies have come under the influence of the Mujahideen, and that is by the grace of Allah, the Most High. And as a result the people discovered the truth about it, its reputation worsened, its prestige was broken globally and it was bled dry economically, even if our interests overlap with the interests of the major corporations and also with those of the neoconservatives, despite the differing intentions.[13]

Now democracy's success or failure is usually judged by reference to the people and society it defines, with outsiders engaged by no other principle but that of convenience. And while such convenience might well translate into relations of mutual advantage among states, the international order cannot itself be democratic without the establishment of a universal state. Above all else, this international order remains a state of nature, with nothing but the fear of reprisal preventing countries from exploiting, oppressing or annihilating each other. Bin Laden, however, holds American democracy to account precisely from the perspective of those outside its demesne. Such a perspective takes humanity itself as its subject, which is why our celebrity terrorist is concerned most of all by the failure of democracies to respect the human rights of those beyond their borders. But his critique of democracy is not limited to the recognition that its citizens' freedom depends upon the unfreedom of others. Instead Osama bin Laden begins his speech by telling us how even the richest and most powerful of democracies can be adjudged failures in a global arena. For example he points out that despite all its might the United States was shaken to its constitutional foundations and led into

---

12   Ibid., p. 4.

13   Ibid., p. 2.

a global war after 9/11 not because of any profound domestic issue but merely by the unexpected actions of a few foreigners:

To preface, I say: despite America being the greatest economic power and possessing the most powerful and up-to-date military arsenal as well; and despite it spending on this war and its army more than the entire world spends on its armies; and despite it being the major state influencing the policies of the world, as if it has a monopoly of the unjust right of veto; despite all of this, 19 young men were able—by the grace of Allah, the Most High—to change the direction of its compass. And in fact, the subject of the Mujahideen has become an inseparable part of the speech of your leader, and the effects and signs of that are not hidden.[14]

In a global arena, Bin Laden seems to be saying, the most insignificant powers and accidental events possess as much political weight as the deepest of domestic concerns, such that it becomes impossible to preserve the integrity of democratic politics within their traditional borders. Whether 9/11 compelled the US to respond militarily by offering it an opportunity to reposition itself globally, or by confronting it with the necessity of protecting its interests, in other words, her subsequent transformation of the world's political landscape possessed what would traditionally be considered a superficial cause, and one that was external to the workings of this mighty democracy. For the paradoxical thing about Al-Qaeda was that its votaries could with their negligible resources create battlefield conditions at heart of a great power, though they could not of course threaten either its government or military in any significant way.

But this means that the terrorist threat, however numerous its potential victims, has never compromised American security from the outside. At most it left open the possibility of an internal transformation in the country's politics, for instance by threatening to erode the electoral support of administrations unable to protect their citizens. Yet it was precisely this negligible militant network that managed to evacuate a great democracy like the United States of its integrity by erasing the line normally drawn in political theory between superficial and weighty causes, or between domestic and international ones. In fact this very inability to sustain the boundaries of a democratic order is what allows Osama bin Laden to speak from inside its crumbling rhetoric, whose

---

14   Ibid., p. 2.

marshalling by the US president, as he points out in the passage quoted above, illustrates more than anything else how the language of democracy has been hijacked by a rag-tag band of amateur terrorists, given that American policy now appears to be dictated by their doings.

Only in the global arena was a negligible force like Al-Qaeda able to subvert the integrity of an immense country like the United States, by forcing it to respond to a barely understood problem beyond the self-proclaimed limits of its democracy. But more than threatening these limits, the global arena is if anything put at risk by democratic politics, which Bin Laden argues have become irrational within its more capacious boundaries. So quite apart from engaging in vast massacres of civilian populations in places like Japan or Vietnam, a democracy like the United States will also compromise the future of humanity itself by ignoring the dangers of climate change to cater to the narrower interests of some among its citizens. As far as Osama bin Laden is concerned, then, democratic politics becomes suicidal in the global arena because it cannot abandon the factionalism that makes it possible in the first place. Rather than blaming the American rejection of the Kyoto Accords on particular interests, in other words, Bin Laden attributes it to the politics of interest that underwrites democracy in general:

In fact, the life of all of mankind is in danger because of the global warming resulting to a large degree from the emissions of the factories of the major corporations, yet despite that, the representatives of these corporations in the White House insist on not observing the Kyoto Accord, with the knowledge that the statistics speak of the death and displacement of millions of human beings because of that, especially in Africa. This greatest of plagues and most dangerous of threats to the lives of humans is taking place in an accelerating fashion as the world is being dominated by the democratic system, which confirms its massive failure to protect humans and their interests from the greed and avarice of the major corporations and their representatives.[15]

While Bin Laden is doing nothing more than trotting out a set of stereotyped popular concerns about climate change, greedy corporations and African poverty in the quotation above, interesting about his reasoning is the fact that democracy rather than the US or even the West is acknowledged to be the rather abstract and structural cause of all this destruction. And this only because the dominant role played by

---

15   Ibid., p. 5.

its factional politics means that democracy is unable to attend seriously to the long-term interests of humanity as a whole. True or false, such a view is manifestly global in dimension, taking as it does the entire human race as its subject. So against the suicidal factionalism of democracy, which he thinks can only sacrifice the long-term future of humanity for short-term corporate interests, Osama bin Laden sets up the virtues of *sharia* or Islamic law. Following the fundamentalist Pakistani thinker Abul Ala Mawdudi, he recommends this law not by demonstrating its intrinsic merits so much as by pointing to the purely formal advantage offered by its archaic character.[16] For the divine law is universal precisely because it happens to be removed from a present-day politics of interest, thus assuming the kind of neutrality that is partial to none:

So it is imperative that you free yourself from all of that and search for an alternative, upright methodology in which it is not the business of any class of humanity to lay down its own laws to its own advantage at the expense of the other classes as is the case with you, since the essence of man-made positive laws is that they serve the interests of those with the capital and thus make the rich richer and the poor poorer.[17]

Like other fundamentalists Mawdudi sought to establish the divine law as state law, to be governed by institutions like courts and the police. Bin Laden, however, has said very little about such institutions, recommending instead the purely civilian, informal and even individual interpretation and application of *sharia* in an almost anarchistic way. What does survive in his thinking from Mawdudi's theory of divine law is its sacrificial nature, something that Osama bin Laden not unexpectedly emphasizes more than his Pakistani predecessor. Mawdudi had made every effort to justify the injunctions of divine law as being more equitable to women, non-Muslims and the poor than Western jurisprudence, only legitimizing the sanguinary punishments of *sharia* as sacrifices necessary to maintain its archaic neutrality after having exhausted the resources of such apologetic. Osama bin Laden, on the other hand, revels in the sacrifices demanded by divine law, which for him illustrate its supremely disinterested and therefore impartial nature. At the end of the day, therefore, both men see the impediments placed in the way of

---

16   See for instance Sayyid Abul Ala Mawdudi, "Islam awr Adl-e Ijtimai", in *Tafhimat*, vol. 3 (Lahore, 1992), p. 156.

17   Imm, pp. 5-6.

women, sectarian minorities and others by this law as sacrifices equivalent in some sense to the military ones required of Muslim men, neither one being avoidable if the law's neutrality was to be safeguarded, its universal claims resting as they did on sheer archaism.

Having detached Islamic law from the grip of the nation-state and emphasized its sacrificial nature, Osama bin Laden has effectively transformed the militant's obedience of *sharia* into an act of sovereignty. For the law is no longer embodied in a set of institutions to which one must submit, but manifests itself in militant acts that possess the force of law in their own right. Yet more than their freedom from institutional authority, what makes these acts sovereign is that they neither claim nor defend any interest, rather destroying interest itself in spectacular gestures of sacrifice that we have seen unite both perpetrators and victims into a single humanity. In other words militant acts are sovereign because they are spendthrift: deriding the protection that law normally extends interests of various kinds to sacrifice life itself as the ground of all interest. In this sense the militant act is law making rather than law abiding, though it be in the most anarchic of ways. I want in the next section to explore the sacrificial meaning of sovereignty in a global arena with no political institutions of its own.

Sovereign acts of terror

In an essay on Europe and the atom bomb published in 1954, Hannah Arendt pointed out that the possibility of destruction on a planetary scale had outdated the old language of sacrifice, together with the courage required for it in times of war.[18] This language had for many centuries defined sacrifice as part of a relationship in which individuals and groups were able to risk their own lives or possessions, and sometimes those of others as well, for some person, people or principles that would survive them all. In other words sacrifice in its political aspect depended upon the survival of that nation, religion or other entity in whose behalf it was made, thus also guaranteeing the immortality of those who would give their lives for it. Indeed the courage of an individual willing to risk

---

18   Hannah Arendt, "Europe and the Atom Bomb" in Jerome Kohn (ed.), *Essays in Understanding: 1930-1954* (New York: Harcourt Brace and Co., 1994), pp. 418-22.

his life for some greater cause only became extraordinary if it stood out from the otherwise ordinary background of things as they always were and would continue to be.

With the atom bomb, however, the relationship between death and survival that had marked the language of sacrifice suddenly lost much if not all of its meaning, since a nuclear war was capable of destroying the possibility of human survival itself at a global level, or at least of altering it radically. And whether or not any political cause survived such a war alongside the victorious peoples and states who upheld it, the use of atomic weapons would certainly obliterate the very background of ordinariness against which the courage of sacrifice stood out and from which it took its meaning. Or as Arendt put it writing about the worst-case scenario of a war that put the survival of the human race in peril:

Courage, under the circumstances of modern warfare, has lost much of its old meaning. By putting in jeopardy the survival of mankind and not only individual life, or at the most the life of a whole people, modern warfare is about to transform the individual mortal man into a conscious member of the human race, of whose immortality he needs to be sure in order to be courageous at all and for whose survival he must care more than for anything else.[19]

While Hannah Arendt was of course describing potentialities that have yet to be realized, her claim that atomic weapons have produced individuals who are self-conscious members of the human race does not require the occurrence of a nuclear war to hold true. And indeed how else are we to define the activists who sacrifice their lives and possessions for world peace, the environment or Islam if not as embodiments of humanity in its own right? For given the institutional invisibility of the human race as a political actor, only such novel forms of sacrificial courage are capable of bringing it into being, though they must do so by undermining the relationship between death and survival upon which sacrifice had traditionally been founded.

Even though Muslim militants, for instance, tend not to be in any doubt of their faith's survival, the fact that its global society, like every other, lacks an institutional presence means that the Muslim community cannot be said to exist politically speaking. Rather than risking their lives for this community, then, our terrorists might actually bring

---

19   Ibid., p. 422.

it into being by acts like suicide bombing, having short-circuited the old link between death and survival in the language of sacrifice by fusing both in their sovereign acts. Arendt lays out the implications of this new and individualized form of sovereignty, in which no real distinction can be drawn between the subject and object of sacrifice, by referring to nuclear war as the possibility that brings humanity to birth in the form of an actor who still stands outside the political world:

With the appearance of atomic weapons, both the Hebrew-Christian limitation on violence and the ancient appeal to courage have for all practical purposes become meaningless, and, with them, the whole political and moral vocabulary in which we are accustomed to discuss these matters.[20]

If all this seems somewhat abstract, let us track the emergence of sovereignty as a new kind of historical practice in the life and thought of Gandhi, who was after all the greatest devotee of its sacrificial form in modern times. While he began with the traditional language of sacrifice as described by Hannah Arendt, the Mahatma enunciated a version of it that was far more complex. Thus sacrificial acts at every level, from fasting and celibacy to passive resistance and even the courting of death, were not simply dedicated to ensuring the survival of some greater cause, but instead at inviting its enemies into different paths of action. In other words sacrifice here established a moral relationship between enemies rather than among the friends to whom its traditional forms were devoted, since for Gandhi it was enmity and not amity that represented the moral relationship at its purest. This is why the Mahatma so regularly recommended attending to one's enemies with more courtesy than to one's own friends and family, even going so far as to advocate sacrificing the latter for the former's goodwill. But such goodwill could only be cultivated by the nonviolent activist deliberately exposing himself to the violence of his enemies, thus forcing them to adopt some other strategy to deal with him. Whether or not this new course of action ended up converting such enemies, then, it certainly forced them to rethink their own narratives of conflict.

Even the sacrificial practices of terrorists, therefore, might conform to Gandhi's principles, however violent they might otherwise be, for such acts are explicitly dedicated to creating a moral relationship be-

20   Ibid., p. 421.

tween enemies, and have indubitably forced those who would oppose them to reformulate their concepts of warfare. But such a reformulation is steeped in panic and yet to assume a political form. In any case the Mahatma was himself not above advocating violence, offered in self-defence or better still in the defence of others, when nonviolent means proved incapable. Though it might represent a lesser form of virtue, he thought that violence was sometimes necessary, if only to prevent the one exercising it as a last resort from sinking to the position of a mere victim, who for Gandhi possessed no moral status whatever. Because sacrifice for Gandhi represented courage at its highest pitch, violence could also be sacrificial, forestalling as it did the cowardice, humiliation and degradation of any victimization too easily accepted. Precisely the moral actor's courage, after all, was required to convert his enemy, or at the very least to alter his behaviour. But what if the sacrificial relationship with an enemy, instrumental despite its careful avoidance of any violence inflicted upon him, were to become impossible?

The Holocaust, followed by the use of the atom bomb, forced the Mahatma to rethink his language of sacrifice, from which he finally eliminated the instrumentality still residing in the relationship between enemies. Gandhi was reluctant in the beginning to accept any alteration of his ideas, and like many during the early stages of the Second World War, unwilling to recognize the utter novelty of Nazism's factory-produced genocide. A troubled correspondence with some of his Jewish admirers and critics in Europe and Palestine, including the eminent Zionists Martin Buber and Judah Magnes, eventually convinced the Mahatma to abandon the notion that nonviolent resistance as an instrumental activity was possible in Germany. While deferring the question of whether nonviolent resistance might convert Hitler to the ways of righteousness, Gandhi still refused to believe as a matter of principle that Germans were all automatons who could only be influenced by the use of force. He therefore counselled Jews who could neither fight nor escape fascism to die with such dignity as they could muster, by inviting rather than merely accepting their immolation in the public and collective repudiation of fascism. And was the Warsaw Ghetto uprising of 1943 not perhaps an example precisely of such an attitude? For this was an uprising dedicated not to the survival of its fighters so much as for "the honour and glory of the Jewish people," the words that comprised its motto.[21]

The following is a passage from Gandhi's first lengthy statement on the pre-war persecution of German Jews, whose publication provoked a furious response from the Nazi press:

If I were a Jew and were born in Germany and earned my livelihood there, I would claim Germany as my home even as the tallest gentile German may, and challenge him to shoot me or cast me in the dungeon; I would refuse to be expelled or to submit to discriminating treatment. And for doing this, I should not wait for the fellow Jews to join me in civil resistance but would have confidence that in the end the rest are bound to follow my example. If one Jew or all the Jews were to accept the prescription here offered, he or they cannot be worse off than now. And suffering voluntarily undergone will bring them an inner strength and joy which no number of resolutions of sympathy passed in the world outside Germany can. Indeed, even if Britain, France and America were to declare hostilities against Germany, they can bring no inner joy, no inner strength. The calculated violence of Hitler may even result in a general massacre of the Jews by way of his first answer to the declaration of such hostilities. But if the Jewish mind could be prepared for voluntary suffering, even the massacre I have imagined could be turned into a day of thanksgiving and joy that Jehovah had wrought deliverance of the race even at the hands of the tyrant. [...] I am convinced that if someone with courage and vision can arise among them to lead them in nonviolent action, the winter of their despair can in the twinkling of an eye be turned into the summer of hope. And what has today become a degrading manhunt can be turned into a calm and determined stand offered by unarmed men and women possessing the strength of suffering given to them by Jehovah. It will be then a truly religious resistance offered against the godless fury of dehumanised man. The German Jews will score a lasting victory over the German gentiles in the sense that they will have converted the latter to an appreciation of human dignity. They will have rendered service to fellow-Germans and proved their title to be the real Germans as against those who are today dragging, however unknowingly, the German name into the mire.[22]

By choosing the manner of their deaths the Jews would demonstrate a courage that released them from the humiliation of being mere vic-

---

21 For this see Hannah Arendt, "The political organization of the Jewish people", in Jerome Kohn and Ron H. Feldman (eds.), *The Jewish Writings* (New York: Schocken Books, 2007), pp. 199-201.

22 M.K. Gandhi, "The Jews", *Harijan*, November 26, 1938. Parenthesis mine.

tims while at the same time proving their title to be the truest of Germans. And the nobility of such a death, thought Gandhi, would have retrospective effect, lending future generations of Jews self-respect while allowing for the eventual conversion of their enemies, who would never again be able to think of these non-victims as alien to Germany. Though he had recommended a similar course of action for the Czechs and even English in the face of Nazi attack, the Mahatma thought that if the unarmed Jews, whom he called the Untouchables of Christianity, were to turn the voluntary sacrifices already being made privately into a public enterprise they would redeem humanity itself. So in a later statement written in response to criticism he had received from the *Jewish Frontier* in New York, Gandhi emphasized the posthumous virtues of *ahimsa* or nonviolence in the face of violence or *himsa*, pointing out that warlike measures offered no more guarantees of security and success than peaceful ones, not least in a situation where Germany's enemies were still hesitating to come to the aid of European Jewry:

I can conceive the necessity of the immolation of hundreds, if not thousands, to appease the hunger of dictators who have no belief in ahimsa. Indeed the maxim is that ahimsa is the most efficacious in front of the greatest himsa. Its quality is really tested only in such cases. Sufferers need not see the result during their lifetime. They must have faith that if their cult survives, the result is a certainty. The method of violence gives no greater guarantee than that of nonviolence. It gives infinitely less.[23]

If the Holocaust had persuaded Gandhi to pare down the instrumental relations created by sacrifice to a bare minimum, the use of atom bombs on Hiroshima and Nagasaki pushed him to reconsider this relationship altogether. And this was because nuclear warfare, like the equally lethal fire-bombing that preceded it, eliminated the proximity between enemies that was necessary for any practice of sacrifice to have effect, though in South Africa and India such practices had retained their efficacy for him even when made available in the press alone. More then proximity, then, it was the bomb's elimination of time that finally rendered the Mahatma's language of sacrifice speechless. For the instantaneous and total character of a nuclear strike allowed its victims no time in which to display their courage, and in doing so to become actors

---

23   M.K. Gandhi, "The Jewish Question", *Harijan*, May 22, 1939.

whose deeds might have some retrospective effect on their descendants and enemies alike. Faced with the possibility of his moral vision being confined to the context of everyday life, or to conventional war at the most, Gandhi decided to cut sacrifice loose from all instrumentality and value it for its own sake, as a practice of sovereignty depending on itself alone.

Speaking to the photojournalist Margaret Bourke-White a few hours before sacrificing his own life to an assassin's bullet, the Mahatma recognized that it would have been impossible for the inhabitants of Hiroshima or Nagasaki to deploy sacrifice, in either its violent or nonviolent aspects, for any instrumental purpose however noble. He therefore wished they had offered themselves up as targets to the American bombers who came bearing their annihilation by refusing to take refuge in shelters or otherwise evade death, and in doing so to offer their murderers the possibility of redemption. For he thought that by remaining victims the residents of these Japanese cities had renounced moral agency for themselves while at the same time denying it to their enemies in the future:

I had asked Gandhiji how he would meet the atom bomb. Would he meet it with nonviolence?

'Ah, ah!' he said. 'How shall I answer that!' The charkha turned busily in his agile hands for a moment, and then he replied: 'I would meet it by prayerful action.' He emphasized the word 'action', and I asked him what form it would take.

'I will not go underground. I will not go into shelters. I will come out in the open and let the pilot see I have not the face of evil against him.'

He turned back to his spinning for a moment before continuing.

'The pilot will not see our faces from his great height, I know. But that longing in our hearts that he will not come to harm would reach up to him and his eyes would be opened. Of those thousands who were done to death in Hiroshima, if they had died with that prayerful action—died openly with that prayer in their hearts—then the war would not have ended so disgracefully as it has. It is a question now of whether the victors are really victors or victims'—he was speaking very slowly and his words had become toneless and low—'of our own lust… and omission. Because the world is not at peace'—his voice had sunk almost to a whisper—'it is still more dreadful…'[24]

While Gandhi's description of sacrifice in the context of nuclear war still possesses a tinge of instrumentality, though of an almost mystical kind, it is clear that a solitary and sovereign element has come to dominate it. But the sovereignty of this sacrifice was not in the least metaphorical, with Gandhi underlining its very substantial reality by suggesting that the Second World War's victors were in their own way victims who had been refused the possibility of redemption by those they killed. Just as with the Holocaust, however, there were many instances of people in Hiroshima who conducted themselves in exactly the way Gandhi favoured, thus doing nothing more than demonstrating the truth of his dictum concerning the everyday character of sacrifice.

Like militants today the Mahatma's efforts to create a moral relationship between enemies ended up redefining sacrifice as a form of sovereignty whose agent's annihilation put the instrumentality of his action in doubt. And this is where the militant and the Mahatma both part ways with the partisans of environmental or pacifist causes, who have done little more than to expand the politics of life and its language of fear from local arenas to a global one.[25] Though separated from Osama bin Laden by a vast gulf, Mohandas Karamchand Gandhi does join him in the rejection of a humanity that is defined by life alone, thus breaking with the politics of states and NGOs alike, all of which take life as their object by invoking its security as an ideal. But the rejection of a politics based on the management of life has as its consequence the rejection of a politics of fear. So both men value the kind of sacrifice that literally volatilizes the body to make its humanity manifest in fearlessness, a quality they value because of the dignity and self-respect it entails. Is it then by stepping out of their bodies in these sovereign acts of sacrifice, violent as well as nonviolent, that human beings might represent

24   Margaret Bourke-White, *Interview With India* (London: The Travel Book Club, 1951), p. 185.

25   In a suggestive article Alex Gourevitch points out that the politics of fear informing the war on terror as much as environmentalism makes for a novel form of global transcendence, in which the importance of locality and the freedom of choice, both characteristic of the democratic tradition, are sacrificed for a planetary politics founded upon the preservation of life alone. See his essay "The politics of fear", in *n+1*, issue 6, Winter 2008.

humanity? Perhaps we can guess at an answer to this difficult question by returning to our point of departure, Karl Jaspers' book *The Future of Mankind*.

The future of an illusion

Reviewing the French translation of Jaspers' text, the literary critic Maurice Blanchot asked why it was that the author's repeated assertions of the atom bomb's absolute novelty were not matched by anything new in his own thought and expository style. While expatiating upon the historical break produced by the bomb, in other words, and calling for a comparable break in our patterns of action and reflection in order to comprehend the originality of the atomic age, Jaspers himself continued to think and act according to the same set of principles and prejudices that had motivated him in the past.[26] Rather than attributing this contradiction to the German philosopher's hypocrisy, however, Blanchot suggested that merely recognizing the startlingly new horizons opened up by the bomb for our moral and political life did not entail comprehending its momentousness. In fact the possibility of a nuclear war remained incomprehensible not only by reason of its global scale, but also because its threat was so extreme as to become nothing more than an empty banality:

If thinking falls back into its traditional affirmations, it is because it wants to risk nothing of itself in the presence of an ambiguous event about which it is not able to decide what it means, with its horrible face, with its appearance as absolute—an event of enormous size but enormously empty, about which it can say nothing save this banality: that it would be better to prevent it.[27]

The same paralysis of thought and action can be seen in people's attitudes towards environmental issues, of course, with terrorism sometimes taking the place of the atom bomb and climate change not only as a source of global fear, but also as the only such threat amenable to control. Whether or not the fear of terrorism displaces that of the nuclear and environmental threats with which it is often paired, what makes

---

26   Maurice Blanchot, " The apocalypse in disappointing", in *Friendship* (Stanford: Stanford University Press, 1997), p. 102.

27   Ibid., p. 104.

these latter incomprehensible is the fact that they threaten an entity, humanity, that according to Blanchot does not yet exist:

On the one hand a power that cannot be, and on the other an existence—the human community—that can be wiped out but not affirmed, or that could be affirmed, in some sense, only after its disappearance and by the void, impossible to grasp, of this disappearance; consequently something that cannot even be destroyed, because it does not exist. It is very probable that humanity would have no fear of this power of the end if it could recognize in it a decision that belonged exclusively to it, on condition thus of being truly the subject and not simply the object of it, and without having to trust to the hazardous initiative of some head of State who is just as foreign to humanity today as formerly the turtle that fell from the sky and crushed his head was to the unfortunate Aeschylus.[28]

Humanity, writes Blanchot, cannot be described as if it were some collective version of the humanist individual, one that has been offered the possibility of suicide by the atom bomb. It can only become this kind of subject posthumously, and exists at the moment in a state of potentiality that not even the global extension of democratic representation is likely to make more real. In its statistical form, therefore, humanity exists because it can be manipulated and even destroyed, while in its individual form it remains unknown. But is it possible to say that here and there humanity does in fact instantiate itself by the individual's sacrifice of humanist subjectivity? If the global Muslim community is seen by terrorists to represent the suffering of humanity itself, and their violence conceived as a series of sacrifices to lend this humanity voice, then the virtues of courage and fearlessness exhibited by this violence can well be defined as the voice of humanity, though one deprived of humanist subjectivity. Having destroyed the body as a subject within which such human virtues could be grounded, and dismissed life itself as the limit of humanity, militant practices like suicide bombing open up a space for the posthuman.

Perhaps it is this posthumanity that is on display in the frequent depictions of martyrs and militants turned into animals. Not the heavenly bodies and houris that are promised to believers in the Quran, then, but figures of birds are what for the most part serve to represent terrorists both living and dead in the verbal and pictorial repertoire of militant

---

28   Ibid., p. 106.

rhetoric. Green birds in particular, which are said in some traditions attributed Muhammad to represent the souls of martyrs fluttering around the divine throne, appear in terrorist writing and photography very frequently.[29] Then there are the birds of prey, eagles, hawks and falcons, which can represent militants living or dead. There are even images like that of the Prophet as a white dove concealed in a cave across which a spider has woven its web, thus throwing off the American bombers depicted flying in the sky outside. The reference here is to the well-known story, mentioned in the holy book itself, of Muhammad escaping his enemies by hiding in a cave over whose mouth a spider has spread its web. Animals like horses are also familiar in militant rhetoric, and sometimes carnivores such as lions, with Osama bin Laden's face superimposed on the head of one such photograph—the terrorist version of Disney's Lion King.[30]

It is not birds and beasts that are anthropomorphized in militant imagery, but rather the reverse, with human beings having become animals in the rhetoric of jihad. And men can take on animal forms in this way because they represent abstract virtues like courage and fearlessness that have been freed from humanist subjectivity as much as from humanitarian statistics to offer us another vision of the world and our place in it. Frightening though this vision might be, it tells us that our traditional notions of humanity are becoming meaningless in a global arena where the humanist subject is being replaced by a statistical aggregate on the one hand, and by a posthuman politics on the other. For if the globalization of militant Islam tells us anything, it is that a planetary politics cannot be conducted with the humanist subject as its foundation, and that the abstract humanity surging into the global arena to take its place might well find instantiation in posthuman

---

29   Among the most famous militant invocations of these creatures are widely circulated audiotapes bearing the title "In the Hearts of Green Birds," which recount the martyrdom of fighters who came from all over the world to Bosnia in the early 1990s. For more recent transcriptions and discussions of these tapes among militants see the following discussion threads on jihadi web forums: http://www.sunniforum.com/forum/archive/index.php?t-8676.html, http://www.ummah.com/forum/showthread.php?t=79293 and http://clearinghouse.infovlad.net/showthread.php?t=10431. I am indebted to Thomas Keenan for drawing my attention to these sites.

30   See "The Islamic imagery project: visual motifs in jihadi Internet propaganda".

forms—of which the sacrificial practices of Muslim militants provide only one example.

INDEX